READING
POSTCOLONIAL
LITERATURE

READING POSTCOLONIAL LITERATURE

From Professional to Non-Professional Practices

HAYLEY G. TOTH

LIVERPOOL UNIVERSITY PRESS

First published 2025 by
Liverpool University Press
4 Cambridge Street
Liverpool
L69 7ZU

This book is freely available on a Creative Commons CC-BY-NC-ND licence thanks to the kind sponsorship of the libraries participating in the Jisc Open Access Community Framework OpenUP initiative.

© Hayley G. Toth 2025, under a Creative Commons Attribution-NonCommercial-NonDerivative licence.

Hayley G. Toth has asserted the right to be identified as the author of this book in accordance with the Copyright, Designs and Patents Act 1988.

All rights reserved. No part of this book may be reproduced, stored in a retrieval system, or transmitted, in any form or by any means, electronic, mechanical, photocopying, recording, or otherwise, without the prior written permission of the publisher.

British Library Cataloguing-in-Publication data
A British Library CIP record is available

ISBN 978-1-83624-313-7 paperback

Typeset by Carnegie Book Production, Lancaster

Contents

Acknowledgements	vii
Introduction	1
1. Reading and the Rushdie Affair	37
2. Reading and Address	73
3. Reading and Non-Understanding	99
4. Popular Reading and Popular Texts	131
Conclusion: Deprofessionalising Postcolonial Studies?	165
Bibliography	185
Index	201

Acknowledgements

This has been something of an itinerant book. It started as a PhD thesis at the University of Leeds, under the supervision of Brendon Nicholls. It gained a chapter on the reception of *Noughts & Crosses*, or the idea for one, in north Leeds, after I taught the novel as a class reader at a number of different schools there. It came with me to the University of Oxford, where it was briefly shelved, while I worked on a very different project. But Oxford became instrumental, for it was there that I reconceived the project and shed some of the comforts of the original thesis. The book was finally finished at Newcastle University. Along the way, it has travelled by plane, train, and automobile, but has for the most part been written in homes in Leeds.

I owe many people my thanks. Thank you to Chloé Johnson and all the team at Liverpool University Press for their support in helping me to get this book into shape, and Rachel Chamberlain at Carnegie Book Production for her invaluable production assistance. I'm grateful to Brendon Nicholls for believing in a version of this project several years ago, and for supporting me as the person to deliver it. Brendon has championed me and this work to anyone who will listen, and remains a steadfast friend and mentor. Thanks, too, to John McLeod and Graham Huggan for their thoughtful critiques over the years, and for modelling what genuine collegiality looks like during our postcolonial events at Leeds. My heartfelt thanks to Merve Emre, who supported me to write this book while working for her, and who taught me so much about writing, criticism, and labour. It was a pleasure to rework this book in light of our conversations about John Guillory, literary reading, and 'the crisis of the humanities,' and to do so with some job security at Oxford. Thanks—for everything. Thanks too to Caroline Koegler, for sustaining a multi-year dialogue with me about professionalism in postcolonial studies, and who invited me to present some of the ideas from this book in Berlin at just the right time. Thanks to colleagues at Newcastle, especially Neelam Srivastava and James Procter, who pushed me to finish this book when I felt that I'd run out of things to say. And thanks to my former English students across north Leeds, who loved and disparaged literature in equal measure, and who reminded me what reading postcolonial literature might do.

I'm fortunate to have a large group of friends, who have shared the many milestones of this project and helped me to unwind over walks, pub quizzes, dinners, bar crawls, birthdays, weddings, and holidays. Thanks to them: you know who you are. Thanks too to my parents Julie and Laszlo, and my brother and sister-in-law Jack and Shaunagh for their support and their repeated attempts to try and understand what this book is about.

Final thanks to Kate Spowage, who has had the displeasure of living, sleeping, and breathing different versions of this book for seven years. Kate read different parts of this book at various stages of the writing process, and the book is better for her feedback. Needless to say, all errors are mine alone. Life gives work meaning, and my life with Kate made the labour of writing this book both possible and rewarding.

Introduction

When postcolonial critics talk about reading, they almost invariably mean the interpretative performance captured and disseminated in journals, books, public lectures, and seminar rooms. In these accounts, reading comes to refer to a professional labour activity. It is a practice that takes particular objects, and which is structured by disciplinary protocols and specific affective and discursive conventions. Its value depends on the disavowal or delegitimisation of reading as it takes place outside of the discipline of postcolonial studies and the profession of literary criticism. The professionalisation of reading in postcolonial studies has beleaguered our understanding of what it is to read postcolonial literature, causing us to confuse the prescription of reading with its description, and, at times, to overstate the political power of reading. This book is about the relationship between professional and non-professional practices of reading postcolonial literature. It is about why and how we read postcolonial literature, and about the different discourses of value that circulate around these acts of reading.

Through literary-sociological enquiry, *Reading Postcolonial Literature* seeks to demystify the ways in which the value of reading postcolonial literature is mediated by the social settings in which reading takes place. At the same time, the book aims to interrogate dominant assumptions about non-professional reading practices as metropolitan, cosmopolitan, liberal, and neocolonial. By examining different contemporary reception contexts, it identifies important continuities between professional and non-professional reading practices. The book presents a new theory of reading postcolonial literature in order to theorise how readers read and value postcolonial literature as a source of cultural and historical knowledge, ethical improvement, and political consciousness. Its central argument is that reception matters in any claims we make about the value of reading postcolonial literature. While engaging with the reception of postcolonial literature challenges some of the established practices and assumptions in the field, the book demonstrates that it also enables us to make a different, stronger case for reading postcolonial literature.

Reading in Postcolonial Studies

How is reading practised and theorised in postcolonial studies? How does reading acquire value? How has the discipline reckoned with the conditions of postcolonial literature's consumption? While the reception of postcolonial literature is relatively understudied and undertheorised, reading is central to the field. Scholars engage in highly professionalised strategies of reading for the purpose of undertaking textual analyses, which they idealise as improving the critical, ethical, or political value of literary interpretation and/or texts. Some scholars have foregrounded the importance of reading by prescribing different ideal reading strategies. There are two discernible trends that have significantly shaped the pursuit of reading as a practice in postcolonial studies. On the one hand, there are scholars who have devised or engaged in professional strategies for reading canonical literary texts in a postcolonial way. Perhaps the most well-known example of this is Edward Said's 'contrapuntal reading,' which refers to a form of colonial discourse analysis that traces the spectre of imperialism and its practices of exploitation in canonical English literature.[1] In *Post-Colonial Studies: The Key Concepts*, Ashcroft, Griffiths, and Tiffin treat Said's work, among others, as exemplary of 'postcolonial reading.' In this tradition, postcolonial reading is "a form of deconstructive reading most usually applied to works emanating from the colonizers."[2] On the other hand, there are postcolonial scholars, including Ashcroft, Griffiths, and Tiffin themselves, who have developed or practised strategies of reading postcolonial literature. This second avenue of enquiry has been highly productive in recent years, and has generated a diverse interpretative repertoire that defies definition as merely 'deconstruction.' As well as Ashcroft, Griffiths, and Tiffin's early articulation of 'symptomatic reading' as a way of "reveal[ing] the discursive formations and ideological forces which traverse the text,"[3] examples include 'responsible reading,' which

---

[1] Edward Said, *Culture and Imperialism* (London: Chatto & Windus, 1993).
[2] Bill Ashcroft, Gareth Griffiths, and Helen Tiffin, *Post-Colonial Studies: The Key Concepts* (Abingdon: Routledge, 2007), p. 173.
[3] Bill Ashcroft, Gareth Griffiths, and Helen Tiffin, *The Empire Writes Back: Theory and Practice in Post-Colonial Literature* (London: Routledge, 2002), p. 83.

represents "a reading that could be said to do justice" to the text,[4] and, more recently, 'reading for resistance,' which promises to "activat[e] the political energies of postcolonial texts to resist, concatenate, and reshape worlds, and, where necessary, begin anew."[5]

These interpretative strategies are prized as more penetrating ('symptomatic reading,' 'contrapuntal reading'), more ethical ('responsible reading'), or more transformative ('reading for resistance'). They derive some of their legitimacy from their perceived distance from the reading practices of non-professional readers. In several important ways, they are different: the reading approaches developed by professional postcolonial critics take up a very specific understanding of reading, where to 'read' is "[t]o study, observe, or interpret (a phenomenon, an object) as though by reading," but "using methodology analogous to literary criticism or interpretation."[6] Understandably, this kind of reading is minimally practised outside of the academic profession. Professional reading tends toward the practice and demonstration of literary criticism because it has the social function of labour. The particular social function of professional reading is one of the reasons that John Guillory argues that "[t]hose of us who are professional readers cannot hope to see our reading practice simply replicated outside the academy".[7] But the representation of professional strategies of reading postcolonial literature as ethically or politically superior casts the practices of non-professionals as exaggeratedly uneducated and conservative. Non-professional readers come to signify a more or less culturally homogeneous community (usually 'Western' or European), whose strategies of textual appreciation and interpretation rob postcolonial literature of its history and its politics. Most often, this devaluing of non-academic forms of reading takes place implicitly, through the valorisation of highly professionalised strategies of reading.

But, at times, scholars award professional reading practices distinction by explicitly defining them in antagonistic opposition to underdeveloped notions of non-professional reading. Derek Attridge, for instance, defines

---

[4] Derek Attridge, "Responsible Reading and Cultural Distance," in *Postcolonial Audiences: Readers, Viewers and Reception*, ed. by Bethan Benwell, James Procter, and Gemma Robinson (London: Routledge, 2012), pp. 234–44 (p. 234).

[5] Elleke Boehmer, *Postcolonial Poetics: 21st-Century Critical Readings* (London: Palgrave Macmillan, 2018), p. 15.

[6] Entry "read," *Oxford English Dictionary*, n.d. <https://www.oed.com> [accessed 7 January 2022].

[7] John Guillory, "The Ethical Practice of Modernity," in *The Turn to Ethics*, ed. by Marjorie Garber, Beatrice Hanssen, and Rebecca L. Walkowitz (New York: Routledge, 2000), pp. 29–46 (p. 33).

'responsible reading' in contradistinction to what he projects as the tendency of amateurs to irresponsibly "reduc[e] the work to an example of pleasurable exoticism."[8] His assumption that non-professional readers practise exoticism is based on an analysis of four book reviews posted on the website of the online retailer Amazon. And although some contributions within this highly selective sample "reflect a preoccupation with cultural difference," as Attridge suggests,[9] his interpretation of the reviews is slightly unforgiving. A more charitable reading reveals that several of the reviews reproduced appear to be engaged in precisely the kind of 'responsible reading' that Attridge champions, albeit rehearsed in a non-professional register. The homogenisation of non-professional readers—as 'Western,' European, metropolitan, or cosmopolitan consumers engaged in exoticisation—belies the diversity of postcolonial literature's non-academic audiences and the eclecticism of their reading practices. "Postcolonial literatures in English," as Graham Huggan points out, "are read by many different people in many different places," and "literary/cultural audiences all over the world are by their very nature plural and heterogenous."[10] Why, then, has the professionalisation of postcolonial studies allowed these caricatures of non-professional reading to flourish?

The fact that professional authority in postcolonial studies is routed through practices of distinction has to do partly with the discipline's existence in the university. The university or school "regulates and thus distributes cultural capital *unequally*."[11] Its role is to "unequally distribut[e] forms of linguistic and symbolic knowledge—ways of reading, writing, and speaking—that underwrite the production and consumption of literature."[12] Within the university, postcolonial studies must at one level concern itself with conferring value upon its practitioners—teacher and student—against the value of its non-practitioners outside the university. This is because cultural capital is relational. "The denial of [...] natural [...] enjoyment," as Pierre Bourdieu writes in *Distinction: A Social Critique of the Judgement of Taste*, secures the "superiority" of particular practices of reading and their practitioners against the practices of another interpretative community:

---

[8] Attridge, "Responsible Reading," p. 235.
[9] Attridge, "Responsible Reading," p. 243.
[10] Graham Huggan, *The Postcolonial Exotic* (London: Routledge, 2001), p. 30.
[11] John Guillory, *Cultural Capital: The Problem of Literary Canon Formation* (Chicago: University of Chicago Press, 1993), ix.
[12] Merve Emre, "Introduction to the New Edition," in *Cultural Capital: The Problem of Literary Canon Formation*, by John Guillory (Chicago: University of Chicago Press, 2023), ix.

"That is why art and cultural consumption are predisposed, consciously and deliberately or not, to fulfil a social function of legitimating social differences".[13] The university, then, formalises a practice of distinction that already obtains in society in every act of cultural evaluation and consumption. The place of postcolonial studies in the university obliges it to participate in practices of distinction, including by delegitimising the everyday reading practices of those outside the university.

If postcolonial studies' instalment of hierarchies of reading bespeaks the socio-institutional conditions of the modern university and the nature of taste as an aspect of social reproduction, it is also the case that these hierarchies of reading reproduce the modern English department's practices of distinction. Professional literature scholars tend to behave possessively about the specialist study of literature as "the most inherently humanizing or importantly political reading practice."[14] Subfields of literary studies such as book history (and those inspired or influenced by the same) are a clear exception to this tendency.[15] In contemporary literary studies, there is growing interest in popular texts, including crime fiction and non-print media like video games, which has generated new insights into non-professional audiences.[16] In any case, the tendency to distinguish professional reading serves particular functions in the discipline of postcolonial studies. The imaginative construction of non-professional readerships provides a rationale for the professionalisation of reading in the field. As Sarah Brouillette argues in her account of the industry of postcolonial writing and criticism:

> [M]ore elite readers often seem to believe that there is a general public engaged in a similar activity (reading), but who practise it *badly*. [...] [A]ny key initial revulsion soon gives way to relief, since the presumed

---

[13] Pierre Bourdieu, *Distinction: A Social Critique of the Judgement of Taste*, trans. by Richard Nice (Cambridge, MA: Harvard University Press, 1984), p. 7.

[14] Sarah Brouillette, "Reading After the University," *Public Books*, 23 November 2022 <https://www.publicbooks.org/reading-after-the-university-english-departments/>.

[15] Many book historians and nineteenth-century scholars are explicitly concerned with histories of reading and circulation, and with non-professional and working-class readerships. For perhaps the best-known example in this critical tradition, see Johnathan Rose, *The Intellectual Life of the British Working Classes* (New Haven: Yale University Press, 2001).

[16] See, for example, my own essay on playing the video game *Disco Elysium* (2019): Hayley G. Toth, "Bad Reading / Bad Gaming," *Post45 Contemporaries*, 8 April 2024 <https://post45.org/2024/04/bad-reading-bad-gaming/> [accessed 9 May 2024].

presence of others gives one a foil against which to define what is right (such as 'complexity') in one's own position.[17]

An amorphous reading public outside of the profession produces value in professional practices of reading and writing postcolonial literature. Professional postcolonial critics to some extent depend on this fictional audience to justify the ethical and political valences of their techniques of interpretation and appreciation. To empirically study non-professional practices of reading postcolonial literature or otherwise query the existence of this fictional audience is therefore to jeopardise the integrity of one of the fantasies that propels the professionalisation of reading and criticism.

The examination of postcolonial literature's reception also challenges dominant understandings of postcolonial literature that locate the possibilities of aesthetic or political resistance in the act of writing. As Bethan Benwell, James Procter, and Gemma Robinson put it in the introduction to their edited collection *Postcolonial Audiences: Readers, Viewers and Reception*, "foregrounding readers, viewers and listeners (ideal or actual) risks compromising some of the more general claims that have been made in the field around the transformative, resistant or subversive capacities of isolated postcolonial texts."[18] To invoke landmark definitions of postcolonial literature, an engagement with reading may undermine claims about postcolonial literature's ability to give voice to the marginalised and formerly colonised,[19] and to "undercut thematically and formally the discourse which supported colonization—the myths of power, the race classifications, the imagery of subordination."[20] Such celebrations of postcolonial literature can only be upheld when the modus operandi is limited to professional reading, and made to stand in for the meaning of the opus (literary work). Put another way, existing definitions of postcolonial literature hold purchase "only when texts are removed from the contingent relations they share with different reading publics, at different historical moments."[21] Postcolonial literature has a particularly contingent relationship with its different reading publics given

---

[17] Sarah Brouillette, *Postcolonial Writers in the Global Literary Marketplace* (Basingstoke: Palgrave, 2011), p. 25.

[18] Bethan Benwell, James Procter, and Gemma Robinson, eds, "Introduction," in *Postcolonial Audiences: Readers, Viewers and Reception* (London: Routledge, 2012), pp. 1–26 (p. 8).

[19] C. L. Innes, *The Cambridge Introduction to Postcolonial Literatures in English* (Cambridge: Cambridge University Press, 2007), p. 4.

[20] Elleke Boehmer, *Colonial and Postcolonial Literature: Migrant Metaphors* (Oxford: Oxford University Press, 2005), p. 14.

[21] Benwell, Procter, and Robinson, "Introduction," p. 8.

that it is "a literary field that is probably not even recognised as postcolonial by many of its readers."[22] Non-professionals, as we will see, scarcely, if ever, refer to literary texts we might call 'postcolonial' as postcolonial literature.

Most of the time, the valorisation of professional reading practices and the conflation of these practices with the meaning of postcolonial literature is implicit. It is encoded in the claims that postcolonial critics make about particular postcolonial texts. These practices of distinction are visible only when postcolonial critics talk explicitly about reading. We can see it at work, for instance, when Derek Attridge insists that "[o]ne's readings are, surely, usually improved by increasing one's knowledge about the cultural context of the work and at the same time scrutinising one's own assumptions for cultural biases".[23] Such 'improvement' requires time and money, or, more specifically, an orientation to literature (as professional waged labour) that non-professional readers cannot readily adopt. We can also see the distinction of professional practices of reading postcolonial literature at work in Elleke Boehmer's recent account of postcolonial poetics. She suggests that "a text's political vision and cultural values are sedimented or concentrated within its figures and structures, and that a postcolonial reading attentive to such figures brings that vision and those values to light."[24] She prizes those forms of reading that excavate the text's 'political unconscious,' to evoke the title of Fredric Jameson's foundational text, from which Boehmer appears to inherit the idea that texts possess political visions that are realisable by (critical) reading. Curiously, she also describes the postcolonial text as "a score for reading," and sees "literary structures not merely as giving shape to our thought as we read; rather they are our thought."[25] Cumulatively then, Boehmer seems to suggest that a symptomatic reading is the most apposite strategy of reading postcolonial literature, and that postcolonial literature compels this kind of reading in its composition. By having postcolonial literature ratify the deployment of professional reading strategies in this way, Boehmer conceals the partiality of her reading approach, which, to deploy James Procter's critique of professional reading, operates within a formalist tradition of "specialist postcolonial reading, whereby politics are 'read off' at the level of the

---

[22] Graham Huggan, "A Preface: Reflections on the Postcolonial Exotic," in *Postcolonial Audiences: Readers, Viewers and Reception*, ed. by Bethan Benwell, James Procter, and Gemma Robinson (London: Routledge, 2012), pp. xiii–xvi (p. xiv).
[23] Attridge, "Responsible Reading," p. 238.
[24] Boehmer, *Postcolonial Poetics*, p. 4.
[25] Boehmer, *Postcolonial Poetics*, p. 7 and p. 2.

aesthetic."[26] This critique is only possible because Boehmer writes explicitly about reading; most often, the promotion of professional reading, and its equation with the work of postcolonial literature, is invisibly inscribed in textual analyses of postcolonial literature. This is to say that Boehmer is not unique in locating the value of postcolonial criticism in its application of professional modes of interpretative enquiry.

The field of postcolonial studies is diverse. Over the last two decades, several scholars have engaged with the production, circulation, and reception of postcolonial literature, and in ways that explicitly challenge the cultural and political priority awarded to individual authors, isolated texts, and specialist reading approaches. Informed by sociological research, scholars including Graham Huggan and Sarah Brouillette have emphasised the materiality of postcolonial literature, raising questions about the larger communications circuit through which postcolonial texts and their authors accrue economic, social, and cultural capital.[27] Scholarship in colonial and postcolonial book history furnishes these accounts with analyses of local literary marketplaces and local readerships, and enjoys new visibility as a result of initiatives like the Postcolonial Print Cultures international research network (co-founded by Neelam Srivastava and Rajeswari Sunder Rajan). If this tradition of scholarship can be called 'materialist' for its attention to postcolonial literature as a material object involving processes of publishing, marketing, distribution, and reading, we can differentiate between this materialist tradition and what can be described as the 'textualist' tradition in which the architects of critical reading strategies tend to operate.

These terms necessarily simplify the breadth of postcolonial scholarship. To ascribe textualism to scholars responsible for the development and application of professionalised reading practices may be unfair, for instance, given that some advocates of symptomatic reading avow Marx, Althusser, and Jameson as influences. In my characterisation of such scholars as textualists, I mean to register their tendency to appropriate Marxism as an aesthetic—a way of reading—and to neglect Marxist principles of social and institutional

---

[26] James Procter, "Reading, Taste and Postcolonial Studies," *Interventions: International Journal of Postcolonial Studies*, 11.2 (2009), pp. 180–98, (p. 182).

[27] Robert Darnton offered the model of the communications circuit as a way of understanding the book publishing industry. See Robert Darnton, "What is the History of Books?" *Daedalus*, 111.3 (1982), pp. 65–83 (p. 68). For a good, updated version of the communications circuit, which takes into account changes in production and consumption, see Padmini Ray Murray and Claire Squires, "The Digital Publishing Communications Circuit," *Book 2.0*, 3.1 (2013), pp. 3–23.

critique.²⁸ My differentiation between textualism and materialism may also struggle to account for the theoretical and methodological eclecticism of postcolonialists like Gayatri Chakravorty Spivak, whose contributions to postcolonial theory attempt to reconcile poststructuralism, subaltern studies, and Marxist political theory.²⁹ But this distinction is useful, I think, because it allows us to describe two critical approaches to reading in postcolonial studies. The first and most dominant, textualism, engages in the professionalisation of reading, and treats individual authors and isolated texts as sites of political and aesthetic resistance, whose complexity requires specialist treatment. The second, materialism, examines the circulation of postcolonial literature (and sometimes criticism). Materialist criticism tends to conclude that increasingly vigilant, self-reflective modes of reading are required to undercut the disproportionate visibility awarded to certain authors, texts, and readerships, and the global culture industry's commodification of cultural difference and its transformation of radical postcolonial politics.

Materialist postcolonial criticism often centres the organisation of the global culture industry in discussions about the value of reading postcolonial literature. Materialist scholars are not simply interested in the fact that publishing tends to be located in metropolitan cities in the Global North. They have recognised, for instance, that independent presses in major Global Northern cities, such as London-based New Beacon Books and Bogle-L'Ouverture, Paris-based Présence Africaine, and Chicago-based Third World Press, have a long history of publishing African and diasporic literatures.³⁰ Peepal Tree Press based in Leeds alone has published over three hundred titles by Caribbean and Black British writers since its establishment in 1985. Nor are materialist critics primarily concerned with the proliferation of local subsidiaries of major multinational publishers and their imperilment of local, independent publishers. Several have drawn attention to the significant role of major multinational

---

²⁸ On the adoption of Marxism as an aesthetic in literary theory, see Aijaz Ahmad, *In Theory: Classes, Nations, Literatures* (London: Verso, 2000), pp. 5–6. For a slightly different account of the appropriation of Marxist critique in postcolonial studies, see Caroline Koegler's account of anti-capitalism as a brand narrative in postcolonial studies. Caroline Koegler, *Critical Branding: Postcolonial Studies and the Market* (New York: Routledge, 2018), pp. 168–89.
²⁹ For one critique of Spivak's attempts to ally her theoretical eclecticism with a practice of institutional critique, see Hayley G. Toth, "Spivak's Planetarity and the Limits of Professional Reading," *Comparative Critical Studies*, 17.3 (2020), pp. 459–78.
³⁰ Ruth Bush and Madhu Krishnan, "Print Activism in Twenty-First-Century Africa," *Wasafiri*, 31.4 (2016), pp. 1–2 (p. 1).

corporations like Penguin in the publication and distribution of books in local and international markets through the work of local subsidiaries.[31] Others have highlighted that the proximity of local, independent publishers to the material and cultural experiences of local writers cannot be taken for granted: their financial dependence on private foreign donors can compromise their visions for creative expression, enlisting them in "spreading liberal capitalist democracy globally."[32] Instead, materialist critics tend to be interested in how the spatial and economic inequalities of global publishing secure the dominance of certain aesthetic and political sensibilities, and thereby create the conditions for the production and circulation of particular texts, and for the primacy of certain kinds of cultural consumption.

Publishers typically pursue postcolonial writing that can be marketed to global audiences (by which I mean professional book reviewers and prize judges, as well as readers). Historically, this has meant the privileging of English-language novels,[33] particularly those that engage in a cosmopolitan imagination of the post-imperial world. It has also overseen investment in writers, such as Salman Rushdie, whose cultural 'hybridity' is thought to lend them a clarity of political vision that is unavailable to stridently nationalist anticolonial writers.[34] The institutionalisation of postcolonial studies has consolidated this vision of postcolonial writing, with the discipline prioritising "novelistic styles which animate a postcolonial identity

---

[31] See Robert Fraser, *Book History through Postcolonial Eyes: Rewriting the Script* (Abingdon: Routledge, 2008), p. 187.

[32] Sarah Brouillette, "On the African Literary Hustle," *Blind Field*, 14 August 2017 <https://blindfieldjournal.com/2017/08/14/on-the-african-literary-hustle/>. See also Caroline Davis's account of the CIA's investment in local book publishing and distribution as part of its strategy for international anti-communist propaganda. Caroline Davis, *African Literature and the CIA: Networks of Authorship and Publishing* (Cambridge: Cambridge University Press, 2020).

[33] Brouillette, *Postcolonial Writers in the Global Literary Marketplace*, pp. 58–59.

[34] See Timothy Brennan, *Salman Rushdie and the Third World: Myths of the Nation* (London: Palgrave Macmillan, 1989), p. 35. Salman Rushdie may exemplify this cosmopolitan postcolonial sensibility, but writers from South Asia and its diasporas more broadly have been highly successful in leveraging their 'hybrid' cultural identities in the aid of promoting liberal visions of cultural admixture. "[W]riting in English, they are available for consecration as embodying a national or supranational voice, unmoored from the more 'minor' perspectives identified with vernacular writing; they are willing to separate politics and aesthetics in the appropriate manner, to act as interpreters of the lands they have left behind, and to deploy a 'semantics of subalternity' attractive to Anglo-American readers." See Brouillette, *Postcolonial Writers in the Global Literary Marketplace*, p. 87.

as fissured, unstable, and multiply located."[35] Publishers also edit and package manuscripts according to the perceived preferences of international audiences. They act as "socio-historical filters through which culture is transmitted," to draw on Ruvani Ranasinha's account of South Asian writing.[36] Through direct editorial intervention and typesetting, together with the preparation of book covers, forewords, and prefaces, publishers produce postcolonial literature as a global commodity and transform writers into cultural authorities.[37]

Writers have assimilated the priorities of publishers and the interpretative horizons of target audiences in order to achieve success, staging representations of cultural difference for the enjoyment of international readers. As Timothy Brennan laments, since Rushdie,

> [s]everal younger writers have entered a genre of third-world metropolitan fiction whose conventions have given their novels the unfortunate feel of ready-mades. Less about an inauthenticity of vision than the context of reception, such novels—typically grouped together in the display cases of library foyers—unjustly come off as a kind of writing by numbers.[38]

For Brennan, postcolonial writing is produced in a way that anticipates its marketing by publishers and its international reception. Building on his account of the cosmopolitan character of postcolonial literature, Sarah Brouillette observes that the most commercially successful postcolonial literature possesses certain formal and political characteristics: "it is English-language fiction; it is relatively 'sophisticated' or 'complex' and often anti-realist, it is politically liberal and suspicious of nationalism; it uses a language of exile, hybridity, and 'mongrel' subjectivity."[39] In short, then, the

---

[35] Benita Parry, "The Institutionalization of Postcolonial Studies," in *The Cambridge Companion to Postcolonial Literary Studies*, ed. by Neil Lazarus (Cambridge: Cambridge University Press, 2004), pp. 66–80 (p. 73).

[36] Ruvani Ranasinha, *South Asian Writers in Twentieth-Century Britain: Culture in Translation* (Oxford: Oxford University Press, 2007), p. 15. On the role of publishers in sanitising, depoliticising, and mythologising African American writing, see also John K. Young, *Black Writers, White Publishers: Marketplace Politics in Twentieth-Century African American Literature* (Jackson: University of Mississippi Press, 2006).

[37] For example, see Huggan, *The Postcolonial Exotic*, pp. 50–55; Young, *Black Writers, White Publishers*; and Anamik Saha, "The Rationalizing/Racializing Logic of Capital in Cultural Production," *Media Industries*, 3.1 (2016), pp. 1–16.

[38] Timothy Brennan, *At Home in the World: Cosmopolitanism Now* (Cambridge, MA: Harvard University Press, 1997), p. 203.

[39] Brouillette, *Postcolonial Writers in the Global Literary Marketplace*, p. 61.

historic prioritisation of cosmopolitan, formally experimental, and niche (but globally accessible) postcolonial literature among publishers has informed the development of postcolonial writing and the conditions of its reception.

While it's easy to criticise postcolonial writers for cooperating with publishers and their target audiences in this way, the insecurity of writing as a profession places increased pressure on writers to behave entrepreneurially, including by writing in a way that anticipates and maximises opportunities for international translation and remediation.[40] Writers' appropriation of foreign values or sensibilities can also be self-conscious and subversive. The construction of an implied cosmopolitan or liberal readership in the text may compel readers to interrogate the prejudices they bring to particular texts. Sarah Brouillette identifies this staging of reception in *We Need New Names* (2013) by NoViolet Bulawayo. The novel is narrated by a young girl named Darling, who has been resettled to a shanty town under the auspices of Operation Murambatsvina, a campaign by the post-independent Zimbabwean government to eliminate informal economic activity and replace 'illegal' dwellings with new, lawful housing solutions. It is estimated that between 650,000 and 700,000 people in Zimbabwe lost their homes, their livelihoods or both as a result of Operation Murambatsvina, but as many as a fifth of Zimbabweans were affected by the policy because its dismantlement of informal economies also impacted legal trade.[41] In her reading of the novel, Brouillette suggests that its self-reflexive representation of economic instability and foreign aid "is less an instance of poverty porn than it is about the conditions of poverty porn's production" in that it "takes as one of its assumptions the prurient and in this case also humanitarian or activist gaze of the developed-world reader-consumer."[42] But to draw on Brouillette's account of 'strategic exoticism' elsewhere, the novel's staging of the humanitarian or activist gaze of the cosmopolitan consumer only "communicates at all because the author and the *actual* reader likely share assumptions about the way culture operates, and concur in their desire to exempt themselves from certain undesirable practices".[43] The novel

---

[40] Sarah Brouillette, "The Rise and Fall of the English-Language Literary Novel since World War II," in *After Marx: Literature, Theory, and Value in the Twenty-First Century*, ed. by Colleen Lye and Christopher Nealon (Cambridge: Cambridge University Press, 2022), pp. 116–30 (p. 128).

[41] Deborah Potts, "'Restoring Order'? Operation Murambatsvina and the Urban Crisis in Zimbabwe," *Journal of Southern African Studies*, 32.2 (2006), pp. 273–91 (p. 276).

[42] Brouillette, "On the African Literary Hustle," unpaginated.

[43] Brouillette, *Postcolonial Writers in the Global Literary Marketplace*, p. 43; original emphasis.

and Brouillette's reading of it rely on the real or imagined existence of a cosmopolitan audience that enjoys *We Need New Names* as poverty porn, and which does not self-consciously recognise the critique of its implied gaze in the text.

And here we arrive at one of the contradictions of materialist postcolonial scholarship. The examination of postcolonial literature's contexts of production, circulation, and consumption takes, as a corollary, the advocacy of self-conscious readings. Sarah Brouillette has criticised this tendency in the work of fellow materialist postcolonial scholar Graham Huggan. She contends: "Much though Huggan himself critiques the notion of authenticity that is key to the posturing of travellers as anti-tourists, in a sense he constructs his own reading practices [...] as more authentic, because they are less commodified".[44] But in the example above and elsewhere in *Postcolonial Writers in the Global Literary Marketplace*, Brouillette distinguishes her reading practices from those of a cosmopolitan audience. Her materialist critique of the industry of postcoloniality does not cause her to disavow the reception of postcolonial literature as complicit, but instead leads her to search for more ethical, even moral, forms of textual interpretation. As John McLeod argues, she "is persistently preoccupied by the matter of conscience in her undaunted attempt to secure viable political leverage—even if [she] does not announce, or perhaps even realize, things as such."[45] Brouillette's sociology of the global literary marketplace forms the background to a new ethics of reading, or, what McLeod describes as, "the (self-)narrativization of the postcolonial critic's guilt-ridden standpoint."[46] That is, Brouillette secures a future for reading postcolonial literature professionally by engaging in institutional and self-critique.

What I want to suggest, then, is that both textualist and materialist approaches distort reading. Textualist criticism secures the value of reading postcolonial literature against an imagined general reading public, whose practices too readily shore up or assimilate cultural difference, or else dehistoricise or depoliticise the representation of empire and the legacies of colonialism. By not addressing postcolonial literature and criticism's conditions of production, textualist criticism moreover produces an overinflated sense of reading postcolonial literature as a form of radical politics. Professional textualist reading practices "highlight the potentiality of reading while distracting us from, or mystifying, not only our own professional

---

[44] Brouillette, *Postcolonial Writers in the Global Literary Marketplace*, p. 21.
[45] John McLeod, "Postcolonial Studies and the Ethics of the Quarrel," *Paragraph*, 40.1 (2017), pp. 97–113 (pp. 109–10).
[46] McLeod, "Postcolonial Studies and the Ethics of the Quarrel," p. 106.

reading practices, but those of readers and literary audiences beyond the academy."[47] Materialist criticism is in this context a kind of corrective: it draws on sociology, book history, and political theory to address postcolonial literature's mediation by the global culture industry, and calls for the symptomatic identification of the socioeconomic and political conditions that structure the experience of reading. Yet, in the end, materialist criticism serves to broker new value for particular kinds of professional reading—those that self-consciously register their implication in the commodification and institutionalisation of a historically specific range of texts. That is to say, materialist critics have sometimes fallen foul of what James Procter calls "the resultant legitimation crisis around the status of literature," occasioned by the growing interdisciplinarity of postcolonialism, which "has placed increasing pressure on professional literary critics to read *harder* and more *earnestly*, with more *suspicion* and *scepticism*, with greater political conviction, in order to demonstrate literature's capacity for transformation."[48] Materialist postcolonial criticism therefore joins textualist criticism in failing to create adequate space for the serious study of non-professional readers. Instead, each disciplinary tradition lends imagined coherence to a community of practice that is socially, culturally, and ideologically discontinuous.

Yet the problem with textualist and materialist accounts of reading postcolonial literature is not just that they locate the value of postcolonial literature in its professional interpretation and appreciation. It is also that they divest reading of its special social significance as a material and textual activity. In failing to account for the material conditions of postcolonial literature's production, textualist postcolonial criticism overestimates the political significance of the reading experience. Textualist accounts of reading "serve to both magnify and mask the implications of reading *itself*. They make exaggerated claims for the political effects of individual literary texts, whose 'aggrandised agency' (Anderson 2006) simultaneously postpones a plausible account of the reader."[49] These claims are based on a fundamental misrecognition of reading as an imaginative, singular encounter that forestalls or disinvents the particular historical formations that determine its occasion. Materialist postcolonial criticism recuperates the materiality of the reading experience. It calls attention to the ways in which reading is structured in advance by, among other things, the globalisation of liberal-democratic values; the dominance of English; the consolidation of an Anglo-American publishing industry and book market; the commercialisation and institutionalisation of a cosmopolitan

---

[47] Procter, "Reading, Taste and Postcolonial Studies," p. 181.
[48] Procter, "Reading, Taste and Postcolonial Studies," p. 196; original emphasis.
[49] Procter, "Reading, Taste and Postcolonial Studies," p. 181; original emphasis.

diasporic sensibility, and the coeval marginalisation of anticolonial and subaltern writing; and the precaritisation and immiseration of postcolonial literature's prospective readers. Consequently, materialist criticism finds little social or political value in reading, unless it is self-consciously scrutinised for its implication in the reproduction of cultural, symbolic, and linguistic capital, and in the maintenance of liberal capitalist democracy. To conclude that reading is only valuable in its symptomatic registration of its own determination by systems of material and discursive inequity is to locate the agency of reading in its governing contexts. As Paul B. Armstrong writes in his critique of contextualist approaches to reading, when "the determinants of meaning are thought to be found elsewhere"—than within individual reading agents and their specific practices of reading—"the initial critical act is to distrust or disregard the experience of reading and to focus attention on contexts whose workings are assumed to be directing, controlling, or determining it even when the reader is unaware of them."[50] In this way, materialist approaches to reading deny the ways that reading can prompt us to change our minds, change how we view the world, or compel us to seek to effect to change in the world. Their registration of reading's determination by global-historical systems and forces becomes a form of determination itself in that it "rob[s] the situation of writing of its historicity by suppressing its futurity"—its "unpredictable destiny in the experiences of readers yet to come."[51] And so, on one hand, with textualist accounts of reading, we have a reader whose material-historical basis ceases to be existential, and becomes cultural and mutable. And, on the other hand, with materialist accounts of reading, we have a reader whose cultural biases are revealed to be historical, material, and inflexible, and which can only therefore be diagnosed.

Few claims can be made about postcolonial literature without an interrogation of the reading practices that secure its cultural, commercial, and institutional value. But, without awarding primacy either to the agency of individual readers or the contexts governing the production, circulation, and consumption of postcolonial literature, what does it mean to read postcolonial literature? What practices and values exist between the optimism of textualist postcolonial criticism and the relative pessimism of materialist postcolonial criticism? How does examining practices of reading postcolonial literature that take place outside the institutional and disciplinary setting which usually organises and remunerates the labour of reading help us to reflect on why we continue to read postcolonial literature?

[50] Paul B. Armstrong, "In Defense of Reading: Or, Why Reading Still Matters in a Contextualist Age," *New Literary History*, 42.1 (2011), pp. 87–113 (p. 90).
[51] Armstrong, "In Defense of Reading," p. 94.

A Theory of Reading Postcolonial Literature

To understand how people interpret and evaluate postcolonial literature, *Reading Postcolonial Literature* articulates a new theory of reading that captures the material and textual nature of reading as it is practised by professional and non-professional readers alike. By theorising how materiality and history mediate readers' modes of interpretation and appreciation, and, conversely, how readers' practices of aesthetic judgement reveal and interrogate the historical formation of their identities and experiences, this book intervenes in the critical prescription of materialist and textualist strategies of reading postcolonial literature. It clarifies the interaction between the politics of reading and the ethics of reading. The book's examination of reading does not advocate or seek to standardise a particular reading practice, but rather seeks to account for the diversity of postcolonial literature's actual reception. At the same time, it attempts to interrogate and clarify the connections between what we do in the classroom and in scholarship, and what takes place outside professional-academic forums.

Reader-response theory is the starting point for my theorisation of how reading postcolonial literature works. Wolfgang Iser offers a sophisticated conceptualisation of how readers differently co-produce the meaning of texts. For Iser, every instance of reading is different because reading is not a process of deciphering the meaning that lies within a text, but is instead a practice of producing meaning which is specific to each reader in the moment of reading. "[I]nterpretation," Iser insists, "is primarily a performative act rather than an explanatory one, although more often than not performance is mistaken for explanation."[52] Reading is not exhaustive. There is not one meaning of a text: for Iser, meaning lies with neither the text, nor the reader, but in the particular negotiation that takes place between them during an instance of reading. "As text and reader thus merge into a single situation," he writes, "the division between subject and object no longer applies, and it therefore follows that meaning is no longer an object to be defined, but is an effect to be experienced".[53] Readers co-produce the meaning (and value) of texts, as well as the meaning (and value) of reading. The horizon of a text is different from that of a reader. A text is also qualitatively different than reality, as it is conceived by readers. These inconsistencies, or what Iser calls 'indeterminacies,'

---

[52] Wolfgang Iser, *The Range of Interpretation* (New York: Columbia University Press, 2000), p. 7.
[53] Wolfgang Iser, *The Act of Reading: A Theory of Aesthetic Response* (Baltimore: Johns Hopkins University Press, 1978), pp. 9–10.

motivate reading and interpretation.[54] As he puts it elsewhere, reading produces a liminal space, which differentiates between reader and text: "Caused by interpretation, the liminal space is bound to contain a resistance to translation, a resistance, however, that energizes that drive to overcome it".[55] To summarise, reading produces differences. Perhaps a text implies a viewpoint that is not a reader's own, stages a world that is unlike a reader's reality, makes novel connections whose significance is not readily apparent to a reader, or sustains a style that defies the interpretative procedures ordinarily adopted by a reader. These differences are not inherent to the text, but are generated by the act of reading, in which each reader engages in a process of translating the text into something meaningful. And so, reading creates differences, but is at the same time the process by which differences are managed.

The production and management of difference is specific to each act of reading. Readers possess different epistemic resources and aesthetic sensibilities after all, and each text rewards different knowledges, interpretative protocols, and emotional attachments. To simplify by way of example, let us take the example of a reader who has read (about) Xiaolu Guo's *A Concise Chinese-English Dictionary for Lovers*,[56] a novel we will meet in more detail later in this book (see Chapter 2). Such a reader will experience Guo's recent novel *A Lover's Discourse*[57] differently than a reader who knows nothing of Guo's fiction. It is not just that the story will be familiar to readers of the first, but, more specifically, knowledge of *A Concise Chinese-English Dictionary for Lovers* might frame their production and apprehension of the meaning of *A Lover's Discourse*. We can see this in Goodreads reviews of the latter: readers describe it as "a variation," "an updated version," or "a retelling" of *A Concise Chinese-English Dictionary for Lovers*. Similarly, readers who have trained in literary reading, who have some knowledge of formal and generic conventions, or who know something of the novel's namesake, Roland Barthes's *A Lover's Discourse: Fragments*,[58] are likely to manage the singularity of *A Lover's Discourse* differently than readers who possess none of this knowledge or experience. Again, Goodreads reviews affirm this: one reader considers Guo's novel as

---

[54] Iser, *The Act of Reading*, p. 24.
[55] Iser, *The Range of Interpretation*, p. 6.
[56] Xiaolu Guo, *A Concise Chinese-English Dictionary for Lovers* (London: Vintage, 2008).
[57] Xiaolu Guo, *A Lover's Discourse* (London: Vintage, 2020).
[58] Roland Barthes, *A Lover's Discourse: Fragments*, trans. by Richard Howard (New York: Hill and Wang, 2001).

an "interesting writing back, even against Barthes," and draws attention to the text's "meta-fictional element [...] about the challenges of representation in literary fiction." The difference of reading is here determined and made traversable by way of the language of literary criticism, or 'writing back.' During reading, then, we draw on our particular knowledges and experiences to produce meaning. In the process, we identify ourselves in a particular way—as experienced readers of a particular author, or as readers schooled in the protocols of professional literary criticism, for example. In doing so, we distinguish ourselves, performing what Bourdieu describes as "[t]he conscious or unconscious implementation of explicit or implicit schemes of perception and apprehension" required for "aesthetic enjoyment."[59]

This process of self-performance and self-distinction does not eliminate a given text's own horizon, but instead helps to create the conditions for producing the meaning of the text. As Iser puts it:

> The manner in which the reader experiences the text will reflect his own disposition, and in this respect the literary text acts as a kind of mirror; but at the same time, the reality which this process helps to create is one that will be *different* from his own (since, normally, we tend to be bored by texts that present us with things we already know perfectly well ourselves). Thus we have the apparently paradoxical situation in which the reader is forced to reveal aspects of himself in order to experience a reality which is different from his own.[60]

Iser here clarifies the relationship between the material-historical and epistemic characteristics of each reader, and the virtual reality of the text. Reading only works insofar as it brings the material into contact with the textual. Reading is motivated by the fact that we have particular knowledges, experiences, orientations, and tastes—and that we have developed them under particular cultural, material, and historical conditions so that they appear to us under certain guises. Enjoying novels, for instance, holds very different associations than it did in the nineteenth century.[61] These characteristics in turn condition the predictions we make when we read, and the

---

[59] Bourdieu, *Distinction*, p. 2.
[60] Wolfgang Iser, *The Implied Reader: Patterns of Communication in Prose Fiction from Bunyan to Beckett* (Baltimore: Johns Hopkins University Press, 1974), pp. 281–82; original emphasis.
[61] On nineteenth-century attitudes about reading novels, see Kate Spowage and Hayley G. Toth, "Reading and Ideology: The Case of the Free Public Libraries Movement," *Journal of Political Ideologies*, 29.3 (2024), pp. 513–32.

different kinds of meaning we are able to derive. But this does not mean that we reproduce ourselves and our particular horizons during reading. Instead, we use our resources to read and produce meaning, and reading in turn suspends, modifies, and reconstitutes those resources. Hence, we frequently talk about being moved by reading, caused to speculate about lives and worlds different than our own, and to wonder whether we haven't previously misunderstood the conditions of our existence.

When the object of reading appears different to us—perhaps it thwarts our routinised habits of interpretation, its unfamiliar reality requires new modes of decoding, or it contains gaps, omissions, or an open ending—we are compelled to use our extratextual resources to sustain reading. Specifically, we are encouraged to synthesise these extratextual resources with what the text makes apparent. In Iser's account, this process is qualitatively different than that described by 'the hermeneutic circle' through which readers self-reflexively arrive at understanding, and where 'understanding' is defined by its proximity to the original intention of a text.[62] As he explains:

> If something nontextual, open-ended, or beyond the reach of one's own stance has to be made manageable, the hermeneutic circle may no longer be adequate. Translating open-endedness into graspability, or entropy into control, is different from translating a text into understanding, or from turning understanding into its application, or from deciphering what its disguises may either hide or reveal. Recursive looping therefore becomes a procedural necessity when it comes to charting open-endedness or controlling entropy; it operates as an input/output interchange or as systemic recursion that allows us to account for the self-maintenance of autonomous systems, particularly living systems such as those of the human organism.[63]

Recursive looping, or recursion, happens in reading situations where the object does not possess a meaning that is available for explication and application. It is an interpretative procedure that is required when an object contains the possibility of different meanings, and whose meanings develop through the practice of recursion itself. To remain with the example of *A Concise Chinese-English Dictionary for Lovers*, let's say that a reader applies their prior experience of reading work by Amy Tan, whose endorsement features prominently on the back cover of Guo's novel, to predict, anticipate, or project the meaning of Guo's novel. Or,

---

[62] See Iser, *The Range of Interpretation*, p. 7 and pp. 41–42.
[63] Iser, *The Range of Interpretation*, p. 8.

a reader draws on their embodied experience as a Chinese immigrant to produce its meaning. These 'inputs' might prove particularly fruitful for interpreting some aspects of the text, and furnish readers' existing ideas and expectations about Chinese-authored literature, Chinese immigration, or femininity and Chineseness. But if reading was simply the procedural determination of new, unfamiliar objects by way of existing knowledge and experience, few people would pursue it—let alone for pleasure. Instead, however useful we find our 'inputs,' and however unconsciously they shape our practices of reading, they remain in some way partial, and do not precomprehend the text before us. This is true even if our 'input' is a prior reading of a given text. And so, recursion takes place between our 'inputs' and what the text returns to us in its 'outputs,' and between our modified 'inputs' and the text's new 'outputs.' It is a process by which a reader alters their frame of reference for apprehending a text in the face of indeterminacy, and so modifies, even enhances, what the text can communicate. As Iser puts it:

> Recursive looping develops as an interchange between input and output, in the course of which a prediction, anticipation, or even projection is corrected insofar as it has failed to square with what it has targeted. Consequently there is—at least potentially—a dual correction: the forward feed returns as an altered feedback loop that in turn feeds into a revised input.[64]

In other words, reading is a kind of negotiation, in which a reader comes to the text with particular ideas and expectations about narrative voice or focalisation, characters, plot, style, etc., as well as how the text conforms or breaks with certain formal or generic traditions, but is repeatedly thwarted by the singularity of the text, and encouraged to revise the kinds of ideas and expectations they project into the text. Recursion is therefore a useful way of thinking about the ways that material and historical conditions are instrumental in the production of the textual meaning, and conversely how textual meaning is materially and historically produced.

While readers may adapt and reconstitute themselves and their knowledges and interpretative procedures in order to sustain reading, they do not become permanently aligned with a horizon in the text, nor are the differences between their particular material-historical vantage point and the textual vantage point of the text eradicated. Instead, reading requires

---

[64] Iser, *The Range of Interpretation*, p. 85.

that we temporarily take up a role. This role is "a selective realization of the implied reader," and can therefore by fulfilled in many different ways.[65] The role taken up by a reader is negotiated by way of recursion, and sits somewhere between their own role and disposition in the world and that of the implied reader. "Generally, the role prescribed by the text will be the stronger," Iser suggests, "but the reader's own disposition will never disappear totally; it will tend instead to form the background to and a frame of reference for the act of grasping and comprehending".[66] In short, the ways that readers traverse or translate a text is predicated on their particular material-historical circumstances, cultural associations, epistemic resources, bodily experiences, and existing relationship to literacy and literary culture. But reading requires the temporary suspension and revision of some of these aspects of a reader's material and historical existence. The implied reader, a structuring device in the text, compels readers, however briefly, to perform as another—to adopt a different subject position than they habitually perform, and to draw knowledge and experience from elsewhere.

Reader-response theory therefore complicates paradigmatic accounts of reading in postcolonial studies. In its pluralisation of reading and meaning, reader-response theory refuses to grant authority to professional judgement. In its account of the interrelation of material and textual processes in reading, where a reader's own position and historically produced disposition can be seen to engage in a dialectical process with the organising structures of a text, belies the prescription of materialist and textualist practices of reading. Its insistence that meaning and value are negotiated by readers and texts together moreover challenges the assumption that postcolonial literature possesses any inherent value that can be assimilated through reading.

Perhaps especially in my account, reader-response theory identifies the politics of reading and the ethics of reading. The ethics of reading refer to the event of reading, in which a reader sustains attention to the singularity of a text and its reorganisation of reality. They depend on close reading: "[their] primary obligation will be or ought to be [...] a love for language, a care for language and for what language can do."[67] Ethics involves the partial inhabitation of a temporary viewpoint in the text, and the concomitant deferral and transformation of a reader's own viewpoint. As such, ethical attention

---

[65] Iser, *The Act of Reading*, p. 37.
[66] Iser, *The Act of Reading*, p. 37.
[67] J. Hillis Miller, "The Ethics of Reading," *Style*, 21.2 (1987), pp. 181–91 (p. 190).

has been described as a "selfless work,"[68] or as a form of self-abandonment.[69] Elsewhere, John Guillory describes ethics as "a practice on the self," where the pursuit of pleasure, ungoverned by any moral code or political imperative, contains the possibility of self-improvement.[70] Ethical engagement happens when we suspend judgement in its moral and aesthetic forms, and when we are obliged to other ways of seeing, knowing, and desiring. As Gayatri Chakravorty Spivak puts it, the ethical is "an interruption of the epistemological, which is the attempt to construct the other as object of knowledge."[71] It is therefore something like the process by which, in Iser's account, a reader selectively realises the function of the implied reader, and takes up a role or disposition that is not their own.

The politics of reading meanwhile name the historical conditions that make reading possible for a particular real reader. They encompass processes of literary production and circulation, such as the location of writers and publishers and their orientation toward certain audiences, whether defined linguistically, geographically, culturally, or socially. Whereas the ethics of reading name a necessarily ahistorical and "disembodied" situation, as Peter D. McDonald points out,[72] the politics of reading refer to the socio-historical situation of reading. They are underpinned by questions such as "Who writes? For whom is the writing being done? In what circumstances?"[73] as well as "who reads[?]", "who publishes?", "for whom is the publishing being done?", and "in what circumstances?"[74] The politics of reading are concerned with the ways that any given reader perceives the world and its objects in particular ways, using interpretative and evaluative tools that are encoded with a material and cultural history. They are about how and why we share our readings, and why some readers and readings possess greater visibility and authority than others. They are therefore also about how the historical organisation of intellectual labour and social life in any given moment interacts with technological innovation (for example, the invention of the codex, the industrial printing press, the internet, social media), and

---

[68] Toth, "Spivak's Planetarity and the Limits of Professional Reading," p. 468.
[69] Mike Marais, "J. M. Coetzee's 'Disgrace' and the Task of the Imagination," *Journal of Modern Literature*, 29.2 (2006), pp. 75–93 (pp. 81–82).
[70] Guillory, "The Ethical Practice of Modernity," p. 39.
[71] Gayatri Chakravorty Spivak, *An Aesthetic Education in an Era of Globalization* (Cambridge, MA: Harvard University Press, 2012), p. 374.
[72] Peter D. McDonald, "The Ethics of Reading and the Question of the Novel: The Challenge of J. M. Coetzee's *Diary of a Bad Year*," *NOVEL: A Forum on Fiction*, 43.3 (2010), pp. 483–99 (p. 489).
[73] McDonald, "The Ethics of Reading," p. 487.
[74] McDonald, "The Ethics of Reading," p. 490.

patterns of cultural differentiation and discrimination that classify readers and readings into particular hierarchies of value. The politics of reading are visible in Iser's account where he argues that reading could not take place without readers engaging their "whole repertoire of historical norms and values," and in his insistence that a "reader's own disposition will never disappear totally" and "will tend instead to form the background to and a frame of reference for the act of grasping and comprehending."[75] We can also observe Iser's interest in the politics of reading in his treatment of processes of canonisation—wherein the authority of the text becomes codependent on the authority of its interpreters—and in his recognition that the secular canon has become a form of cultural capital.[76]

Reader-response theory does not treat the politics of reading and the ethics of reading as different strategies of reading, nor as different concerns for reception theorists. Rather, it tacitly suggests that the ethics of reading and the politics of reading are dialectically related. For Iser, reading is a socio-historically situated practice between a reader with a particular horizon or disposition, and a text with a particular genealogy of production and circulation. It is political. Yet, reading is also singular and arresting: its occasion involves the translation of the self and the self's horizon into a different register, and implicates the reader in the temporary performance of an unfamiliar viewpoint. It is ethical. This is not a paradox. The registration of the politics of reading is routed through the ethics of reading, or the re-recognition of the self through the othering horizon of the text. Conversely, participation in the ethics of reading depends on the politics of reading, or on the self-awareness and self-possession that makes self-translation and self-transformation possible. To adapt Iser's own description of reading as dialectical, "the familiar facilitates our comprehension of the unfamiliar, but the unfamiliar in turn restructures our comprehension of the familiar."[77] Put another way, the political conditions of our existence mediate our engagement with the situation of the text to which we are ethically obliged, but our ethical attention to the text's reconstitution of ourselves and the world transforms how we understand the political conditions of our existence. The politics of reading therefore provides access to the ethics of reading, and the ethics of reading structures the politics of reading.

How can we conceptualise the dialectical interaction of politics and ethics in practices of reading? If readers are somewhat coherent, politically speaking, but impermanent ethically speaking, and if these two states of the

---

[75] Iser, *The Act of Reading*, p. 37.
[76] See Iser, *The Range of Interpretation*, pp. 13–40.
[77] Iser, *The Act of Reading*, p. 94.

self are mutually constitutive, what sense does it make to speak of a reader? What does any of this mean for our understanding of reading postcolonial literature? Here, I want to draw together the insights of reader-response theory, and notions of the ethics and politics of reading, to present a new theory of readers that can account for their interaction with postcolonial literature. Because reading engages in politics and ethics, and therefore both invokes the self and its horizon at the same time as it transforms this self and its horizon, it is useful to think of reading as producing a self-in-the-world and a reading self. The self-in-the-world denotes readers as cognate, corporeal agents that are accustomed to performing a particular range of subject positions. The reading self refers to the personas and viewpoints we adopt when we read. They are each interfaces through which we produce meaning. The self-in-the-world possesses a specific range of affective, interpretative, and evaluative resources, developed through formal and informal education, cultural experiences, and habits of discursive engagement. Its resources provide the reader with legibility as a subject. And its mode of interpretation is mediated by these resources, which structure its forms of enquiry about the world and the way it understands itself in the world. The reading self, by contrast, is a moving and flexible horizon. One of its functions is to perform a particular version of the implied reader, but it also imaginatively actualises different viewpoints in the text (such as that of the narrative focaliser). It participates in the production of the text world. It lends the text's vision reality by making novel meanings and connections according to the ontic, epistemic, and aesthetic procedures that become apparent during the time flow of reading.

By differentiating between these two subjects of reading, I'm advancing Iser's own suggestion that it is "tenable" to think of reading as concerning two selves, because reading involves a tension between the performance of the self and the partial performance of the implied reader.[78] In his development of Iser's proposition that reading produces two selves, Paul B. Armstrong has clarified that

> [t]he performance of roles brings about a splitting or doubling that differentiates subjectivity from the subject positions it enacts. The necessity of *playing* a role makes reading (like any other norm-governed social activity) a doubled experience of "me" and "not me" in which the self is paradoxically present to itself only by acting *as* another.[79]

[78] Iser, *The Act of Reading*, p. 37.
[79] Armstrong, "In Defense of Reading," pp. 95–96; original emphasis.

To use my terms, reading involves the self (as self-in-the-world), but it is also a performance of the self (as reading self). The self-in-the-world and the reading self represent different vantage points from which to apprehend the text. The self-in-the-world engages with the text materially—as a material object, whose contents are mediated by the historical and political conditions of the present, including the socioeconomic and linguistic arrangement of literary production, circulation, and consumption. The reading self engages with the text textually—as an aesthetic and discursive object that communicates in a different register, presents objects that have no prior ontic existence or epistemic protocols, or else represents objects that are unfamiliar to readers, or in a way that is unfamiliar.

By distinguishing between the self-in-the-world and the reading self, I don't mean to suggest that some readers use the self-in-the-world to read, while others use the reading self. The self-in-the-world and the reading self are not categories of readers. Rather, they are conceptual devices that allow us to clarify what takes place when a reader practises reading. Readers do not advance in interpretation and evaluation using either the reading self or the self-in-the-world. Instead, they draw on the faculties of both. We might think of the reader as a composite subject that is not separate from the textual object, but instead enters into different relations with the text as the self-in-the-world and the reading self are engaged. The self-in-the-world and the reading self exist in dialectical tension. They interact and affect one another, mutually constituting their viewpoints during reading. The self-in-the-world makes assumptions about the textual object, drawing on its store of knowledge, and embodied and cultural experience to produce expectations from the book's cover, or the author's name. The social occasion of the text's reception is important here. It matters what motivates reading, where reading happens, and the values and beliefs about reading to which readers have access. Such circumstances play a role in the self-in-the-world's expectations of reading and predictions of a text. As Jenni Ramone has argued, culture may not determine reading, or else readers with a shared cultural background would all read the same way, but it is "economically located: readers who share a location's economy will understand the function of reading to be dependent upon that local economy," and their position within it.[80] The reading self adopts these expectations and priorities to produce meaning. But, when a text brings the reading self up short, presenting something which does not accord with a frame the reading self has assumed on behalf

---

[80] Jenni Ramone, *Postcolonial Literatures in the Local Literary Marketplace* (London: Palgrave Macmillan, 2020), p. 244.

of the self-in-the-world, the liminal space between reader and text becomes visible. The reading self returns to the self-in-the-world, and compels it to revise its assumptions and the affective, ontic, and epistemic resources on which they were based. With a modified set of expectations about the text's meaning, the reading self returns to the text to resume reading. The reading self and the self-in-the-world together develop an interstitial vantage point from which to proceed with interpretation. As this recursion takes place, the self-in-the-world is unmoored, and caused to transform its resources and the ways in which it applies them during reading. Consequently, it gains new critical distance with which to reassess its historically produced knowledge and cultural experience, and the particular discourses of morality and value it brings to bear during reading. This model of the reader helps to elaborate Iser's claim that the reader "sets the work in motion and so sets himself in motion, too."[81] The self-in-the-world situates the text in a particular way to project and precomprehend its meaning. The reading self transacts these expectations, but also uses them to identify indeterminacies. Through indeterminacy, or difference, the text obliges the reading self to return to the self-in-the-world, which must now transform the horizon through which it interprets the text, and through which the reading self's ethical attention is mediated.

Readers may at times be less inclined, or less prepared, to engage in ethical and political transformation. But some form of translation and transformation must always occur for reading to take place. That is, readers must both produce the liminal space of difference, and seek to traverse it. Iser uses the term 'colonisation' to metaphorically refer to reading practices which seek to exert the authority of the self over the text. "Whenever the presuppositions of the register are superimposed on the subject matter," he writes, "the liminal space is colonized by the concepts brought to bear".[82] Such practices eliminate any differences between reader and text in such a manner as to produce the text as predictable, calculable, and self-affirming. For Iser, this is not reading at all. "Such a colonization," he argues, "converts interpretation into an act that determines the intended meaning of the subject matter. When this happens, interpretation ceases".[83] Hence, this book insists that while partial and selective reading, not reading, and non-understanding may be disavowed by professional postcolonial critics, they remain practices of reading all the same in that they quite clearly respond to the text as different from the self.

[81] Iser, *The Act of Reading*, p. 21.
[82] Iser, *The Range of Interpretation*, p. 151.
[83] Iser, *The Range of Interpretation*, p. 151.

As you read this book, then, my theory of reading asks that you suspend investment in any particular, professional practices of reading postcolonial literature in order to observe that what we do as professionals is specific, but also belongs to a social practice that is performed by others—by non-professionals. For both professional and non-professional readers, the act of reading is productive: it produces meaning and value. It is recursive: it involves the application of locally specific understandings of reading (as labour or leisure, or as entertaining or informative, for instance), and reader-specific knowledge, experience and desires, and the periodic interrogation, transformation, and revision of those resources. Reading is both material and textual, organised by the ethics of reading and the politics of reading. A model of a discontinuous reading subject, with a reading self and a self-in-the-world, helps us to comprehend the material-textual, ethical-political character of reading. The concepts of the reading self and the self-in-the-world also capture the ways that reading is a kind of performance through which we instantiate ourselves and roleplay others and other viewpoints.

On Method and Structure

Reading Postcolonial Literature tests and refines this theory of reading by applying it to four reception contexts. I use my theory of reading to analyse and re-evaluate professional and non-professional practices of reading different postcolonial texts. Each chapter collates and close reads reading data already available in the public domain, hosted by world media, critical studies, and social media platforms. My purpose is not to be exhaustive, but rather to be illustrative. In looking at social media platforms as sites for non-professional reading, I follow the example of reading scholars, who have analysed practices of reading on online social reading sites like Goodreads in order to locate and understand the practices of non-professional readers, who otherwise "constitute a nonruling group with limited access to having a voice on mainstream media, and low visibility and authority within the formal institutions of literary culture."[84] As Federico Pianzola has recently argued:

> Digital social reading spaces and practices are often seen as a way to participate in cultural discussions otherwise dominated by a small or

---

[84] Beth Driscoll and DeNel Rehberg Sedo, "Faraway, So Close: Seeing the Intimacy in Goodreads Reviews," *Qualitative Inquiry*, 25.3 (2018), pp. 248–59 (p. 249).

elite group of readers, namely individuals belonging to the publishing and media industries, and to educational institutions.[85]

Platforms like Goodreads and Amazon customer reviews remain hierarchically organised, and not all readers and reviews accrue value equally. Readers who demonstrate cultural capital or perform authority on these platforms, for example, can influence others' public performances of reading (if not the way they read privately).[86] In recent times, there have been instances where influential reviewers have secured a negative consensus about particular texts, and even successfully called for the revision or withdrawal of certain books.[87] But, as Simone Murray argues in *The Digital Literary Sphere: Reading, Writing, and Selling Books in the Internet Era*, "Social media has certainly rendered reviewing more democratically accessible and interactive than the traditional print reviewing paradigm".[88] For this reason, social media platforms like Goodreads and Amazon customer reviews have proved popular with non-professional readers who wish to talk about their experiences of reading particular texts.[89]

For critics of amateur book reviewing, the notion of an interpretative and cultural democracy generates "fears of radical cultural relativism: kneejerk judgments by an ignorant, unqualified mass; the reduction of nuanced critique to crude quantitative measures; and the potential for online systems to be 'gamed' in various ways."[90] And certainly, the quantitative values conferred upon literature on platforms like Goodreads and Amazon

---

[85] Federico Pianzola, "Sociality and Seriality in Digital Reading: Two Extra Memos for this Millennium," in *The Routledge Companion to Literary Media*, ed. by Astrid Ensslin, Julia Round and Bronwen Thomas (Abingdon: Routledge, 2023), pp. 479–89 (p. 483).

[86] DeNel Rehberg Sedo, "'I Used to Read Anything That Caught My Eye, But…': Cultural Authority and Intermediaries in a Virtual Young Adult Book Club," in *Reading Communities from Salons to Cyberspace*, ed. by DeNel Rehberg Sedo (New York: Palgrave Macmillan, 2011), pp. 101–22 (pp. 108–10).

[87] See Chiara Bullen, "'Your Bookshelf Is Problematic': Progressive and Problematic Publishing in the Age of COVID-19," in *Bookshelves in the Age of the COVID-19 Pandemic*, ed. by Corinna Norrick-Rühl and Shafquat Towheed (Sham: Palgrave Macmillan, 2022), pp. 69–92.

[88] Simone Murray, *The Digital Literary Sphere: Reading, Writing, and Selling Books in an Internet Era* (Baltimore: John Hopkins University Press, 2018), p. 113.

[89] Amazon established its customer reviews platform in 1997. Goodreads was founded in 2006 and purchased by Amazon in 2013. For a critical account of Amazon's monopoly on the sale and consumption of books, see Mark McGurl, *Everything and Less: The Novel in the Age of Amazon* (London: Verso, 2021).

[90] Murray, *The Digital Literary Sphere*, p. 112.

customer reviews hold little to no analytical value. At the time of writing, *A Concise Chinese-English Dictionary for Lovers* has a mean score of 3.55 out of 5 stars on Goodreads, which tells us that it is of very similar quality to the second instalment of the *Twilight* saga *New Moon* by Stephenie Meyer (3.58 out of 5 stars). On Amazon, the product has an average rating of 4.3 out of 5 stars, based on over four hundred global reviews, which makes it quantitively the same as a portable ball pump I bought from the online retailer back in May 2023. But the assumption that non-professional readers make crude pronouncements about literature, that they have a shallow or deficient understanding of literature, and that they constitute a uniformly ignorant reading public, belongs to a tradition of abstraction similar to that which dominates discussions of world and postcolonial literature's audiences.

My treatment of these platforms as proxies for non-professional reading is necessary, because non-professional reading otherwise tends to take place privately. As John Guillory has argued, one of the things that distinguishes professional and lay reading is that "lay reading is largely a *solitary* practice. Its scenes of communal reading are seldom formally organized, but rather occur by chance or in an ad hoc manner."[91] Professional reading, by contrast, is intensely public. As Guillory puts it:

> [T]his reading is a *communal* practice. Even when the scholar reads in privacy, this act of reading is connected in numerous ways to communal scenes; and it is often dedicated to the end of a public and publishable 'reading.' It envisions an audience of students or scholars, in the classroom or in print. These performed 'readings' thus submit to the response and judgment of other professional readers.[92]

The comparative study of professional and non-professional practices of reading postcolonial literature therefore requires that we either focus on a slightly deprofessionalised version of professional practices of reading (for example, by examining the private, unpublished reading practices of professionals), or on a relatively professionalised brand of non-professional reading (for instance, by exploring the public or published reading practices of non-professionals). This book takes the latter approach, through a comparative analysis of the public, published readings of professionals and non-professionals, unsolicited by myself or any research team, and already available in the public domain. It yet recognises that the platforms through which non-professional readers make their reading practices

---

[91] Guillory, "The Ethical Practice of Modernity," p. 32; original emphasis.
[92] Guillory, "The Ethical Practice of Modernity," pp. 31–32; original emphasis.

public mediate their discursive engagement. On Amazon customer reviews and Goodreads, for instance, users are encouraged to be evaluative, and are obliged to award texts a particular numeric value (from one to five stars). These platforms also operate as social networks in which users "perform their identities as readers,"[93] including by forming connections with other users. This is most explicit on Goodreads, where users can publicly 'like' or comment on other readers' reviews, and 'follow' or 'friend' other users. Amazon customer reviews, by contrast, is more of an additional online social reading facility that complements the site's primary e-commerce service, by providing Amazon with free, user-generated content to better sell products. Many Amazon reviewers nonetheless use the service in a similar way to Goodreads users, performing as readers as often as consumers, with the aim of demonstrating their relationship to reading and book culture as well as any given text.

The performance of non-professional reading practices on these platforms is therefore qualitatively different from private practices of non-professional reading, in that it is structured by different motivations, social goals, and discursive conventions. But analysing these performances of non-professional reading as practices of reading is viable, I think, because the performance of professional reading is similarly mediated by its social function, which is to demonstrate expertise and authority before different publics for (potential) remuneration. Academic literary criticism and non-professional book reviewing have in common that they are both socially mediated performances of reading. My analysis of different kinds of public practices of reading postcolonial literature therefore enables the discussion of reading as a social activity. Through the study of such performances of reading, we can observe how professional and non-professional practices of reading alike serve social goals, from the performance of identity to cultural distinction. To talk about reading in the seminar room or book club, or to write about reading in a journal article or customer review is to make the experience of reading legible as a social practice.

When I analyse the reading practices shared by non-professional readers on social media platforms, I protect their privacy by not disclosing their usernames. This approach corresponds with that of Beth Driscoll and DeNel Rehberg Sedo, who argue that, although such data is "publicly visible" and "available for analysis," users "most likely did not expect their reviews to be aggregated and studied" when they originally posted them.[94]

---

[93] Lisa Nakamura, "'Words with Friends': Socially Networked Reading on *Goodreads*," *PMLA*, 128.1 (2013), pp. 239–43 (p. 240).

[94] Driscoll and Rehberg Sedo, "Faraway, So Close," pp. 250–51.

Where non-professional readers choose to indirectly identify themselves in the body of the review text—for example, as a regular or lapsed reader, as a student or teacher, or by a particular nationality, ethnicity, race, gender, or religious affiliation—I treat these performances of identity as inseparable from the performance of reading, and as part of my object of analysis. As we will see, non-professional readers frequently call attention to the role of aspects of their identity in the aesthetic and moral judgements they make about different texts. They also evoke their identity in discussions about what motivates their reading, as well as in commentaries on the value of reading in general and of reading particular texts.

Chapter Breakdown

Each chapter of this book focuses on the reception of a single text with the aim of discussing a single theoretical issue about reading in postcolonial studies. Cumulatively, they seek to challenge our assumptions about reading in postcolonial studies, and demonstrate that the further study of reading in the discipline can enrich our understanding of what reading postcolonial literature is and does for its readers. My chosen texts are all novels, and share a relationship to London. Salahuddin Chamchawala and Gibreel Farishta hurtle toward ('Proper') London from the sky at the beginning of *The Satanic Verses*. Zhuang 'Z' Xiao Qiao arrives in London to study English at the beginning of *A Concise Chinese-English Dictionary for Lovers*. The unnamed narrator of *Harare North* claims asylum in Britain, and subsequently resides in Brixton, London. And while the setting of *Noughts & Crosses* is ill-defined, it has been firmly relocated to London by the television adaptation *Noughts + Crosses* released in March 2020. Each of them was also first published by an imprint or division of Penguin or Random House, which merged in 2013 to form the major multinational publisher Penguin Random House. *The Satanic Verses* was first published by Viking (at the time owned by Penguin); *A Concise Chinese-English Dictionary* was originally published by Chatto & Windus (at the time an imprint of Random House); *Harare North* was first published by Johnathan Cape (an imprint of Random House); and *Noughts & Crosses* was published by Doubleday (a division of Random House). In these ways, they are archetypal examples of postcolonial literature, and their reception has the potential to shed light on the reading and reception of postcolonial literature more broadly.

Chapter 1 revisits the reception of *The Satanic Verses*. Often referred to as 'the Rushdie affair,' the reception of Salman Rushdie's *The Satanic Verses* remains "the most notorious instance of postcolonial reading to date."[95] Its reception was both extreme and extremely public. It was spectacularised by book burnings and bans, protests and counterprotests, and the Iranian Ayatollah's pronouncement of the fatwā. Over forty years later, the book and its author remain highly controversial, as testified by the recent attempted murder of Salman Rushdie at the Chautauqua Institution in Chautauqua, New York in August 2022. Against the prevailing narrative of the Rushdie affair, according to which the novel's reception exemplified and exacerbated cultural and religious differences, I argue that the text's divisive reception clarifies the different registers of professional and non-professional reading communities. Non-professional readers, including faith leaders, religious organisations, and religious scholars, criticised the novel for its depiction of Islam, with several arguing that fiction should not be permitted to defame and defile the Prophet—still less be celebrated for doing so. These critics of *The Satanic Verses* represent reading as a material practice, involving particular selves-in-the-world whose cultural, religious, and aesthetic sensibilities are liable to be mocked, offended, and delegitimised by the text's revisionist history. Literary professionals, including writers, scholars, and critics, tended to defend the novel by appealing to its fictional form, and by insisting that fiction is protected by the right to free speech, including the right to offend. By imbibing this specific vision of the literary with cultural and political significance, supporters of the novel made defences of *The Satanic Verses* available for co-optation by politicians about the place of Muslims and Islam in Britain and the world. But their primary argument was that the reading is a textual practice, wherein each reader's reading self is compelled to suspend conceptions and self and world in the face of the singularity or literariness of the text. In my account of professional and non-professional practices of reading *The Satanic Verses*, I trace how readers fail to sustain these orthodoxies of reading—where materialist accounts of the text as bad history rely on textual practices, and where textualist accounts of the novel as magic realist literary fiction depend on a material imaginary. I argue that rethinking the Rushdie affair as a debate about reading is useful for three key reasons. First, it helps to clarify the performative nature of reading, where identifying as a reader or non-reader, or talking about a text in a particular way can be understood as a way of performing the self, and of communicating and connecting with different social groups. Second, it helps to account for variety in the novel's reception, including examples of religious, non-professional defences of the text, and secular, professional criticisms

---

[95] Benwell, Procter, and Robinson, "Introduction," p. 17.

of the text. In doing so, it complicates assumptions about the relationship between reading and identity that flourished during the Rushdie affair, and which have persisted in critical and news media reflections on the novel's reception. Third, and finally, it serves to illustrate that, notwithstanding the claims that readers make about reading, reading is not uniformly a material or textual activity, but always involves the dialectical engagement of the self-in-the-world and the reading self.

Building on Chapter 1's elaboration of the complex relationship between reading postcolonial literature and identity, Chapter 2 explores reading and address through a focus on the reception of Xiaolu Guo's translational novel *A Concise Chinese-English Dictionary for Lovers*. It argues that critics have dismissed the novel's readership as 'Western' or 'English-speaking' through a focus on its addressed audience, or implied reader. This has in part to do with such accounts' engagement with theories of translation. Theories like Lawrence Venuti's, I show, presume an explicit and direct relationship between translation and reading, and implicitly suggest that the interpretative and ideological work performed by translation can only be revealed and overcome by professional reading practices. On the basis that Venuti is capable of behaving as a reader, not an addressee—of practising a reading that is not implied—Chapter 2 makes the case that other readers might also negotiate the question of address in their own reading practices. By looking at professional and non-professional practices of reading *A Concise Chinese-English Dictionary for Lovers*, I draw attention to the ways that readers differently negotiate their own identity and that of the addressee through the experience of reading the text and its protagonist. By contrast with professional postcolonial critics, non-professional readers regularly relate to the novel's protagonist as real. This realist aesthetic, I show, is reparative in that it intervenes in the text's elliptical naming of the protagonist. But it also comes with risks: for several non-professional readers, the experience of being frustrated in their desires and expectations of relation produces disidentification with the protagonist, and disappointment in the book and its author. It leads one non-professional reader to criticise the novel for addressing a literary-professional audience that rewards difficult, 'clever' fiction.

Developing Chapter 2's conclusions about the perceived 'difficulty' of postcolonial literature, Chapter 3 focuses on reading experiences of difficulty. It identifies non-understanding as a key point of continuity between professional and non-professional practices of reading postcolonial literature. In its analysis of the reception of *Harare North* by Brian Chikwava, this chapter considers how and why readers respond in different ways to the difficulty of postcolonial literature, and ultimately makes a case for the legitimacy of non-understanding as a reading practice. I first explore readers' different interpretations and appreciations of the novel's narrative voice. Non-professional readers frequently attribute the text's difficulty to its narrative voice, which they variously describe as 'Zimbabwean,' 'pidgin,' and 'Shona.' With reference to Krishnan (2014) and Ndlovu (2016), I draw attention to a dominant critical view according to which such responses represent exoticist or orientalist modes of perception, typical of non-professional, non-African readers. I dispute such simplifications of the relationship between reading and identity. I highlight that the narrative voice's cultural and geopolitical coordinates are corroborated by paratextual features such as the book's cover and blurb, as well as epitextual phenomena such as Chikwava's receipt of the Caine Prize for African Writing five years before the publication of *Harare North*. I furthermore show that such interpretations are not solely the preserve of an exoticising and othering cosmopolitan audience, but are also enacted by amateur and professional readers who self-identify as African or Zimbabwean. While African and Zimbabwean scholars praise the 'authenticity' of the narrative voice, Zimbabwean non-professional readers critique its staged authenticity in insightful ways. Through an analysis of the identity claims made by readers to support their interpretations of the narrative voice's cultural, linguistic, and geographic associations, I demonstrate that, although professional credentials or local and national identity are often leveraged to authorise readings, there is no clear consensus among readers—professional, Zimbabwean, or otherwise. Thus, I develop Benwell, Procter, and Robinson's assertion that readers come to possess 'reading identities'[96] by highlighting that readers' interpretations exceed (institutional) group membership as well as cultural and geopolitical coordinates. I make the case that reading is partial, based on processes of selection, prioritisation, and elimination. Non-understanding, I conclude, defies critical definition as reading failure, and should instead be understood as a form of reading (and a valuable one) in and of itself.

From my concern in Chapter 3 with the viability of non-professional interpretative protocols like non-understanding for reading postcolonial literature, I move in Chapter 4 to explore the reception of a text primarily read by non-professional readers. I begin by arguing that postcolonial studies has tended to overlook popular culture, and to associate popular

---

[96] Bethan Benwell, James Procter, and Gemma Robinson, "'That May Be Where I Come from but That's Not How I Read': Diaspora, Location and Reading Identities," in *Postcolonial Audiences: Readers, Viewers and Reception*, ed. by Bethan Benwell, James Procter, and Gemma Robinson (London: Routledge, 2012), pp. 43–56 (p. 45).

cultural consumption with aesthetic vulgarity, cultural vacuity, and political compromise. I develop Stuart Hall's definition of 'the popular' as a struggle to argue that reading is an important avenue through which the relationship between a popular cultural form and the dominant culture is expressed. I proceed to explore the reception of *Noughts & Crosses* as a site of competing popularities, in which non-professional readers, including cultural and educational organisations, have rearticulated the novel's relationship to the state and the nation in the process of elaborating its educational value. While these non-professional actors have significantly influenced the reception of *Noughts & Crosses*, readers on online social media platforms, I show, regularly flout established interpretative frameworks to complicate the novel's perceived didactic value. *Noughts & Crosses* may be popular. It may originate with the national-popular case of Stephen Lawrence's murder. It may have achieved mass, commercial popularity with the help of educational and cultural agencies. And it may have secured state popularity in the process of the latter. But, in the absence of a professional readership, non-professional readers continue to criticise and renegotiate the novel's popularity, and its purported didactic function. Perhaps professional postcolonial critics will never pay popular texts the same attention as their 'literary' counterparts. But they should, I conclude, for while popular literature itself can be deceptive and politically compromised, its audiences are not fools, and often make perceptive critiques of the cultural hollowness and ideological work of popular texts.

In this book's conclusion, I perform a cursory sociological analysis of postcolonial studies as a discipline, with the aim of clarifying the challenges and possibilities of the UK higher education context. I first offer an account of how the discipline's understanding of reading is mediated by political change and institutional interpretations of government policy. Institutional responses to the managed 'crisis of the humanities,' I argue, have not challenged the priority awarded to reading in postcolonial studies, but have rather expanded upon the discipline's own evaluation of professional reading to define the study of postcolonial literature as culturally and economically valuable in a global job market. While materialist and sociological scholarship has enabled critiques of the discipline's professionalisation of reading, its methods and conclusions have been neglected in its circulation and reception. I focus on the anthology as a site of disciplinary reproduction, where sociological critiques of the discipline can be incorporated as part of the professional interpretative repertoire of postcolonial studies. I conclude by suggesting that the discipline's own mediation by issues of production, circulation, and reception (and larger structuring political-economic forces) compels us to read the discipline. Drawing once again on my theory of reading, I consider what it means to read postcolonial studies, not as the reading self who merely assimilates its singular authority, but as both the reading self and the self-in-the-world. If, for the reading self, the discipline's claims about reading are compelling, for the self-in-the-world, they are specific—historically imperative at different times, and socially meaningful in the context of professionalisation and institutionalisation, but also different than the claims we might make about reading in general, or about reading postcolonial literature outside of the university. Our students can help us in reading the discipline, for their position as neither professionals nor non-professionals gifts them the ability to denaturalise what we take for granted about reading in postcolonial studies.

Reading Postcolonial Literature therefore addresses itself to teachers as well as researchers of postcolonial literature. This is a book that asks its readers to consider whether existing approaches to the study of reading postcolonial literature adequately engage with the conditions of postcolonial literature's global circulation and reception, especially in the context of the discipline's claims about the power of reading and of individual postcolonial texts. Postcolonial studies has left important questions about reading unanswered, and curtailed the pursuit of still other questions by taking for granted the authority and distinctiveness of professional reading practices. This book scrutinises assumptions about reading that, if not specific to postcolonial studies, have been articulated in specific ways in the discipline to delegitimise non-professional reading practices. This book seeks to model new ways of thinking about and teaching the relationship between professional and non-professional practices of reading postcolonial literature, and invites new ways of relating to our students that recognises their value as cultural intermediaries between the discipline and its complicated outside.

CHAPTER 1

Reading and the Rushdie Affair

On 12 August 2022, Salman Rushdie was attacked as he was being introduced at a speaking engagement at the Chautauqua Institution in Chautauqua, New York. More than a thousand people had gathered in the institution's open-air amphitheatre to listen to the author in conversation with Henry Reese. Reese, alongside his wife, visual artist Diane Samuels, co-founded City of Asylum, a non-profit organisation in Pittsburgh, Pennsylvania that provides sanctuary to exiled writers. Reese and Samuels were inspired to found City of Asylum after hearing Rushdie refer to the Cities of Asylum network in Europe during a talk in Pittsburgh in 1997, and Rushdie and Reese had since become friends. During the attack, the author sustained around a dozen stab wounds.[1] Reese was also injured as he held down the assailant's legs to prevent him inflicting further harm upon the author.[2] Rushdie was left permanently blind in his right eye, and continues to receive physical therapy for nerve damage on his left hand. In an exclusive interview with the *New York Post* from the Chautauqua County Jail, five days after the attack, his attacker, Hadi Matar, from Fairview, New Jersey, said that he had watched many lectures by the author on YouTube, and didn't like him. Matar claimed that Rushdie had

---

[1] In an exclusive interview with *The New Yorker*, Rushdie said that he may have been stabbed as many as fifteen times, but interviewer and writer David Remnick writes that the author was stabbed around a dozen times: David Remnick, "The Defiance of Salman Rushdie," *The New Yorker*, 6 February 2023 <https://www.newyorker.com/magazine/2023/02/13/salman-rushdie-recovery-victory-city> [accessed 28 February 2023].

[2] Bevan Hurley, "Salman Rushdie Moderator Henry Reese Reveals Black Eye and Knife Wound from Attack on Author," *Independent*, 18 August 2022 <https://www.independent.co.uk/news/world/americas/salman-rushdie-henry-reese-attack-author-b2147766.html> [accessed 28 February 2023].

attacked Islam and Muslims.³ Drawing on excerpts from that interview, several media outlets from around the world ran similar headlines: "Sir Salman Rushdie Attack Suspect 'Only Read Two Pages' of *Satanic Verses*" (*BBC*), "Salman Rushdie Attack Suspect Says He Only Read Two Pages of *Satanic Verses*" (*Independent*), "Hadi Matar Breaks Silence on Salman Rushdie Attack, Says Read Only Two Pages of *The Satanic Verses*" (*DNA*), "Salman Rushdie Attacker: 'I Only Read Two Pages of His Book'" (*Al Bawaba*), "'I Don't Like Him': Salman Rushdie's Alleged Attacker Claims He's Only Read Two Pages of Satanic Verses" (*Deadline*).⁴ The attack on Salman Rushdie became legible, if neither understandable nor defensible, through Matar's discursive engagement with *The Satanic Verses*. Whether perceived as dishonest or defiant, the assailant's refusal to read the text came to signify both his intolerance and the illegitimacy of his beliefs.

The attempted murder of Salman Rushdie over thirty years after the publication of *The Satanic Verses* brings into sharp relief the seriousness of the novel's reception, as well as the ways that the Rushdie affair endowed reading and not reading with cultural and political significance. Reading and the refusal to read were each attached to distinctive and opposing identities. At the same time, the mediation of the attack by international news media, and the consequential role played by the social media platform YouTube (at least, according to Rushdie's attacker), recalls the iterative character of

---

3 Steven Vago and Ben Kesslen, "Salman Rushdie Attacker Praises Iran's Ayatollah, Surprised Author Survived: Jailhouse Interview," *New York Post*, 17 August 2022 <https://nypost.com/2022/08/17/alleged-salman-rushdie-attacker-didnt-think-author-would-survive/> [accessed 28 February 2023].

4 "Sir Salman Rushdie Attack Suspect 'Only Read Two Pages' of *Satanic Verses*," *BBC*, 18 August 2022 <https://www.bbc.co.uk/news/entertainment-arts-62588666> [accessed 28 February 2024]; Graeme Massie, "Salman Rushdie Attack Suspect Says He Only Read Two Pages of *Satanic Verses*," *Independent*, 17 August 2022 <https://www.independent.co.uk/news/world/americas/crime/salman-rushdie-attack-hadi-matar-satanic-verses-b2147081.html> [accessed 28 February 2024]; Caroline Frost, "'I Don't Like Him': Salman Rushdie's Alleged Attacker Claims He's Only Read Two Pages Of *Satanic Verses*," *Deadline*, 19 August 2022 <https://deadline.com/2022/08/salman-rushdie-alleged-attacker-hadi-matar-read-two-pages-satanic-verses-1235096009/> [accessed 28 February 2024]; *DNA* Web Team, "Hadi Matar Breaks Silence on Salman Rushdie Attack, Says Read Only Two Pages of *The Satanic Verses*," *DNA*, 18 August 2022 <https://www.dnaindia.com/world/report-hadi-matar-breaks-silence-on-salman-rushdie-attack-says-read-only-2-pages-of-the-satanic-verses-2977430> [accessed 28 February 2024]; "Salman Rushdie Attacker: 'I Only Read Two Pages of His Book'," *Al Bawaba*, 18 August 2022 <https://www.albawaba.com/node/salman-rushdie-attacker-%E2%80%98i-only-read-two-pages-his-book-1487905> [accessed 28 February 2024].

the original debate about the novel as it played out in newspapers, radio broadcasts, and television journalism. Certainly, the Rushdie affair of the late 1980s travelled slower than news of his attack in 2022. As Rushdie himself reflected in a recent interview with *The New York Times*, timed to coincide with the publication of his new memoir, *Knife: Mediations After an Attempted Murder* (2024), in the late 1980s, "the most sophisticated method of transmission was the fax machine, and that kept the lid on it [the affair] to some degree."[5] But, the increasing globalisation and socialisation of news since the Rushdie affair did not simply ensure that news of Rushdie's attack reached a larger audience more quickly, but that the event acquired an immediacy and dramatic proximity that never obtained in coverage about *The Satanic Verses* or its reception. On the day of the attack itself, twenty-four-hour news channels presented remote viewers with amateur photography of the aftermath, hastily captured by live audiences in the amphitheatre on smartphones. Matar was identified quickly, and his jailhouse interview five days after the attack gifted audiences the opportunity to know his disinterest in the novel intimately. Yet for all the differences between the mediation of the original debate about *The Satanic Verses*, and the hypermediated coverage of Rushdie's attack, the latter ensured primarily that Matar could be dismissed as a non-reader of the novel, and that conclusions could be redrawn about the religious fanaticism and intolerance of *The Satanic Verses*' (non-)reading communities. In this way, media coverage of the attack on Rushdie revived the discursive parameters of the Rushdie affair, including the ascription of *The Satanic Verses*' critics as Muslim non-readers, the assignation of identity with deterministic power over practices of reading and not reading, and the tendency to generalise about (non-)reading communities based on the actions and beliefs of individuals. Rushdie himself has played a key role in translating the attack through the dominant tropes of the affair. For instance, in the same interview with *The New York Times*, the author reiterated that *The Satanic Verses*' critics were "almost universally" non-readers.[6]

It is in this context that this chapter returns to the Rushdie affair, with the aim of complicating the relationship between reading and identity that it established, and which has been refurbished over thirty years later in news coverage of the recent attack on the author. I revisit the reception of the novel through an engagement with international news and media publications,

---

[5] The Ezra Klein Show, "Salman Rushdie Is Not Who You Think He Is," *The New York Times*, 26 April 2024 <https://www.nytimes.com/2024/04/26/opinion/ezra-klein-podcast-salman-rushdie.html> [accessed 14 May 2024].

[6] The Ezra Klein Show, "Salman Rushdie Is Not Who You Think He Is."

letters, and academic publications (including Rushdie's own essays). My aim in this chapter is not to uncover practices of reading *The Satanic Verses* that were marginalised in debates about the novel or its reception, but rather to reinterpret practices of reading the novel that held great influence over the public imagination of the Rushdie affair. One of my main sources in this chapter is *The Rushdie File*, edited by Lisa Appignanesi and Sara Maitland, which attempts to collate "the best and most representative materials that fairly and fully reflect all points of view."[7] In revisiting practices of reading the novel and media coverage of its reception, I trace the ways that readers and commentators established a relationship between reading and identity. It was not simply that reading became predictable by religious or cultural affiliation, but that religious or cultural belief was seen to compel and organise practices of reading.

I complicate this dominant narrative of the Rushdie affair by suggesting that in fact one of the major divisions in the reception of the novel was between literary professionals, whose secular humanist values made them easy allies of the political and punditry class in Britain, and non-professionals, including faith leaders, members of religious organisations, and religious scholars, whose expectations of recognition and relation became sources of displeasure and offence. Using my original reading model, I argue that critical (often non-professional) readers tended to materialise *The Satanic Verses,* and to express concern about the ways that the text undermines the originary narratives of Islam as well as Islamic religious practices. Upon encountering reimagined events from Islamic history and stereotypes of the Prophet and his followers, such readers' reading selves are moved to enlist the knowledges and experiences of their selves-in-the-world, which project the text as harmfully inaccurate. The materialist reading practices of critical readers leads them to engage in a politics of reading that questions both Rushdie's ability to write as a native informant and the cultural market for Islamophobia. Supportive (often professional) readers, by contrast, tend to textualise the narrative, and to draw attention to its generic status as fiction. Such readers short-circuit the role of their selves-in-the-world in the experience of fictionality and literariness, and emphasise the reality-suspending activities of their reading selves. Both critical and supportive readers yet struggle to sustain these orthodoxies of reading. Their commentaries at times signal the hybrid character of reading. Despite affirming that reading is either material or textual, readers on both

[7] Lisa Appignanesi and Sara Maitland, *The Rushdie File* (Syracuse: Syracuse University Press, 1990).

sides of the debate in practice adopt and describe practices of reading that are both material and textual. The Rushdie affair, I conclude, is instructive for thinking about practices of reading postcolonial literature, for it reveals the complex relationship between reading and identity, and the historic deployment of professional identity as a practice of distinction.

The Rushdie Affair: From Social Conflict to Cultural Conflict

In a 1989 essay for *The Bookseller*, Rushdie reflected that, in writing the novel, his aim was not to shore up atavistic or static notions of identity, but rather to consider how new forms of selfhood emerge through the theme of migration. He wrote:

> I did not want to write a kind of sociologically based fiction about how terrible it is today for black people in England. I wanted to write a novel which at its most fundamental level is about metamorphosis— the nature of it, the process by which it happens, its effect on the metamorphosed self and on the world around it, and its link with the act of travelling. Not least because the pressures exerted by migration are one of the classic contemporary locations of metamorphosis—what I call 'translation': a carrying across of the self into another place and another language. I am fascinated by how the classic roots of the self in language, society and place are disrupted by the act of migration: you suddenly find yourself in a new culture with different rules, and a new language, and for a while you flounder. The self is forced to find different principles on which to invent itself. That's what I was really trying to write about.[8]

Rushdie here celebrates the fluidity and flexibility of identity. Migration is, for the author, a lens through which practices of self-reinvention become visible. Accordingly, *The Satanic Verses*, at least on one level, depicts the migration and transformation of its central protagonists Saladin Chamcha(wala) and Gibreel Farishta. It is ironic, then, that one of the legacies of the Rushdie affair was the reproduction of cultural identities, and the refurbishment of patterns of cultural differentiation. The novel's highly publicised reception

[8] Salman Rushdie, quoted in Bhikhu Parekh, "The Rushdie Affair and the British Press," in *Text Wars: Communication, Censorship, Freedom and Responsibility*, ed. by Hilda David and Francis Jarman (Oxford: Oxford University Press, 2021), pp. 62–85 (p. 63).

made available ways of performing identity through practices of reading. By the time that the novel was published in Britain in 1988, one could express not only cultural and political beliefs, but cultural membership simply by stating that they had read the novel or intended to do so. How did *The Satanic Verses* become an object of identity construction? What performances of identity did the Rushdie affair make possible? What performances of identity did the debate about the novel conceal?

Shortly after *The Satanic Verses* was published in the UK, and before its global circulation, identity categories were emerging before its prospective readers. Syed Shahabuddin, a member of the Lok Sabha (the House of the People, the lower house of India's bicameral legislature), successfully campaigned for the book to be banned in India on the grounds that it posed a threat to public order. In an article for *Times of India* published on 13 October 1988, Shahabuddin addressed Rushdie directly:

> You are aggrieved that some of us have condemned you without a hearing and asked for the ban without reading your book. Yes, I have not read it, nor do I intend to. I do not have to wade through a filthy drain to know what filth is. My first inadvertent step would tell me what I have stepped into. For me, the synopsis, the review, the excerpts, the opinions of those who had read it and your gloatings were enough. Rushdie "the Islamic scholar, the man who studied Islam at university" has to brag about his Islamic credentials, so that he can convincingly vend his Islam wares in the West, which has not yet laid the ghost of the crusades to rest, but given it a new cultural wrapping which explains why writers like you are so wanted and pampered.[9]

In this much-cited passage, Shahabuddin defiantly identifies as a non-reader of *The Satanic Verses*. He also identifies as a Muslim: his use of the first person plural ("You are aggrieved that some of *us* have condemned you") responds directly to Rushdie's letter to Prime Minister of India Rajiv Gandhi of 7 October 1988, republished in various newspapers, in which Rushdie complained that "[t]he book was banned after representations by two or three Muslim politicians including Syed Shahabuddin, MP, and Khurshid Alam Khan, MP [...] whom I do not hesitate to call extremists, even fundamentalists" and who "have attacked me and my novel while stating that they had no need actually to read it."[10] In Rushdie's account, Shahabuddin and others' vehement lobbying against the novel was explicitly determined by

---

[9] Syed Shahabuddin, quoted in Appignanesi and Maitland, *The Rushdie File*, p. 39.
[10] Salman Rushdie, quoted in Appignanesi and Maitland, *The Rushdie File*, p. 34.

their identities as Muslims, even extremists. He argued moreover that their refusal to read the text granted them no authority over its meaning. Rushdie made the same claim many years later in his 2024 interview with *The New York Times*. Paraphrasing Shahabuddin, whom he called "one of the leaders of the Indian Muslim protest against the book," the author expressed his astonishment to Ezra Klein that "that was the kind of attitude: You don't need to read it. It's just filth".[11] For Rushdie and contemporary commentators such as Kenan Malik, Prime Minister Gandhi and the Indian National Congress had conceded to a factional minority by banning the import of the novel.[12] Yet, in the passage above, Shahabuddin is not only speaking as a Muslim or as a non-reader, but also as a local, non-professional reader. He scolds Rushdie for peddling old stereotypes of Islam for the enjoyment of consumers in Britain. In the same article, he derided the fawning coterie of literary critics in India that had rushed to celebrate the book's foreign acclaim almost as if it was their own. He wrote:

> What is shocking is not the protest of the "irreverent minority" but the Anglicised elite for whom a book by a writer of Indian origin nominated, sorry, shortlisted for the highest literary award in the *Vilayet* by the sahibs themselves—all pukka Sahibs, mind you—is the height of achievement and the mark of merit.[13]

Shahabuddin ridicules an elite intellectual class in India for investing in the authority of the Booker Prize to measure literary excellence. He uses the language of colonial India to accentuate the deference of Indian intellectuals toward the prize and its white, upper-middle-class judges.[14] Later in the article, Shahabuddin put it more explicitly, naming the production and

[11] The Ezra Klein Show, "Salman Rushdie Is Not Who You Think He Is."
[12] Kenan Malik, "Exploding the Fatwa Myths," *The Guardian*, 9 February 2009 <https://www.theguardian.com/commentisfree/2009/feb/09/religion-islam-fatwa-khomeini-rushdie> [accessed 29 November 2018].
[13] Syed Shahabuddin, quoted in Appignanesi and Maitland, *The Rushdie File*, p. 37.
[14] In 1988, the judges of the Booker Prize were former Labour Party Leader Michael Foot (educated at Oxford), author Sebastian Faulks (educated at Cambridge), radio producer and film critic Phillip French (educated at Oxford), writer and journalist Blake Morrison (who completed his PhD at University College London in 1977), and writer Rose Tremain (educated at the Sorbonne and the University of East Anglia, and Professor of Creative Writing at the University of East Anglia [UEA] while serving as a judge). Sharon Norris has discussed the prevalence of Oxbridge and UEA graduates on the judging panels of the Booker Prize. See Sharon Norris, "The Booker Prize: A Bourdieusian Perspective," *Journal for Cultural Research*, 10.2 (2006), pp. 139–58, (pp. 145–46).

circulation of the text as a form of "'literary colonialism'" that India will not endure, "not even under the deafening and superb orchestration of your liberal band."[15] No matter how enthusiastically 'liberals' might 'bang the drum' for Rushdie, Shahabuddin was not to be deterred in his critique of the novel.

There is little doubt that Syed Shahabuddin's intervention in the Rushdie affair propelled his political career, including as a representative for the Muslim minority in India. But, at the heart of the debate that would become the Rushdie affair, he identified a divide not just between Muslims and non-Muslims, but also between a non-professional audience who failed to see literary merit in the fantastical and ahistorical treatment of the Prophet Muhammad, and a professional community of readers who bowed before migrant writers like Rushdie. Shahabuddin's construction of this division between professional and non-professional readers of *The Satanic Verses* responded to Rushdie's own representation of the debate about the novel. In his letter to Rajiv Gandhi, the author boasted that "just about every leading Indian newspaper and magazine has deplored the ban as, for example, a 'philistine decision' (*The Hindu*'s editorial) or 'thought control' (the title of the *Indian Express*'s leader)." He added, "It is not for nothing that such eminent writers as Kingsley Amis, Harold Pinter, Stephen Spender and Tom Stoppard have joined International Pen, Index on Censorship and India's own association of publishers and booksellers in condemning the decision."[16] Rushdie leveraged the cultural capital of literary professionals, including award-winning English authors and playwrights, against an uncredentialed 'philistine' class, too ignorant to recognise the magnificence of the novel, who supported its proscription. Despite the complexity of Shahabuddin's identity claims, his early intervention became known primarily for anticipating the "nastiness" that would characterise the Rushdie affair.[17] The construction of him as a Muslim non-reader furthermore anticipated the connection that readers and commentators would make between the Islamic faith and the refusal to read.[18]

The UK Action Committee on Islamic Affairs (UKACIA) was one of the main actors involved in the production of a Muslim non-readership of *The Satanic Verses* in Britain. The organisation was founded by Muhammad Manazir Ahsan (Director of the Islamic Foundation of Leicester) and

---

[15] Shahabuddin, quoted in Appignanesi and Maitland, *The Rushdie File*, p. 40.
[16] Rushdie, quoted in Appignanesi and Maitland, *The Rushdie File*, p. 35.
[17] Daniel Pipes, *The Rushdie Affair: The Novel, the Ayatollah, and the West* (New York: Birch Lane Press, 1990), p. 20.
[18] Pipes, *The Rushdie Affair*, p. 20.

Muhammad Hashir Faruqi (editor of *Impact International*, a Muslim current affairs magazine published fortnightly) on 11 October 1988, fifteen days after the publication of the novel in the UK. The UK Action Committee on Islamic Affairs attempted to represent the interests of major Islamic organisations.[19] According to a letter circulated on 28 October 1988 by its convenor Mughram Al-Ghamdi to Muslim organisations and mosques in Britain, it aimed to coordinate a Muslim response that would secure the book's proscription, a public apology, and the payment of damages to an agreed Islamic charity in Britain.[20] In its political representation of British Muslims, the UK Action Committee on Islamic Affairs simplified the relationship between religious belief and reading practices, and strategically presented a united Muslim viewpoint on the text. In his letter, Al-Ghamdi encouraged Muslim ambassadors to "approach your local M.P.'s [sic] and police chiefs and tell them that the publication of this book has angered and outraged Muslims enormously."[21] The organisation assumed the responsibility and authority to speak for British Muslims, and suppressed Muslim responses other than anger and outrage. It transformed British Muslims into a coherent political community through an appeal to a shared affective economy. This affective economy was furnished and reproduced in retrospective accounts of the UK Action Committee on Islamic Affairs' role in the Rushdie Affair, such as that of its co-founder M. Manazir Ahsan and scholar Abdur Raheem Kidwai. In *Sacrilege Versus Civility: Muslim Perspectives on* The Satanic Verses *Affair* (1993), Ahsan and Kidwai recall that "[w]ith one voice," the committee "guide[d] the Muslim community in their efforts to express their anger and hurt."[22]

In many ways, the position of the UK Action Committee on Islamic Affairs reflected that of its co-founder, Muhammad Hashir Faruqi. In his

---

[19] In her account of the UK Action Committee on Islamic Affairs, Khadijah Elshayyal has argued that "there was no real consensus that it was to be *the* official representative or umbrella body for Muslim groups in the UK." See Khadijah Elshayyal, *Muslim Identity Politics: Islam, Activism and Equality in Britain* (London: I.B. Taurus, 2018), p. 86; original emphasis. Based out of London Central Mosque in Regent's Park, London, and partly funded by actors and organisations overseas, including Saudi Arabia, the Committee was necessarily unable to capture the diverse views of Muslim groups up and down the country.

[20] Mughram Al-Ghamdi, quoted in Appignanesi and Maitland, *The Rushdie File*, pp. 47–48.

[21] Al-Ghamdi, quoted in Appignanesi and Maitland, *The Rushdie File*, p. 48.

[22] M. Manazir Ahsan and Abdur Raheem Kidwai, *Sacrilege Versus Civility: Muslim Perspectives on* The Satanic Verses *Affair* (Leicester: The Islamic Foundation, 1993), pp. 26–27.

editorial for *Impact International*, published on 28 September 1988 before the establishment of the organisation, Faruqi wrote that "The Muslim community in Britain [...] is shocked and outraged beyond any describable measure by the unprecedented enormity of this sacrilege and by the fact that a so far respectable publisher, Penguin, has been insensitive enough to lend its name in this extreme profanity".[23] His production of the shock and outrage of British Muslims informed the UK Action Committee on Islamic Affairs' own representation of British Muslims' anger and outrage. Faruqi's criticism of Penguin for publishing *The Satanic Verses* moreover foreshadowed one of the organisation's main demands: that the publisher "immediately withdraw and pulp all copies [...] as well as to undertake not to allow to be published any future editions of this sacrilege."[24] Yet, at the same time as he identified as a Muslim and made representations on behalf of an imagined community of British Muslims, Faruqi, like Syed Shahabuddin, spoke as a non-professional against the insularity of a professional intellectual class of Rushdie devotees. Warning British Muslims to pursue the book's proscription and reparations "through all civilised and legitimate means," rather than through violence, Faruqi instructed readers of *Impact International* to "please leave Mr Salman Rushdie all to himself and to his charmed circle of 'literary critics.'"[25] Faruqi mocked Rushdie as a narcissist, whose audience was solely made up of professional readers. Through the use of scare quotes, he questioned the authority of literary critics to decide what constitutes cultural value. In this way, Faruqi characterised Rushdie's detractors, including himself, as not just members of a Muslim community, but also a non-professional community, whose lack of cultural and symbolic capital lent them a clarity of perspective unavailable to the 'charmed' professional.

The professional status of Rushdie and his supporters, in contrast to the non-professional position of many of *The Satanic Verses*' most ardent critics, was not explicitly addressed by the UK Action Committee on Islamic Affairs. However, it was a line of defence pursued by Viking (the imprint of Penguin that published the novel) and the Penguin Group itself in response to calls from Islamic organisations (including the UK Action Committee on Islamic Affairs) and members of the public to withdraw the novel from sale and pulp all copies. Responding directly to Iqbal Sacranie, the Joint Convenor of the UK Action Committee on Islamic Affairs, Viking's editorial director called *The Satanic Verses* "a purely literary work" that "has received the highest possible praise: in London, the *Sunday Times* called it 'a masterpiece'

---

[23] M. H. Faruqi, quoted in Appignanesi and Maitland, *The Rushdie File*, p. 48.
[24] Al-Ghamdi, quoted in Appignanesi and Maitland, *The Rushdie File*, p. 47.
[25] Faruqi, quoted in Appignanesi and Maitland, *The Rushdie File*, p. 49.

and in India, the *Indian Post* described it as 'wondrous and uplifting.'"[26] A statement by the Penguin Group similarly insisted that the novel was "a work of fiction" that "has been enthusiastically received by reviewers and literary critics" and reproduced the same two quotes from reviews of the book. The Penguin Group added that the shortlisting of *The Satanic Verses* for the Booker Prize, "Britain's foremost award for literary fiction," together with its receipt of the Whitbread Award, testifies to its quality.[27] Viking and Penguin suggested that the book's extraordinary acclaim among literary professionals did not reflect the cultural solipsism of an intellectual class, but rather transparently signified the merit of *The Satanic Verses* as a work of literary fiction. It was implied that the cultural and social capital of professional readers endowed their readings with greater value, in such a way as to secure greater interpretative authority for professional praise over non-professional criticism.

If the early debate about *The Satanic Verses* was structured by the performance of intersectional social, cultural, and religious identities, by 1989 the Rushdie affair was acted out and narrated by the antagonistic performance of religious and secular identities. The purported disagreement between Muslim and secular readers moreover came to be understood as a much larger struggle between Islam and secular liberalism. The book burnings in January 1989, organised by the Bradford Council of Mosques, secured the attention of national media, and significantly shaped how previous and future contributions to the debate would be understood. As Tariq Modood argues, "as far as the national media is concerned, nothing had happened prior to the Bradford book-burning demonstration of 14 January."[28] An article for the *Independent* dated 16 January 1989 compared the protesters to "the Inquisition and Hitler's National Socialists," and defended the novel on the grounds that "[i]t is hardly likely that the worthy and liberal-minded *literati* who sat on the panels awarding these prizes would have thought so highly of a book which was overtly blasphemous, even of another faith".[29] The professional and political credentials of the novel's champions remained important, then. But they were no longer contrasted with the apparent philistinism of its critics. Instead, they were distinguished from the fanatical faith of a 'foreign' Muslim population. "It may indeed be thought," wrote

---

[26] Viking Editorial Director, quoted in Ahsan and Kidwai, *Sacrilege Versus Civility*, p. 319.

[27] The Penguin Group, quoted in Ahsan and Kidwai, *Sacrilege Versus Civility*, p. 320.

[28] Tariq Modood, "Religious Anger and Minority Rights," *The Political Quarterly*, 60.3 (1989), pp. 280–84 (p. 280).

[29] *Independent*, quoted in Appignanesi and Maitland, *The Rushdie File*, p. 55.

the *Independent*, "that Muslims are furnishing further moral parables about Islam by attacking Rushdie's fictional creation, not only through the Islamic world [...] but in Britain".[30] The article presupposes the existence of an Islamic world, and contrasts it with Britain, thereby questioning the authority of Islam in Britain. It is implied that protests, including book burnings, might be expected in 'the Islamic world,' but they have no place in a Christian / secular Britain.

The Bradford book burnings gained new significance and attention following Ayatollah Khomeini's pronouncement of the infamous fatwā on 14 February 1989.[31] Media coverage of the Bradford protest and the fatwā lent disproportionate significance to the Muslim identity of *The Satanic Verses*' critics. Such coverage conveyed that faith in Islam determined reading practices, and produced not just protesters or the Iranian Ayatollah, but *all* Muslims as intolerant actors interested in inciting or participating in violence. Scholarly criticism on the Rushdie affair reproduced this interpretation. Islam came to be understood as a threat to free speech, whose claims were 'foreign' and held no jurisdiction over cultural production, circulation, and consumption in Britain. In a 1989 pamphlet titled *Sacred Cows*, writer Fay Weldon explicitly blamed the fundamentalism of Islam for the furore of the Rushdie affair. Reflecting on the initial indifference of liberal Britons toward the novel and its increasingly divisive reception, she described the Ayatollah's fatwā as a kind of 'wake-up call' and implored readers to "[p]lease let us not go to sleep again".[32] For Weldon, the fatwā alerted secular liberal Britons like herself that Islam, and the Qur'anic text around which its belief system is organised, posed a direct threat to the freedoms of secular liberalism. In the pamphlet, she describes the Qur'an as "this rigid set of rules for living, perceiving and thinking," which "gives weapons and strength to the thought police—and the thought police are easily set marching, and they frighten."[33] In doing so, Weldon adapted Rushdie's own account of the organisation of Islam. In a 1989 essay for *The New York Review of Books*, Rushdie complained that "a powerful tribe of clerics has taken over Islam. These are the contemporary Thought Police".[34]

Weldon equated death threats levelled against Rushdie with the imperilment of British society, writing:

---

[30] *Independent*, quoted in Appignanesi and Maitland, *The Rushdie File*, p. 55.
[31] See Modood, "Religious Anger and Minority Rights."
[32] Fay Weldon, *Sacred Cows* (London: Chatto & Windus, 1989), p. 9.
[33] Weldon, *Sacred Cows*, p. 5 and p. 7.
[34] Salman Rushdie, "The Book Burning," *The New York Review of Books*, 2 March 1989, np.

> "Kill, kill, kill Rushdie" does not to me mean deep hurt and anger at Rushdie, it means a plague on you and all your works, on your rotten society: a society so appalling even the rules for living and believing laid down for hot-climate living by a sixth-century poet/warrior/businessman living in a primitive and largely illiterate society seems preferable to any you lot—that's us lot—have to offer. A plague on your folly, your arts, your alleged freedom of speech—*what about us?*[35]

Islam is here presented as a way of life that ought to be obsolete. It is consigned to a past geohistorical and cultural moment in which it was, perhaps, appropriate. Weldon presumes the existence of a coherent British society ("us lot") that enjoys cultural and political freedom under the rule of secular liberalism. And she contrasts this British society with a fanatical Muslim community committed to curbing cultural and artistic freedoms. In this way, Weldon implicitly represents Muslims as foreign—an extraneous, menacing threat to the imagined British society to which she belongs.

In the wake of the fatwā, several writers and critics joined Weldon in denouncing Islam. Malise Ruthven, for instance, described Islam as a kind of fascism, and contrasted it unfavourably with both secular liberalism and Christian fundamentalism.[36] Elsewhere, he echoed Weldon's description of protests against the novel as "primitive,"[37] calling protesters "utterly *foreign*," "like men from the sticks, irredeemably provincial."[38] Playwright Harold Pinter led a group of British writers, literary agents, and publishers to 10 Downing Street to petition then-Prime Minister Margaret Thatcher for an end to what he described as "an intolerable and barbaric state of affairs." Pinter was explicitly addressing the fatwā, but his letter to the British government made a connection between Ayatollah and Muslims more generally, in insisting that "'The Government ... should confront Iran with the consequences of its statement and remind the Islamic community that it cannot incite people to murder.'"[39] In a letter to *The New York Review of Books*, published on 16 March 1989, a group of literary and cultural critics, including Edward Said and Gayatri Chakravorty Spivak, offered a less critical account of Islam, and a less homogenising account of Muslims. They nonetheless affirmed the Rushdie

---

[35] Weldon, *Sacred Cows*, p. 14.
[36] See Malise Ruthven, *A Fury for God: The Islamist Attack on America* (London: Granta, 2002), p. 38 and p. 207.
[37] Weldon, *Sacred Cows*, p. 9.
[38] Malise Ruthven, *A Satanic Affair: Salman Rushdie and the Rage of Islam* (London: Chatto & Windus, 1990), p. 1; original emphasis.
[39] Murtagh, quoted in Appignanesi and Maitland, *The Rushdie File*, p. 81.

affair as a conflict between religious fundamentalist and secular liberal values. "We deplore and regret this sort of thing," Said, Spivak, and their fellow critics wrote about the threats of violence levelled against Rushdie, "and we reaffirm our belief in universal principles of rational discussion and freedom of expression."[40] They awarded their argument professional and cultural-religious authority, speaking "[a]s writers and scholars from the Islamic world," even as they promoted the "universality" of post-Christian, secular-liberal values. In this way, the public counter-demonstrations and interventions of literary professionals monumentalised cultural and religious differences between *The Satanic Verses*' reading communities. They had the effect of precluding a rational, secular critique of the novel or its author.

While the fatwā, and to a lesser extent the Bradford demonstration, mediated the production of two coherent and opposed reading communities, it was not the case that practices of reading dramatically changed or became more united after 14 February 1989. There remained insufficient agreement among the novel's readers to justify the narration of the Rushdie affair as a conflict between Muslims and non-Muslims, or between religious fundamentalism and secular liberalism. As Ruvani Ranasinha has suggested, "[d]evout Muslims were not unequivocal about either Rushdie or the Ayatollah's *fatwa* [...] Nor was it the case that all those offended by Rushdie's text supported the *fatwa* and the book burnings".[41] Some Muslims did not support the book's proscription.[42] Others were moved to denounce Islamism and support the right to free speech.[43] Islamic organisations were also not uniformly in support of either the Bradford book burnings or the fatwā. The Chair of the Islamic Society for the Promotion of Religious Tolerance denounced Khomeini's statement and the violence it endorsed,[44]

---

[40] Edward Said and others, "Antithetical to Islam," *The New York Review of Books*, 17 February 1989 <http://www.nytimes.com/1989/02/17/opinion/l-antithetical-to-islam-121589.html> [accessed 31 January 2017].

[41] Ruvani Ranasinha, "The Fatwa and its Aftermath," in *The Cambridge Companion to Salman Rushdie*, ed. by Abdulrazak Gurnah (Cambridge: Cambridge University Press, 2007), pp. 45–59 (p. 48; original emphasis).

[42] See Talal Asad, "Ethnography, Literature, and Politics: Some Readings and Uses of Salman Rushdie's *The Satanic Verses*," *Cultural Anthropology*, 5.3 (1990), pp. 239–69 (pp. 244–45).

[43] For example, see Anouar Abdallah, *For Rushdie: Essays by Arab and Muslim Writers in Defense of Free Speech* (New York: George Braziller, 1994) and Fawzia Afzal-Khan, "Here Are the Muslim Feminist Voices, Mr. Rushdie!" *Television and New Media*, 3.2 (2002), pp. 139–42.

[44] Hesham El-Essawi, quoted in Appignanesi and Maitland, *The Rushdie File*, pp. 77–78.

while the UK Action Committee on Islamic Affairs "neither sanctioned nor approved of" the Bradford Council of Mosques' organisation of the book-burnings.[45]

Non-Muslims, too, offered secular criticisms of the novel. Even after the fatwā, Roald Dahl complained about the treatment of Rushdie "as some sort of hero."[46] In a letter to the *Times* dated 28 February 1989, he argued that the flagrancy with which Rushdie had offended Muslims under the auspices of freedom of expression threatened "the very proper principle" of free speech.[47] "In a civilised world," Dahl argued, "we all have a moral obligation to apply a modicum of censorship to our own work in order to reinforce this principle of free speech".[48] John Le Carré agreed, telling *The New York Times* in May 1989 that "I don't think it is given to any of us to be impertinent to great religions with impunity".[49] Le Carré's criticism of Rushdie saw the two authors enter into a decade-long public feud, in which Rushdie would accuse Le Carré of being a "Philistine," and Le Carré in response would mock Rushdie's "self-canonisation."[50] Practices of reading remained diverse, then. A secular critique of the novel and its author was possible. And a critique of the elitism, arrogance, and paternalism of Rushdie, and the philistinism of his detractors remained available. But, after the publicised book burnings in Bradford, and after the fatwā, the identity of *The Satanic Verses*' readers was highly circumscribed, and their reading practices were increasingly generalised and caricatured by supportive readers. The social conflict that characterised the early debate (and which Rushdie and Le Carré pursued in its later stages) between a professional, Anglophone or Anglophile literary class and a non-professional class and its interpellated political and religious agents, was overwritten by what would become the dominant narrative of the Rushdie affair as a conflict between secular liberalism and Islam. "The

---

[45] Seán McLoughlin, "The State, New Muslim Leaderships and Islam as a Resource for Public Engagement in Britain," in *European Muslims and the Secular State*, ed. by Jocelyne Cesari and Seán McLoughlin (London and New York: Routledge, 2005), pp. 55–69 (p. 59).

[46] Roald Dahl, quoted in Appignanesi and Maitland, *The Rushdie File*, p. 200.

[47] Roald Dahl, quoted in Appignanesi and Maitland, *The Rushdie File*, p. 200.

[48] Roald Dahl, quoted in Appignanesi and Maitland, *The Rushdie File*, p. 200.

[49] John Le Carré, quoted in Rachel Donadio, "Fighting Words on Sir Salman," *The New York Times*, 15 July 2007 <https://www.nytimes.com/2007/07/15/books/review/15donadio.html> [accessed 29 October 2019].

[50] Guardian Research Department, "November 1997: Rushdie and le Carré in Literary Spat," *The Guardian*, 12 November 2012 <https://www.theguardian.com/theguardian/from-the-archive-blog/2012/nov/12/salman-rushdie-john-le-carre-archive-1997> [accessed 19 September 2017].

dispute," as Peter Morey reflects, "is now frozen and canonized as being about freedom of expression versus nascent Islamic fundamentalism".[51]

The Rushdie Affair as Reading Conflict

And so, the Rushdie affair became a durable epitext that concealed and transformed its object—the reception of *The Satanic Verses*. As Fischer and Abedi have argued, "the Rushdie affair [...] generates differentiated audiences" and is a "highly charged social text that gets people to further enact the conflicts it describes" between rational criticism and religious authority.[52] To read or otherwise discuss the novel today, as then, is to take a position within this conflict, and to identify oneself to others in a particular way. And any act of reading the novel is mediated by those public acts of reading and discussion that came before. As Talal Asad puts it, "all these utterances (writings), and others about the context, are intertexts that readers bring to bear on the novel."[53] With *The Satanic Verses*, then, we have a peculiar case where the object of reading is always both the novel and its reception. In these circumstances, what value did interlocuters invest in reading? What reading practices can be uncovered and reconstructed in their writings about the novel and its reception? How does a focus on the purported reading practices of the text's readers complicate the relationship between reading and identity, and help us to diversify the debate about the novel?

We know that the Rushdie affair vested reading with the capacity for subject constitution, in the sense that the performance of reading was practised and understood as a performance of identity. But contributors to the multi-authored narrative of the Rushdie affair also distinguished between reading and not reading. Critics of *The Satanic Verses* and of Rushdie were commonly constructed as non-readers. It was argued that, by not reading the novel, such critics forfeited any right or authority to criticise it. Rushdie himself regularly sought to delegitimise his critics by calling them non-readers. Recall his letter to the Indian Prime Minister dated 7 October 1988, in which he disparaged Syed Shahabuddin and Khurshid Alam Khan

---

[51] Peter Morey, *Islamophobia and the Novel* (New York: Columbia University Press, 2018), p. 5.
[52] Michael M. J. Fischer and Mehdi Abedi, "Bombay Talkies, the Word and the World: Salman Rushdie's *Satanic Verses*," *Cultural Anthropology*, 5.2 (1990), pp. 107–59 (p. 108).
[53] Talal Asad, *Genealogies of Religion: Discipline and Reasons of Power in Christianity and Islam* (Baltimore: John Hopkins University Press, 1993), p. 276.

for criticising the novel while refusing to read it.⁵⁴ In an interview recorded on 27 January 1989, and broadcast by Channel 4 on 14 February 1989, the author continued to dismiss critics of his novel as non-readers, telling the interviewer that "Almost all the people who are being so insulted and provoked and disgusted have not really read the book".⁵⁵ Literary professionals at the time made similar claims about the text's critics. In their own letter to the Indian PM Rajiv Gandhi, dated 20 October 1988, Dom Moraes and Adil Jussawalla petitioned for the ban against the novel's importation to India to be lifted, arguing that "the ban was ill conceived and hastily executed, a sop offered to a handful of people, who themselves have not read the book."⁵⁶ In an article for the *Evening Standard* dated 3 March 1989, writer Nadine Gordimer similarly produced critics of *The Satanic Verses* as non-readers. Gordimer expressed her alarm at a Muslim demonstration in South Africa against a proposed visit by Salman Rushdie in November 1988 to talk about censorship. Speaking about the protest and death threats levelled against the author and those who had been involved in inviting him to the country, she wrote: "And all of this, of course, by people who had not read the book. I know, because I had the only copy in the country, a proof sent to me by his American publisher".⁵⁷ Scholarly commentaries on the Rushdie affair have since reproduced *The Satanic Verses'* critics as non-readers. In his 1999 book-length account of Salman Rushdie, Damian Grant chooses to "set aside [...] the merely expletive attacks from those who have never actually read the work" in his discussion of the novel's reception.⁵⁸ In his account of Shahabuddin's intervention in the debate, Kenan Malik claims that "Like virtually all of Rushdie's opponents, Shahabuddin had not actually read *The Satanic Verses*".⁵⁹ The delegitimisation of the novel's critics as non-readers is also visible in contemporary postcolonial studies scholarship. Following the publication of Rushdie's memoir *Joseph Anton* (2012), the *Journal of Commonwealth Literature* released an online special issue dedicated to *The Satanic Verses*. In their introduction to the special issue, which collates articles on *The Satanic Verses* and Rushdie previously published in the journal, Claire Chambers and Susan Watkins state that

---

⁵⁴ Salman Rushdie, quoted in Appignanesi and Maitland, *The Rushdie File*, p. 34.
⁵⁵ Rushdie, quoted in Appignanesi and Maitland, *The Rushdie File*, p. 23.
⁵⁶ Dom Moraes and Adil Jussawalla, quoted in Appignanesi and Maitland, *The Rushdie File*, p. 41.
⁵⁷ Nadine Gordimer, quoted in Appignanesi and Maitland, *The Rushdie File*, p. 196.
⁵⁸ Damian Grant, *Salman Rushdie* (Devon: Northcote House, 1999), p. 16.
⁵⁹ Kenan Malik, *From Fatwa to Jihad: The Rushdie Affair and Its Legacy* (London: Atlantic Books, 2009), p. 15.

"Most of the protesters against *The Satanic Verses* hadn't read the book, or had only read photocopies of decontextualized excerpts from its notorious 'Jahilia' section".[60]

Certainly, some critics of the novel hadn't read it, or not in its entirety. Not only was *The Satanic Verses* frequently read in excerpt, but it was also read by both critics and supporters in absentia through the Rushdie affair. In an article dated 7 March 1989 for the *Independent*, a version of which was delivered as a lecture at Cornell University on 1 March 1989, writer Graham Swift complained about the politicisation of the novel by non-readers on both sides of the debate.[61] In his brief account of the Rushdie affair, John Gabriel similarly highlighted that "initial western responses" were "not so much to the novel itself, but to the wave of protests that its publication had provoked amongst Muslim communities, both in Britain and internationally."[62] The fatwā, together with protests and counterprotests around the world, secured the notoriety of the book and its author. Practices of reading *The Satanic Verses* were mediated by the infamy of its reception. As Robert Fraser argues, "[b]y 1990, in the West at least, for everyone who had read one of [Salman Rushdie's] books, a thousand had heard of him. In Asia, where his work was subjected to widespread bans and censorship, the discrepancy was still more extreme".[63] In some cases, then, the Rushdie affair supplanted *The Satanic Verses* as the object of discursive engagement, or else in other cases retroactively modified readers' responses to the text.[64]

Importantly, the Rushdie affair also transformed the act of not reading into a form of identity construction and interpretative performance. As Benwell, Procter, and Robinson have argued in their account of the symmetries between the reception of *Brick Lane* by Monica Ali and the reception of *The Satanic Verses*, "not reading is more usefully thought of as a particular *kind* of discursive engagement with cultural objects that is always meaningful, productive of meaning, in excess of nothing."[65] To identify as a non-reader of *The Satanic Verses* was to make a claim about the moral or aesthetic vacuity

---

[60] Clare Chambers and Susan Watkins, introduction to the "Online Special Issue: *The Satanic Verses*," *Journal of Commonwealth Literature*, n.d. <http://journals.sagepub.com/page/jcl/collections/online-special-issue-satanic-verses> [accessed 24 November 2023].

[61] Graham Swift, quoted in Appignanesi and Maitland, *The Rushdie File*, p. 202.

[62] John Gabriel, *Racism, Culture, Markets* (London: Routledge, 1994), p. 24.

[63] Robert Fraser, *Book History through Postcolonial Eyes: Re-writing the Script* (Abingdon: Routledge, 2008), p. 184.

[64] For examples, see Asad, "Ethnography, Literature, and Politics," pp. 242–47.

[65] Bethan Benwell, James Procter, and Gemma Robinson, "Not Reading *Brick Lane*," *New Formations* 73 (2011), pp. 90–116 (p. 92; original emphasis).

of the text, and to participate in the "expression of a desirable and principled identity."⁶⁶ Consider the identity work that Syed Shahabuddin's explicit identification as a non-reader performs. His refusal to read *The Satanic Verses* serves to distinguish him from what he identifies as the implied audience of the novel: 'Western', neocolonial consumers and an "Anglicised elite" whose tastes track those of the Booker Prize committee. Through not reading, Shahabuddin constructs himself as a more discerning cultural critic, capable of independently concluding that the novel is "filth."⁶⁷ Shahabuddin's judgement here exemplifies the way that "[n]ot reading might be best understood as part of a continuum of reading, rather than reading's opposite".⁶⁸

An appreciation for the interpretative and discursive work performed by not reading allows us to re-evaluate both critical and supportive responses to *The Satanic Verses*. It legitimises the well-documented, partial, and selective reading practices and elective non-reading of critical respondents to the novel—"the vocal 'non-readers' who constitute a significant interpretative community" but who "remain routinely sidelined in literary and sociological discussions of the Rushdie affair."⁶⁹ But at the same time it validates the less well-documented, partial and selective reading practices of the text's supporters. For, as Talal Asad has argued,

> *The Satanic Verses* draws on a wide variety of literary texts, reproduces words and phrases from half a dozen languages, and alludes to as many national and religious settings. In what sense precisely can Western readers who have little familiarity with these multiple references be said to have read the book?⁷⁰

In these terms, how can any readers claim to have read the book? Asad questions what we mean by 'reading,' asking whether it's possible, or even desirable, that all readers read and understand every aspect of *The Satanic Verses*. In his words, "To demand that the act of 'reading' must always conform to an a priori norm of skills and knowledges is perhaps arbitrary".⁷¹

---

⁶⁶ Benwell, Procter, and Robinson, "Not Reading *Brick Lane*," p. 95.
⁶⁷ For quoted material, see Syed Shahabuddin, quoted in Appignanesi and Maitland, *The Rushdie File*, pp. 37–39.
⁶⁸ Benwell, Procter, and Robinson, "Not Reading *Brick Lane*," p. 95.
⁶⁹ Ranasinha, "The Fatwa and its Aftermath," p. 46.
⁷⁰ Asad, "Ethnography, Literature, and Politics," pp. 247–48. Parekh makes a similar point about the intelligibility of the novel's Bombayite style and ethos to foreign readerships. See Bhikhu Parekh, "Between Holy Text and Moral Void," *New Statesman and Society*, 24 March 1989, pp. 29–33 (p. 30).
⁷¹ Asad, "Ethnography, Literature, and Politics," p. 248.

Reading always involves acts of selection, prioritisation, and elimination (see Chapter 4 for a detailed account of reading as non-understanding). And these processes are mediated by the resources of what I have called the self-in-the-world, and its recursive exchanges with the reading self and the text. In this chapter, then, I discuss readers and non-readers alike as 'readers' in recognition of the discursive work performed by not reading, and the partiality of reading in general. When we examine contributions to the debate as practices of reading, rather than just performances of identity or political interventions, both supportive and critical readers can be seen to make particular claims about the ontic and discursive ambit of literature, and about practices of reading. Some aspects of these different visions of literature and reading are structured by the secular and religious beliefs of the novel's reading communities. As others have argued, secular liberalism and Islam differently impute the role of literature, and so the Rushdie affair effectively rehearsed an old conflict between different epistemological systems, or what Peter Morey, drawing on the work of Talal Asad, calls "rational criticism" and "religious authority."[72] Religious belief vests literature, or scripture, with sacred power, and reading, or hermeneutics, with the capacity for exegesis; whereas secular liberalism awards literature "pseudosacred status,"[73] and reading and criticism is prized in those forms that reproduce its "modern transcendent power."[74] But these accounts perhaps lend too much authority to secular and religious belief in predicting and determining reading practices. If we work backwards, beginning with how critics and commentators described *The Satanic Verses* and the experience of reading, the Rushdie Affair can be seen as conflict of reading and interpretation, as much as a social, cultural, or religious conflict.

We know that critical readers frequently argued that *The Satanic Verses* ridiculed the sacred history of Islam. Importantly, for such readers, the text was not fictional, but counter-historical, and therefore political. For example, in a review of the novel published in the 28 October–10 November 1988 edition of *Impact International*, Director-General of the Islamic Academy in Cambridge, Syed Ali Ashraf, complained that Rushdie had "intentionally and deliberately distorted the history of the Blessed Prophet and his Companions," including by giving the novel's prophet "the name that vicious missionaries in the Middle Ages used to give to the Prophet (peace be upon him) only in order to tell people that he was not writing a history."[75] For Ashraf, *The*

---

[72] Morey, *Islamophobia and the Novel*, p. 36.
[73] Morey, *Islamophobia and the Novel*, p. 39.
[74] Asad, "Ethnography, Literature, and Politics," p. 293.
[75] Ashraf, quoted in Appignanesi and Maitland, *The Rushdie File*, p. 19.

Satanic Verses compels a historical, materialist practice of reading that both situates the text's depiction of the fictional religion of 'Submission' in relation to the real history of Islam, and consequently identifies where the text is untruthful, and where it caricatures and orientalises the real protagonists of Islamic history. Elsewhere in the review, he suggests that the text demands to be read and criticised not just as a history, but as "an anti-Islamic theory in the guise of a novel."[76] Ashraf argues that the book's premise, as a work of fiction, disguises Rushdie's motives to ridicule Islam. His materialist practice of reading inspires a politics of reading through which his self-in-the-world interrogates Rushdie as a secular writer.

In an article for *New Statesman & Society*, published shortly after the fatwā, Bhikhu Parekh similarly concluded that the text was not a work of fiction, but a "fantasised history."[77] As he puts it, "Rushdie fantasises and redefines real, recognisable men and women and does not create wholly new characters and images. [...] *The Satanic Verses*," he continued, "is thus a work of fantasy, not of pure fiction, or an imaginatively reinterpreted but not a radically reconstituted reality".[78] Parekh is clear that this kind of work has advantages in being able to clarify migrant consciousness and interrogate individuals' role in historical movements. More than once, he suggests that aspects of *The Satanic Verses*' treatment of Islam form part of a "legitimate literary inquiry."[79] But fantasised history also has risks: "If a writer is not careful, he or she can end up treating recognisable men and women as *mere* objects of fantasies, as people whom he knows better than they do themselves, as *manipulable* material for the free play of his imagination" and so "become not just disrespectful and irreverent, but supercilious and dismissive, a shade crude, even perhaps exhibitionist, scoring cheap points off half-real characters."[80] For Parekh, writers have a responsibility to respect the reality of historical actors, especially in the knowledge that fictionalised characters drawn from history can be (mis)recognised as real people. To ethicise, or roleplay, 'real' historical actors, and permit readers as reading selves to do so, Parekh implies, is to diminish these real people's historical and political agency. In *Be Careful with Muhammad!: The Salman Rushdie Affair* (1989), Shabbir Akhtar commends "the Hindu writer Bhikhu Parekh" for clarifying the text's

---

[76] Ashraf, quoted in Appignanesi and Maitland, *The Rushdie File*, p. 19.
[77] Parekh, "Between Holy Text and Moral Void," p. 30.
[78] Parekh, "Between Holy Text and Moral Void," p. 30.
[79] See Parekh, "Between Holy Text and Moral Void," pp. 31–32.
[80] Parekh, "Between Holy Text and Moral Void," p. 30; original emphasis.

distortion of Islamic history.[81] He pursues a similar criticism of the text. "Rushdie does not explore, in a fictional context, the religious mind or religious attitudes in general," Akhtar argues. Instead, "[t]he characters in *The Satanic Verses* are real historical personalities of the Islamic tradition— redefined, re-assessed, their motives and actions radically if imaginatively reinterpreted".[82] Akhtar implies that, while a fictional exploration of religious belief might have been worthy of aesthetic and ethical attention, *The Satanic Verses* fails to merit such practices of reading on account of its misrepresentation of the real historical protagonists of Islam.

For critics of *The Satanic Verses*, then, the text obligates an acutely materialist practice of reading. Their practices of reading produce the text as 'fantasised history,' to use Parekh's term, because they possess the knowledge of Islamic history to recognise the Prophet Muhammad, Mecca, Islam, and the disputed history of the Satanic Verses, among other things, in Mahound, Jahilia, 'Submission,' and the occasion of the Satanic Verses respectively. Reading *The Satanic Verses* is not, for these readers, a purely textual or imaginative experience to be pursued by the reading self, because the text presents objects that have a prior ontic existence and epistemic protocols. Their reading selves recruit the self-in-the-world, whose knowledge locates Islamic referents in the text, and whose aesthetic tastes, moral sensibilities, and political beliefs are tested by the debauchery of the fantasised prophet, the convenience of both God's and Mahound's divine interventions, and the orientalism of the text's naming procedures.

Since the Rushdie affair, several critics have re-evaluated the debate, and concluded that critics of the novel at the time raised legitimate questions of its claims to fictionality. In her book-length study, titled *An Attempt to Understand the Muslim Reaction to The Satanic Verses* (1999), Victoria La'Porte, for instance, has suggested that, "because of its close associations to real historical events," the novel "cannot lay claim to be pure fiction and thus have all the safeguards pure fiction is entitled to."[83] Anshuman Mondal has similarly argued that "Rushdie does not always violate the conventional historical record relating to the first years of Islam".[84] He

---

[81] Shabbir Akhtar, *Be Careful with Muhammad!: The Salman Rushdie Affair* (London: Bellew Publishing, 1989), p. 4.

[82] Akhtar, *Be Careful with Muhammad!*, p. 5.

[83] Victoria La'Porte, *An Attempt to Understand the Muslim Reaction to The Satanic Verses* (Lewiston: Edwin Mellen Press, 1999), p. 119.

[84] Anshuman A. Mondal, "'Representing the Very Ethic he Battled': Secularism, Islam(ism) and Self-Transgression in *The Satanic Verses*," *Textual Practice* 27.3 (2013), pp. 419–37 (p. 425).

continues: "it may well be the relative proximity of his account of the formation of Islam to the orthodox sacred history that precipitated such emotional turbulence in contemporary Muslim (non)readers."[85] Mondal unhelpfully reproduces the idea that critical readers had sometimes not read the novel. His sense that *The Satanic Verses*' critics were driven by emotional conflict furthermore furnishes an understanding of critical readerships as philistines, untutored in the protocols of intellectual debate. Yet, Mondal also insightfully considers whether the text's staged historicity might explain, if not justify, experiences of the text as offensive. Taken together, La'Porte's and Mondal's contemporary accounts demonstrate that it is possible to understand critiques of *The Satanic Verses* as reading practices, and to inhabit the interpretative and evaluative logics of those reading practices without sharing the cultural and religious identity of the novel's most vocal critics. A self-in-the-world that sacralises Islamic history might generate a particular affective response to the text's representation of Islam, but a self-in-the-world that merely possesses a knowledge of the historical formation of Islam can recognise that the novel invites historical comparison with the real, sacred history of Islam.

To turn now to supportive readers, we find that early readers of the novel regularly called attention to *The Satanic Verses*' discursive status as a work of fiction. The same readers often suggested that, as fiction, the text demanded a particular kind of discursive engagement, characterised by ethical attention, if not aesthetic reverence. In an article for the *Indian Post* (published on 2 October 1988, and republished in *The Rushdie File*), Nisha Puri described *The Satanic Verses* as Rushdie's "most ambitious fictional endeavour."[86] Contrasting the author favourably with James Joyce, Puri continued: "Rushdie remains buoyantly accessible to anyone who responds to all that is good and living in the supreme fictions offered by literary genius".[87] By suggesting that *The Satanic Verses* is intelligible to any reader with good taste, Puri not only naturalises literary excellence and Rushdie's genius, but at the same time contributes to an understanding of the novel's critical respondents as uncultured readers, incapable of recognising 'good' fiction when they see it. Other supportive readers also affirmed the literary quality of *The Satanic Verses*. At the award ceremony for the Whitbread Prize in 1988, Fay Weldon described the novel as a work of literary fiction so "magnificent" that it "defies any but the most timid of souls *not* to give it a

---

[85] Mondal, "'Representing the Very Ethic he Battled,'" p. 425.
[86] Nisha Puri, quoted in Appignanesi and Maitland, *The Rushdie File*, p. 9.
[87] Nisha Puri, quoted in Appignanesi and Maitland, *The Rushdie File*, p. 9.

prize."[88] By insisting on the literary quality of *The Satanic Verses*, early readers implicitly insisted that it merited the literary attention of literary readers.

Interestingly, in her Whitbread Prize speech, Fay Weldon was not criticising the timidness of critical readers, whose sensibilities were offended by the book, but rather the timidness of "the English literary establishment."[89] And she recalls feeling vindicated in her sense of the national literary establishment's obsequious commitment to formally conventional fiction by white authors when Rushdie was denied the Booker Prize. Yet, that the book was shortlisted for the prize in the first place was a consequence of the involvement of a political actor, rather than any literary establishment figure. As Asha Rogers has uncovered, it was former Labour Party leader Michael Foot, who acted as chair of the judging panel for the Booker Prize in 1988, who secured a place for *The Satanic Verses* on the shortlist, not necessarily because he enjoyed the book as literary fiction, but rather with the aim of "us[ing] the Booker's public platform to promote the value of free expression."[90] In this sense, it didn't matter that Rushdie didn't win. By successfully getting *The Satanic Verses* on the Booker Prize shortlist, Foot secured increased publicity for both the novel and the cause of free speech.

Weldon's criticism of the literary establishment's failure to award Rushdie the Booker Prize in 1988 is also curious because Rushdie has generally found an amenable critical audience among literary professionals (including prize judging panels), thanks in no small part to what Aijaz Ahmad describes as "a certain complicity of a shared starting point between the author and his critics, generated largely by the very conditions in which the idea of a 'Third World Literature' has arisen."[91] Rushdie's celebration of migrant consciousness and self-exile, and his individualisation of historical struggle, Ahmad argues, have "become the manifest common sense of the metropolitan intelligentsia, dutifully reproduced in the literary productions and pronouncements of 'Third World intellectuals' located within that milieu."[92] Weldon's characterisation of the national literary establishment as antagonistic toward writers like Rushdie therefore feels a little outdated, for Rushdie's writing has been enthusiastically embraced by the publishing, prize and critical industries.

---

[88] Weldon, *Sacred Cows*, p. 37; original emphasis.
[89] Weldon, *Sacred Cows*, p. 37 and p. 38.
[90] Asha Rogers, *State Sponsored Literature: Britain and Cultural Diversity after 1945* (Oxford: Oxford University Press, 2020), p. 136.
[91] Aijaz Ahmad, *In Theory: Classes, Nations, Literatures* (London: Verso, 2000), p. 142.
[92] Ahmad, *In Theory*, p. 130.

Hence, for Bhikhu Parekh, it is not the literary establishment's, but Rushdie's "timid obeisance to the latest literary and political fashions" that ought to be scrutinised, for the author "enjoyed the uncritical support of a literary establishment obsessed with 'terrifying singularity.'"[93] Rushdie's early work belongs to a privileged tradition of 'Third World writing,' characterised by

> a harsh questioning of radical decolonisation theory; a dismissive or parodic attitude towards the project of national culture; a manipulation of imperial imagery and local legend as a means of politicising 'current events'; and a declaration of cultural 'hybridity'—a hybridity claimed to offer certain advantages in negotiating the collisions of language, race and art in a world of disparate peoples comprising a single, if not exactly unified, world.[94]

Rushdie's role in the canonisation of post-nationalism is visible too in postcolonial studies. As James Procter has argued, "his writing played an extraordinary and unparalleled constitutive role in the very formation of postcolonial theory, whose vocabularies of hybridity and migration register the taint of his presence."[95] Fay Weldon's prizing of the novel as literary fiction is therefore highly particular to the historical literary milieu of the time: the emergence of 'Third World literature,' and the beginning of its transformation into postcolonial writing through the professionalisation of Rushdie's writing as postcolonial theory. Weldon's defence of *The Satanic Verses* serves to confer value on both this new writing, and on particular modes of cultural judgement and appreciation. This is important, because while supporters of *The Satanic Verses* often obliquely mobilised the protections of free speech, they neither derived nor pursued legal authority, but instead sought the intellectual authority to define literature and reading. As Talal Asad has argued in his account of the Rushdie affair, "*Professional* critique [...] has less

---

[93] Parekh, "Between Holy Text and Moral Void," p. 31 and p. 33.
[94] Brennan, *Salman Rushdie and the Third World: Myths of the Nation* (London: Palgrave Macmillan, 1989), p. 35. On the political scepticism of Rushdie's late style, see Ágnes Györke, "Rushdie and Globalization," in *Rushdie in Context*, ed. by Florian Stadtler (Cambridge: Cambridge University Press, 2023), pp. 182–92 and Peter Morey, "Rushdie and Globalization," in *Rushdie in Context*, ed. by Florian Stadtler (Cambridge: Cambridge University Press, 2023), pp. 318–28.
[95] James Procter, "'The Ghost of Other Stories': Salman Rushdie and the Question of Canonicity?" *A Black British Canon?*, ed. by Gail Low and Marion Wynne-Davies (Basingstoke: Palgrave Macmillan, 2006), pp. 35–49 (p. 44).

to do with the right of free speech than with the reproduction of intellectual disciplines and the aesthetics and ethics that go with them".[96]

In the wake of the fatwā, defences of *The Satanic Verses* as fiction became more urgent. The Ayatollah criticised the book as one which had been "compiled, printed and published in opposition to Islam, the Prophet and the Koran [sic]."[97] After Khomeini's decree, the book's status as fiction became its best defence. At a conference held at the Institute of Contemporary Arts in London on 19 March 1989, at which writers, critics, and media professionals reflected on the cultural questions raised by the Rushdie affair, the chair of the opening session, 'Truth and Fiction,' deemed it important to reiterate that *The Satanic Verses* was a work of fiction. "The spark which ignited this fire is a serious and ambitious work of imaginative fiction. I think it's very important to say this," BBC 2 Controller Alan Yentob said, "because looking at some of the correspondence in the pages of our newspapers, one would imagine that this book was simply written as a provocative act and that it has no serious purpose".[98] Yentob suggested that letters to the national media had misrepresented *The Satanic Verses* as a treatise against Islam. When he defined *The Satanic Verses* as fiction, he had a particular kind of fiction in mind. He evaluated the novel through the emerging paradigm of 'Third World Literature,' praising its ability to traverse different cultures and literary traditions. Rushdie "has always seen himself as part of two worlds," Yentob noted, and his writing "explores the gap between cultures" and combines European and Indian forms of storytelling.[99] By setting the tone of the 1989 conference on the Rushdie affair in such a way, he therefore naturalised the appreciation of Rushdie as a native informant on the immigrant experience, and his works as exemplary of a new tradition of writing.

Rushdie himself regularly defended *The Satanic Verses* as fiction. He called upon critics to pay attention not to 'fictional' accounts of the book in the national and international press, but to "the [book] I actually wrote."[100] Rushdie reified a distinction between truthful accounts of the novel, and deceptive ones. In his writing on the affair, the definition of *The Satanic Verses* as a work of fiction had clear implications for practices of reading.

---

[96] Talal Asad, "Freedom of Speech and Religious Limitations," in *Rethinking Secularism*, ed. by Craig Calhoun, Mark Juergensmeyer, and Johnathan VanAntwerpen (Oxford: Oxford University Press, 2011), pp. 282–97 (p. 292).
[97] Ayatollah Khomeini, quoted in Appignanesi and Maitland, *The Rushdie File*, p. 68.
[98] Yentob, quoted in Appignanesi and Maitland, *The Rushdie File*, pp. 179–80.
[99] Yentob, quoted in Appignanesi and Maitland, *The Rushdie File*, p. 180.
[100] Salman Rushdie, *Imaginary Homelands: Essays and Criticism 1981-1991* (London: Granta, 1991), p. 397.

"Fiction uses facts as a starting-place and then spirals away to explore its real concerns, which are only tangentially historical," Rushdie wrote in an essay about the Rushdie affair titled "In Good Faith."[101] "Not to see this," he continued, "to treat fiction as if it were fact, is to make a serious mistake of categories. The case of *The Satanic Verses* may be one of the biggest category mistakes in literary history".[102] The author affirms the fictional quality of *The Satanic Verses*, and insists that fiction requires appropriate treatment, capable of negotiating its "tangentially historical" character. Across the essay, Rushdie distinguishes between fact and fiction in order to differentiate between his and his supporters' apposite practices of reading the text as fiction, and critics' misguided practices of reading the text as (bad) history. As Anshuman A. Mondal has argued, by contrast with *The Satanic Verses*, "In Good Faith" "articulates a more 'empiricist' notion of history in which facts are facts, and historiography and fiction occupy radically different, even opposed discursive terrains."[103] Yet one might dispute the extent to which avowed atheists like Rushdie or Fay Weldon appreciate and experience the reality of the Prophet Muhammad, and the events described in the Qur'an and the Hadith.[104] For secular readers, what discursive terrain would Islamic history occupy? What kind of reality would their reading practices award the historical protagonists of Islam? On what epistemic and affective resources would their selves-in-the-world draw?

Rushdie has spoken often about his intentions with *The Satanic Verses*, with the aim of establishing that he and his work have been misread. "[T]he character 'Salman the Persian,'" he insists, is "named not to 'insult and abuse' Muhammad's companion Salman al-Farisi, but more as an ironic reference to

---

[101] Rushdie, *Imaginary Homelands*, p. 409.

[102] Rushdie, *Imaginary Homelands*, p. 409.

[103] Mondal, "'Representing the very ethic he battled,'" pp. 423–24. For scholarship on *The Satanic Verses*' ambiguous treatment of fact and fiction, and its foregrounding of processes of narrativisation and historiography, see also Vijay Lakshmi, "Rushdie's Fiction: The World Beyond the Looking Glass," in *Reworlding: The Literature of the Indian Diaspora*, ed. by Emmanuel S. Nelson (New York: Greenwood Press, 1992), pp. 149–55 and Grant, *Salman Rushdie*, p. 3 and pp. 74–76.

[104] Weldon revealed that she had become a Christian in 2006: see Stuart Jeffries, "Lie Back and Think of Jesus," *The Guardian*, 5 September 2006 <https://www.theguardian.com/world/2006/sep/05/gender.religion> [accessed 29 February 2024]. Rushdie suggested that he had converted to Islam in "Why I Have Embraced Islam" (1991), but later removed the essay from subsequent editions of *Imaginary Homelands* and replaced it with "One Thousand Days in a Balloon," an essay deploring the conservatism of what he calls "Actually Existing Islam." In the essay "In Good Faith," Rushdie identifies as "a secular, pluralist, eclectic man." Rushdie, *Imaginary Homelands*, p. 405.

the novel's author".¹⁰⁵ "The purpose of the 'brothel sequence,'" he continues, "was not to 'insult and abuse' the Prophet's wives, but to dramatize certain ideas about morality; and sexuality, too": "[t]hat men should be so aroused by the great ladies' whorish counterfeits says something about *them*, not the great ladies, and about the extent to which sexual relations have to do with possession".¹⁰⁶ And elsewhere, in defence of his use of the name Mahound for the text's fictionalised Prophet, Rushdie argues that "[c]entral to the purposes of *The Satanic Verses* is the process of reclaiming language from one's opponents".¹⁰⁷ I'm less interested here in evaluating the fidelity of each of these claims, than in how they express Rushdie's investment in authorial intention. He implicitly identifies himself as the best reader of his work: the further a reader gets from Rushdie's own reading practice, the less accurate their reading practice becomes. How far can we say that Rushdie is an accurate reader of *The Satanic Verses*? What would an accurate reading look like? Certainly, the author is not a comprehensive reader of the text. In *Joseph Anton: A Memoir* (2013), an autobiographical account of the Rushdie affair and his time in hiding under the name 'Joseph Anton,' the author continues to make claims about *The Satanic Verses*' real meaning. Writing of himself in the third person, he argues:

> his Prophet was not called Muhammad, lived in a city not called Mecca, and created a religion not (or not quite) called Islam. And he appeared only in the dream sequences of a man being driven insane by his loss of faith. These many distancing devices were, in their creator's opinion, indicators of the fictive nature of his project.¹⁰⁸

Rushdie is right that Mahound does not share Muhammad's name, that Jahilia is not Mecca, and that Submission is not Islam. He is also correct that Mahound is only present in the chapters titled 'Mahound' and 'Return to Jahilia.' Both chapters are conveyed as dreams: the first opens with an extended passage narrating Gibreel Farishta's sleeping and dreaming state; the latter is interrupted by the phrase "And Gibreel dreamed this:" shortly

---

¹⁰⁵ Rushdie, *Imaginary Homelands*, p. 399.
¹⁰⁶ Rushdie, *Imaginary Homelands*, pp. 401–2; original emphasis.
¹⁰⁷ Rushdie, *Imaginary Homelands*, p. 402.
¹⁰⁸ Salman Rushdie, *Joseph Anton: A Memoir* (London: Vintage, 2013), p. 75. Rushdie makes a similar argument in the following essays: Salman Rushdie, "My Book Speaks for Itself," *The New York Times*, 17 February 1989, p. 39; Rushdie, quoted in Appignanesi and Maitland, *The Rushdie File*, p. 44; and Rushdie, *Imaginary Homelands*, pp. 397–403.

after it begins and features expressions throughout which emphasise the narrative's fictitiousness.[109] Yet, it isn't clear that the purpose of the dream sequences is to distance events from reality. *The Satanic Verses*' treatment of the reality of dreams and the fantastical quality of reality encourages readers to reconsider the relationship between dream and reality, history, and fiction. Consider Gibreel's early confession to Saladin on the hijacked flight that he fears sleep because he suffers vivid dreams in which he appears as the archangel Gibreel:

> and I don't mean interpreting a role, Spoono, I am him, he is me, I am the bloody archangel, Gibreel himself, large as bloody life. [...] Gibreel was sweating from fear: 'Point is, Spoono,' he pleaded, 'every time I go to sleep the dream starts up from where it stopped. Same dream in the same place. As if somebody just paused the video while I went out of the room. Or, or. As if he's the guy who's awake and this is the bloody nightmare. His bloody dream: us. Here. All of it.'[110]

Gibreel worries that his reality is not real, but dreamed, nightmarish. He is disquieted by the reality of his dreams, and wonders whether the archangel Gibreel isn't the real, 'awake' one, and he and his reality is the dream, or the fiction. At least among those readers who are attentive to the text's sustained confusion of reality and dream, then, the dream sequences do not establish the fictitiousness of Mahound, Jahilia, and Submission, or their distance from reality, but instead produce their discursive ambivalence. The text's metafictional reflections on reality and fiction compels the reading self to adopt a flexible and movable sense of the text world that can accommodate the possibility that Gibreel and the cast of 'Proper London' characters are merely the players of an intratextually authenticated reality (the founding of Submission in Jahilia). At least in this sense, the text invites the self-in-the-world to use its archive of knowledges, experiences, and tastes to adjudicate the material reality of Jahilia, not 'Proper London.'

Both supportive and critical readers therefore make claims about *The Satanic Verses* in a way that reveals their very different practices of reading. Critical readers experience the text as (a)historical: they use the knowledge of their selves-in-the-world to produce the text's proximity to the real history of Islam, and they sometimes use the affective repertoire of their selves-in-the-world to comprehend this proximity as offensive and salacious. They tend

---

[109] Salman Rushdie, *The Satanic Verses* (London: Vintage, 2006), see pp. 91–92, 363, 370, 372, 376, 390, 393, 394.
[110] Rushdie, *The Satanic Verses*, p. 83.

to conceal the role of their reading selves in the recursive transformation of the text's referents into the real referents of Islamic history. Supportive readers experience the text as literary fiction: they delight in the singularity of the text, using their reading selves to co-produce the text's fictional objects, and to make novel connections between its literary inquiries and broader cultural and philosophical questions. At the same time, they tend to conceal the role of the selves-in-the-world in their appreciation of the text–selves-in-the-world which have at their disposal specific knowledges and values, including a secular liberal orientation toward literature as a transcendent object, and metropolitan tastes that value Rushdie's brand of 'Third World Literature.' Where many of the Rushdie affair's contributors and analysts have charted a fairly straightforward relationship between reading and identity, including by producing critics of the text as Muslim non-readers, my account shows that actual practices of reading *The Satanic Verses* were far more complex. Both critics and supporters upheld orthodoxies of reading, but these cannot be easily predicted by religious or cultural affiliation.

The Ethics and Politics of Reading *The Satanic Verses*

What unites supporters and critics of *The Satanic Verses* is not only the partiality of their practices of reading, but their difficulty sustaining such orthodoxies of reading. That is to say, if critical readers tend toward materialist reading practices that comprehend the text as (bad) history, and if supportive readers tend toward textualist reading practices that appreciate the text as literary fiction, both critics and supporters can at times be seen to undertake inverse reading practices. In so doing, they introduce inconsistencies in their avowed practices of reading, and concede the possibilities of other practices of reading *The Satanic Verses*. This is significant because the text's audiences have, since the Rushdie affair, been considered opposed and divided—by interpretation if not identity. Inconsistencies in the reading practices of *The Satanic Verses*' critics and supporters register the essential hybridity of reading as a practice which brings the material into contact with the textual, and engages both the ethics and politics of reading.

Given the dominant tendency among critical readers to describe *The Satanic Verses* as history, and to criticise it in that discursive register as an unfaithful and obscene account of the beginning of Islam, it is surprising to find that several critical readers at the same time offer a literary appraisal of the text. For instance, President of Iran Ali Khamenei (who would later become Ayatollah Ruhollah Khomeini's successor as the Supreme Leader of

Iran) explicitly defined *The Satanic Verses* as fiction. Three days after the Ayatollah announced the fatwā, and during his second sermon at Friday prayers at Tehran University, Khamenei told listeners, "The book is of course a fictional novel; it is a story".[111] He proceeded to evaluate its merit using a literary register, stating that "[a]side from being a sin in the eyes of the law, religion and humanity, this dirtying of literature and arts was an ugly deed".[112] President Khamenei complained that, as well as desacralising the Prophet Muhammad and his wives and companions, *The Satanic Verses* had befouled the institution of literature. His admission illuminates the textualist reading practices that underpin even materialist practices of reading the text. His reading self, we can deduce, first undertakes a partial performance of the implied reader, and actualises different, intratextual perspectives and objects to produce the narrative and the text world. But his self-in-the-world possesses the knowledge to identify resemblances between the text's viewpoints and referents and those of Islamic history, and moreover deploys moral and aesthetic values that produce the text as an offence against not only Islamic, but literary sensibilities.

The text is profane, then, not simply because it flouts the sanctity of Islam and the Prophet, but because it defiles the arts. Khamenei spoke with some reverence about the institution of literature, claiming that it must have been the work of "the Great Satan [USA] or one of his surrogates, where one member of the British royal literary society was forced to write a book."[113] A secular investment in the authority of institutions like the Royal Society of Literature (RSL) to consecrate literary genius causes Khamenei to conclude that Rushdie, a fellow of the RSL since 1983, must have been possessed by the devil to have written *The Satanic Verses*. "For a person to taint the shining period of history which is admired by one million human beings in the world, to receive some money or to become famous," Khamenei concluded, "is one of the basest deeds that a writer could commit".[114] The sacrilegious treatment of Islamic history remains a cause for criticism, but not because Rushdie ought to honour or practise religious faith, but rather because there are moral expectations that literary writers should not seek to shock audiences for money or fame. Hence Khamenei implored not Muslims, but "the world's literary men and scribes and those involved in the field to

---

[111] Ali Khamenei, quoted in Appignanesi and Maitland, *The Rushdie File*, p. 73.
[112] Khamenei, quoted in Appignanesi and Maitland, *The Rushdie File*, p. 73.
[113] Khamenei, quoted in Appignanesi and Maitland, *The Rushdie File*, p. 73. Rushdie was elected as a fellow of the Royal Society of Literature in 1983.
[114] Khamenei, quoted in Appignanesi and Maitland, *The Rushdie File*, p. 73.

banish this ugly and evil person."[115] For Khamenei, it was the literary field to which Rushdie didn't belong, and to which the president appealed for help in proscribing the author.

Within his materialist and religious critique of the text, Shabbir Akhtar also offered a literary account of its flaws in much the same way as Khamenei. "[M]any parts of *The Satanic Verses* defy comprehension and tire even the sympathetic reader", Akhtar argued.[116] On this basis, he twice qualified his account of the novel with the phrase "in so far as [the text] is intelligible."[117] For Akhtar, the book is badly written: it strains under the weight of its spatio-temporal collisions between seventh-century Jahilia, present-day Bombay, and contemporary London. He gives the impression that, had the book been more coherent, and had Rushdie sought to guide audiences toward comprehension, *The Satanic Verses* might have held his interest. But, instead, Akhtar complains that "Rushdie is often self-indulgent, caring little for the reader puzzled by the complexity or incoherence—whichever sounds better—in some of the passages".[118] Like Khamenei, then, Akhtar embeds a literary critique within his religious critique of the text. In doing so, he exemplifies the hybrid character of reading, where a materialist critique of the text as bad history is only possible insofar as an ethics of reading has taken place, and has compelled a politics of reading that makes connections between textual representation and material practice. Akhtar's criticism brings to bear not only his religious sensibilities, but his view of the author's personality and intent, a sense of the market for literary fiction, and an awareness of the extent to which literary fiction is distinguished by its difficulty.

A final example of the textualist character of otherwise materialist criticisms of the text can be found in Syed Ali Ashraf's early review of the novel for *Impact International*. We saw earlier that Ashraf's principal issue lies with Rushdie's intention to distort the history of Islam and the sacred image of the Prophet Muhammad. But he also takes Rushdie to task for the formal and tonal inconsistencies of the text. "The method that he has adopted to achieve his goal [of 'preaching an anti-Islamic theory'] is also confusing and unsuccessful from the literary point of view", Ashraf writes.[119] He complains that the magic realist style of the text fails to be believable, and that the text renders characters unsympathetically. "[W]hen we go a bit deep into his characterisation we notice that nearly all these characters are

---

[115] Khamenei, quoted in Appignanesi and Maitland, *The Rushdie File*, p. 73.
[116] Akhtar, *Be Careful with Muhammad!*, p. 17.
[117] See Akhtar, *Be Careful with Muhammad!*, p. 3 and p. 14.
[118] Akhtar, *Be Careful with Muhammad!*, p. 17.
[119] Ashraf, quoted in Appignanesi and Maitland, *The Rushdie File*, p. 20.

repeating the same side of human nature I shall term satanic, i.e. the world of passions and lusts and selfishness not for a moment relieved by a desire to struggle with such devilish enchantments."[120] The absence of 'goodness' in the text is, for Ashraf, not merely a religious offence, but a secular literary one. His desire for ethical engagement—for attachment, and immersion—is thwarted by *The Satanic Verses'* immoral code. To draw on the language of my theory of reading, the experience of reading the text is unsatisfying precisely because it relies on the suspension of the self-in-the-world's moral and aesthetic preoccupations, as well as its formal preferences. Ashraf's practice of reading is here revealed as intimately textualist: his reading self attends to the singularity of the text's register, but its engagement in the ethics of reading is consequently transformed, or comprehended, by a politics of reading that quantifies the text's distance from reality unfavourably by an extratextual moral horizon. Ashraf exhibits a desire for relation that marks out the non-professionalism of his reading practice (on non-professional reading and relatability, see Chapter 2).

Like critical, materialist readers, supportive, textualists readers also find it difficult to sustain their orthodoxies of reading. Recall that one of the common defences of *The Satanic Verses* is that it is fiction, and that its textual referents do not directly correspond with any historical or religious referents outside the text. John Walsh articulates this defence clearly in his article for the *Sunday Times*, dated 19 February 1989. "Rushdie's constant emphasis on ambiguity should discourage readers from making hard-and-fast correspondences between his fiction and the real world", Walsh writes.[121] After providing a brief summary on *The Satanic Verses'* controversial passages, he continues: "At no point in these imaginings does Rushdie refer to the prophet Muhammad by name, nor to the city of Mecca, nor to the Sheria law [sic], nor anything directly concerned with Islamic faith".[122] Walsh, then, insists on the fictionality of the text, and indicates that any reading that identifies Islamic referents in the text is a partial reading, or misreading. Yet, he himself locates the history of Islam in the text. Notwithstanding the apparent "ambiguity" of the narrative—its refusal to name Islam as its object of inquiry—Walsh argues that "Rushdie's narrative thrust is to re-imagine, through the dreams of the film star [Gibreel], the beginnings of Islamic culture".[123] While he advocates for an ethics of reading that attends to the singularity of Mahound, Jahilia, and 'Submission,' he himself engages in a

---

[120] Ashraf, quoted in Appignanesi and Maitland, *The Rushdie File*, p. 21.
[121] Walsh, quoted in Appignanesi and Maitland, *The Rushdie File*, p. 25.
[122] Walsh, quoted in Appignanesi and Maitland, *The Rushdie File*, p. 26.
[123] Walsh, quoted in Appignanesi and Maitland, *The Rushdie File*, p. 26.

politics of reading that actualises the text's referents as those of Islamic history. He overcomes indeterminacy through an appeal to a material history.

As the self-appointed ideal reader of his work, Rushdie perhaps surprisingly also engages in a more hybrid—that is to say, material and textual—practice of reading than he often solicits. His essay "In Good Faith" may reify a distinction between fact and fiction, but at the same time it contends that the narrative's referents are both factual and fictional. Quoting the palinode that occurs throughout *The Satanic Verses*, Rushdie tells us:

> Jahilia [...] both 'is and is not' Mecca. Many of the details of its social life are drawn from historical research; but it is also a dream of an Indian city (its concentric street-plan deliberately recalls New Delhi), and, as Gibreel spends time in England, it becomes a dream of London too. Likewise, the religion of 'Submission' both is and is not Islam.[124]

He suggests that the novel's dream sequences are not merely fictional but combine elements of reality. In doing so, he authorises a materialist practice of reading the text's dream sequences as fantasised and transmogrified history.

Rushdie might not treat Islam with reverence, then, but he does treat it in the text. To the question "How much of [the novel's engagement with the Qur'an] was based on historical fact?", posed by an interviewer for *Bandung File* in early 1989, Rushdie replied: "Almost entirely. Almost everything in those sections—the dream sequences—starts from an historical or quasi-historical basis [...] I studied [Muhammad's life] as an historian".[125] His admission here makes it difficult to claim that *The Satanic Verses* occupies only the fictional discursive realm. Rushdie describes adopting a historical and literary register to interrogate the formation of Islam and the sanctity of the Prophet Muhammad. This is significant because it legitimises critical readers' practices of reading the text materially and historically as an unfaithful and orientalist rendition of Islamic history. To take only the example of Jahilia, what do we make of its homophonic resemblance to Jāhilīyah (جاهلية, which translates as 'ignorance'), an Islamic concept that refers to the period before the Qur'anic revelation and birth of Islam. For some readers, Jahilia undoubtedly compels material-historical practices of reading the text as 'bad' or offensive history. In the excerpts above, Rushdie does not contest such practices of reading, but explicitly affirms them. Readers whose selves-in-the-world possess knowledge of the name

---

[124] Rushdie, *Imaginary Homelands*, p. 409.
[125] Rushdie, quoted in Appignanesi and Maitland, *The Rushdie File*, pp. 21–22.

for pre-Islamic Arabia can project this into the text in the place of Jahilia, and their practice of doing so positions them closer in reading practice to Rushdie, *The Satanic Verses*' ideal reader, not further away. Is knowledge of Islam a requisite for reading the text, then? Does it enhance the reading experience, or change its quality? In an interview for the *Observer*, published on 25 September 1988, Sean French asked something similar: "Isn't there a risk that your readers won't know about Islam?"[126] Rushdie replied in the following way:

> Well, of course, many of the book's readers *will* know about Islam—they may not be white. To my mind, that varied reading of my books has been true of everything I've written. To simplify: in England people read *Midnight's Children* as a fantasy, in India people read it as a history book. But if you know nothing of Islam the novel still ought to work at the level of pure story. It's about the beginning of a religion—the questions of temptation, of compromise.[127]

By his own admission, Rushdie oversimplifies the reading practices of his audiences in a way that plots a deterministic relationship between national identity and reading. The acknowledgement that his works invite different reading practices and different interpretations is nonetheless important. *Midnight's Children* can be read both as a partition narrative and as a fantasy, Rushdie tells French, just as *The Satanic Verses* can be read as a retelling of Islamic history and as a 'universal' story of faith and doubt. The former—a historically informed practice of reading—is subtly valorised, with latter, textualist practice of reading the text as "pure story" offered by Rushdie as something of a consolation for his English readerships.

A careful analysis of practices of reading *The Satanic Verses* shows us that neither supportive nor critical readers offer coherent strategies of interpreting and evaluating the novel. Avowedly materialist or historical practices of reading do not simply draw on the religious knowledge or belief of their selves-in-the-world to read the novel, but also evaluate the novel as fiction. Likewise, Rushdie and supportive readers do not sustain a purely textualist practice of reading the novel as fiction, but instead insist on its relationship to the early history of Islam. Before the Rushdie affair, Rushdie showed an awareness that different readerships would engage with *The Satanic Verses* in different ways, precisely because readers possess different knowledges and affinities to Islam.

---

[126] Sean French, quoted in Appignanesi and Maitland, *The Rushdie File*, p. 7.
[127] Rushdie, quoted in Appignanesi and Maitland, *The Rushdie File*, pp. 7–8; original emphasis.

Conclusion

By revisiting the Rushdie affair as a reading conflict between professional and non-professional readers, this chapter has demonstrated that reading is not wholly determined by identity. Certainly, practices of reading *The Satanic Verses* represent performances of identity, where even to speak as a reader is to make claims about the text's merit and one's own literary proficiency and belonging. But identity does not predict practices of reading. Even professional and non-professional status does not adequately characterise the novel's divided reception. Professional and non-professional readers did tend to adopt opposing positions in the debate about the novel, in part because they were speaking in different registers. However, not only were there exceptions to this trend, but both supportive professionals and critical non-professionals had less coherent interpretations of the novel than is remembered either by critical accounts of the Rushdie affair or recent reflections on the debate in light of the attack on Rushdie. In this way, the Rushdie affair is instructive for thinking about how practices of distinction have concealed the continuities between professional and non-professional practices of reading postcolonial literature. Following the attempted murder of Rushdie in 2022, there is a risk that we as writers and critics further entrench distinctions between ourselves and an imagined public outside that threatens our work and our lives. This risk is intensified by today's increasingly fast-moving information economy, which, as we've seen, has simplified the connections between Rushdie's attacker and the putative antagonists of the Rushdie affair. It strikes me that now, as then, it would be a mistake to confuse the actions of one individual for the beliefs of a whole group.

CHAPTER 2

Reading and Address

For Xiaolu Guo, making art is a kind of self-exile. Born in China in 1976, Guo grew up in a small fishing village in the eastern province of Zhejiang. The persecution of artists following the Chinese Communist Revolution, which resulted in the establishment of the People's Republic of China in 1949, had a formative effect on young Guo, who remembers her father's internment at a prison camp for his work as a traditional landscape ink painter, and her brother's participation in the student-led demonstrations at Tiananmen Square, Beijing, in 1989.[1] She trained as a filmmaker at the Beijing Film Academy before taking up a British Council scholarship at the National Film School in London in 2002. Her first documentary film *The Concrete Revolution* (2004) attracted the anger of the Chinese government for its depiction of the rural construction workers who were dispatched to Beijing to prepare the city for the 2008 Beijing Olympics. She was briefly deported after her British visa ran out, but successfully returned to Britain three months later, and now resides in Hackney with her husband and their daughter.[2] Britain has therefore become a place of literal sanctuary for Guo. But it is in the English language that Guo has found artistic refuge. In a panel conversation for the Asia Society with Isaac Stone Fish, she has talked about the imaginative possibilities of writing in English: "[For] immigrant writers like me, you know, it's my decision—a choice—to use my second language because actually I found a much more free, free space, you know. I can write without self-censorship".[3] Writing in English, Guo suggests, has

---

[1] Xiaolu Guo and Maya Jaggi, "Xiaolu Guo: 'Growing up in a Communist Society with Limited Freedom, You're a Spiky, Angry Rat,'" *The Guardian*, 30 May 2014 <https://www.theguardian.com/books/2014/may/30/xiaolu-guo-communist-china-interview> [accessed 24 April 2023].
[2] Guo and Jaggi, "Xiaolu Guo."
[3] Xiaolu Guo, quoted in Asia Society, "Why Xiaolu Guo Writes in English," YouTube, 9 November 2017 <https://www.youtube.com/watch?v=MOzigblC1mk> [accessed 24 April 2023].

freed her from state censorship, and the kind of self-censorship it compels. She yet remains uninterested in linguistic mastery: "I live with my broken language and it's my pride to use that broken language. There's tiny escape maybe for artists [who] use different language", Guo says, "maybe live in different places, or use different form to work as artists. [...] I do think you need to find your own space, and a certain artistic language".[4]

Often formally challenging and linguistically innovative, Guo's English-language writing frequently treats issues of translation and intercultural communication. *A Concise Chinese-English Dictionary for Lovers*, her third novel and first published in English, has encouraged critical accounts of its exploration of translingual and transcultural communication,[5] its dramatisation of linguistic translation,[6] and its reflections on the relationship between linguistic translation and sociocultural translation.[7] The novel follows twenty-three year old protagonist and narrator, Zhuang Xiao Qiao—or Z, as she becomes known—for the duration of her year-long stay in London, where she learns English at a private language school. The protagonist's trip and her education are funded by her parents who believe that an education in English will enable her to expand their shoe-making business in China. In London, she meets an older Englishman, known only as 'you,' with whom she falls in love, and who causes her to reflect on linguistic and cultural differences. She ultimately returns to China, not

---

[4] Guo, quoted in Asia Society, "Why Xiaolu Guo Writes in English."

[5] Annalisa Oboe, "Language, Eros and Culture in Xiaolu Guo's *A Concise Chinese-English Dictionary for Lovers*," in *The Tapestry of the Creative Word in Anglophone Literatures*, ed. by Antonella Riem Natale, Maria Renata Docle, Stefano Mercanti, and Caterina Colomba (Udine: Forum Editrice Universitaria Udinese, 2013), pp. 267–79; Angelia Poon, "Becoming a Global Subject: Language and the Body in Xiaolu Guo's *A Concise Chinese-English Dictionary for Lovers*," *Transnational Literature*, 6.1 (2013), pp. 1–9; Ania Spyra, "On Labors of Love and Language Learning: Xiaolu Guo Rewriting the Monolingual Family Romance," *Studies in the Novel*, 48.4 (2016), pp. 444–61; Guiliana Ferri, "The Master's Tools Will Never Dismantle the Master's House: Decolonising Intercultural Communication," *Language and Intercultural Communication*, 22.3 (2022), pp. 381–90 (p. 385).

[6] Fiona Doloughan, "Text Design and Acts of Translation: The Art of Textual Remaking and Generic Transformation," *Translation and Interpreting Studies*, 4.1 (2009), pp. 101–15; Rachael Gilmour, "Living between Languages: The Politics of Translation in Leila Aboulela's *Minaret* and Xiaolu Guo's *A Concise Chinese-English Dictionary for Lovers*," *Journal of Commonwealth Literature*, 47.2 (2012), pp. 207–27; Rachael Gilmour, *Bad English: Literature, Multilingualism, and the Politics of Language in Contemporary Britain* (Manchester: Manchester University Press, 2020), pp. 168–204.

[7] Fiona Doloughan, "The Construction of Space in Contemporary Narrative," *Journal of Narrative Theory*, 45.1 (2015), pp. 1–17.

to work in her hometown as planned, but to live in Beijing. Written in the first person through the focalisation of the protagonist, the narrative observes the register of a diary, but contains the stylistic features of a dictionary. Most episodes are named for a target word or phrase that she encounters and learns within the episode. In this way, it is a kind of vernacular dictionary, in which the protagonist's gradual acquisition of English is indexed by both her explicit acquisition of a target word or phrase, and the stylistic transformation of her first-person narration from a 'non-standard' prosaic English to a more 'standard' and sometimes poetic form of English.

This chapter explores the reception of *A Concise Chinese-English Dictionary for Lovers* by Xiaolu Guo through an engagement with professional responses published in journal articles and books, and non-professional responses published online on social reading platforms. It aims to intervene in professional speculation about non-professional readers' affinity to any national or linguistic context. That is, where scholars have suggested that novels like Guo's address a 'Western' or 'native' audience, and either affirm or interrogate cultural and linguistic biases, I insist that this addressed audience must be differentiated from the actual readership of *A Concise Chinese-English Dictionary for Lovers*. Non-professional practices of reading the text significantly differ from professional practices of reading the text, particularly in the ways they invest in self-identification and in identification with the protagonist as real. Yet their reading practices defy definition as nationalist or nativist, and at times explicitly draw attention to the gap between the text's addressed audience and its actual readers. By differentiating themselves from the audience constructed and addressed by the novel, non-professional readers in fact behave more like professional readers than is commonly assumed. Both readerships insist on their difference from any addressed audience. Professional readers tend to deter (self-)recognition as the culturally or linguistically nativist audience addressed by the text through the self-reflexive identification of the novel's addressed audience, and the association of this addressed audience with a non-professional readership. But non-professional readers, too, demonstrate an awareness of the novel's addressed audience, and their practices of reading seek to forge new forms of relating to the text, its protagonist and its author that are not anticipated by the novel.

Reading and Address

In their analyses of *A Concise Chinese-English Dictionary for Lovers* as translational literature, scholars have considered the implied audience of the novel. Fiona Doloughan has suggested that the text is "directed towards an English-speaking audience, and one which by and large assumes little knowledge of China or Chinese other than stereotypical representations on the part of the reader."[8] For Doloughan, the novel challenges this English-speaking audience to overcome their attachment to monolingualism. Sneja Gunew puts its slightly differently. She argues that the protagonist's often humorous linguistic and cultural misunderstandings only communicate because Guo shares with readers greater knowledge of English than her protagonist. "These misconceptions," as she puts it, "create a number of instances of dramatic irony, thus forging a complicitous relationship with a more 'knowing' reader".[9] Where Gunew uses 'complicity' descriptively, Flair Donglai Shi uses the term evaluatively to criticise Guo's cooperation with foreign, 'Western' publishers and their target audiences. "Xiaolu Guo," he argues, in his account of the book cover of her third English-language novel *UFO in Her Eyes* (2009), "has complied with western market forces to some extent, and thus she may be accused of portraying a negative image of China for the sake of performing a certain kind of anti-establishment criticality for her western viewers and readers".[10] In his comparative analysis of the Chinese, Taiwanese, and British editions of *A Concise Chinese-English Dictionary for Lovers*, Shi similarly argues that the cover of the British edition of her 2007 novel engages in the "reductive representation of the racial/national Other."[11] What interests me here is not so much Shi's account of the covers of Guo's books as exoticist, but his sense that the book covers respond to and satisfy the tastes of 'Western' audiences. To be a 'Western' reader in his account can seem to mean engaging in reading practices that produce foreign cultural

---

[8] Fiona Doloughan, "Translation as a Motor of Critique and Invention in Contemporary Literature: The Case of Xiaolu Guo," in *Multilingual Currents in Literature, Translation and Culture*, ed. by Rachael Gilmour and Tamar Steinitz (New York: Routledge, 2017), pp. 150–67 (p. 160).
[9] Sneja Gunew, *Post-Multicultural Writers as Neo-Cosmopolitan Mediators* (Anthem Press, 2017), p. 93.
[10] Flair Donglai Shi, "Reborn Translated: Xiaolu Guo as World Author," *Kritika Kultura*, 36 (2021), pp. 166–94 (p. 185).
[11] Flair Donglai Shi, "Translating the Translational: A Comparative Study of the Taiwanese and Mainland Chinese Translations of Xiaolu Guo's *A Concise Chinese-English Dictionary for Lovers*," *Translation and Literature*, 30 (2021), pp. 1–29 (p. 14).

products as allegorical and their authors as 'native informants.' Shi concludes that translational fiction like *A Concise Chinese-English Dictionary for Lovers* is limited in its ability to challenge the authority of English and the discourses of linguistic, literary, and cultural value that circulate around it. Such works, he argues, "may challenge the so-called native reader's demand for fluency, but will in no way jeopardize the anglophone text's comprehensibility as a consumable literary object."[12]

While it's useful to reflect on the complicity of fiction like Guo's with the structural inequities of the global literary marketplace, which secures the disproportionate circulation and translation of English-language works, the notion that there exists a 'native reader' who demands a particular performance of linguistic competence during reading stereotypes the reading practices of first-language English speakers. First-language speakers come to signify agents of monolingual discourse in their cultural engagements. In fairness, the concept of the 'native reader' is not Shi's, but Rebecca L. Walkowitz's, in whose work 'native readers' are not quite those who require the replication of 'standard' or idiolectic linguistic practices in the texts they read, but "those who assume that the book they are holding was written for them or that the language they are encountering is, in some proprietary or intrinsic way, theirs."[13] She uses the term to distinguish the cultural and ideological work performed by translational literature, which inhibits native fluency and "interferes with the novel's traditional role as an instrument of monolingual collectivity."[14] By reproducing Walkowitz's argument, Shi nonetheless affirms the existence of a 'native readership,' whose nativist practices are ideologically, but not materially, impeded by the translational character of texts like *A Concise Chinese-English Dictionary for Lovers*.

In their identification of the English-speaking or 'Western' audience for Guo's novel, these critical arguments illuminate the ways in which scholarship in world and postcolonial literary studies has prioritised what Michael Allan calls "the question of address" over "the question of reading." In "Reading with One Eye, Speaking with One Tongue: On the Problem of Address in World Literature," Allan suggests that studies of the formation of national readerships and cosmopolitan readerships alike "tend to skirt the full potential of the nonnational reader, or perhaps more precisely, the reader

---

[12] Shi, "Translating the Translational," p. 27.
[13] Rebecca L. Walkowitz, *Born Translated: The Contemporary Novel in an Age of World Literature* (New York: Columbia University Press, 2015), p. 6.
[14] Walkowitz, *Born Translated*, p. 46.

who is not addressed explicitly by a literary work."[15] By focusing on who a text addresses at the expense of who actually reads a text, such scholarship on reading in postcolonial and world literature studies risks delimiting the reception of literature. As Leah Price has argued, "some of the most interesting cases [of reading] are those in which the implied reader differs sharply from what we know about the empirical audience."[16] To mistake a text's address, or implied reader, for its actual readers, is therefore to forget that readers frequently and unpredictably read texts intended for others. It is also to obscure how readers' reading selves selectively realise the function of the implied reader (see Introduction, pp. 20–21).

A work's actual and future readers are approximated by its address. We can see this at work in Lawrence Venuti's influential work on the invisibility of translation, which has been taken up widely in world and postcolonial literary studies, and which is cited by both Flair Donglai Shi and Rebecca L. Walkowitz in their accounts of translational literature. Venuti argues that there are two distinctive methods of translation: domestication, "an ethnocentric reduction of the foreign text to target-language cultural values, bringing the author back home," and foreignisation, "an ethnodeviant pressure on those values to register the linguistic and cultural difference of the foreign text, sending the reader abroad."[17] He is clear that a tradition of domestication is dominant in Britain and the United States, and moreover that it has produced domestic readerships that are "aggressively monolingual, unreceptive to the foreign, accustomed to fluent translations that invisibly inscribe foreign texts with English-language values and provide readers with the narcissistic experience of recognizing their own culture in a cultural other."[18] But, while he may use the language of reading and readerships to criticise the prevalence of domestication, Venuti is more properly speaking not of the question of reading, but of the question of address: that is, the ways that publishers, editors, writers, translators, and reviewers cooperatively produce a text's audience, imposing limits on its address.

Reading is always mediated by address. Someone who doesn't read, or doesn't read English, for instance, is neither addressed by *A Concise*

---

[15] Michael Allan, "Reading with One Eye, Speaking with One Tongue: On the Problem of Address in World Literature," *Comparative Literature Studies*, 44.1–2 (2007), pp. 1–19 (p. 5 and p. 3).

[16] Leah Price, "Reading: The State of the Discipline," *Book History*, 7 (2004), pp. 303–20 (p. 305).

[17] Lawrence Venuti, *The Translator's Invisibility: A History of Translation* (London: Routledge, 2004), p. 20.

[18] Venuti, *The Translator's Invisibility*, p. 23, p. 15.

Chinese-English Dictionary for Lovers, nor able to join its readership. But reading also exceeds address. As Michael Allan demonstrates in his analysis of Jean-Paul Sartre's preface to Frantz Fanon's *Les damnés de la terre* (translated into English as *The Wretched of the Earth*), Sartre recognises that he is not addressed by Fanon's original text, but reads it anyway; in doing so, and by preparing the work's preface, Sartre produces a new address for Fanon's work: European (especially French) readers.[19] Venuti's own practices of reading exemplify the difference between the text's address and its readers. When he advocates a strategy of symptomatic reading to uncover the cultural and ideological work performed by both domestication and foreignisation, Venuti purposefully behaves as a reader who is not addressed by the translation, and performs a practice of reading that is explicitly neither compelled, nor precomprehended by the text. "This sort of reading," Venuti says of symptomatic reading, "can be said to foreignize a domesticating translation by showing where it is discontinuous" and to "uncove[r] the domesticating movement involved in any foreignizing translation by showing where its construction of the foreign depends on domestic cultural materials."[20] By his own account, then, Venuti's critique of domestication slightly misrepresents the relationship between a text's address and its readerships, and underestimates readers' ability to identify, but not necessarily identify *with*, the addressed audience.

Perhaps Venuti's endorsement of symptomatic reading betrays his investment in the professionalisation of reading as a solution to the problem of translation. "It is in academic institutions, most importantly," he argues, "that different reading practices can be developed and applied to translations".[21] But if Venuti is capable of a critical practice of reading that registers how translation resemiotises cultural difference, and which recognises his own role in the constitution of the domestic and the foreign, then what's to say that other readers aren't also capable of the same? And are we to believe these readers, or readers-to-come, only reside in academic institutions? How does a reorientation toward reading and its negotiation of textual address contest existing ideas about domestic or native readerships? The language of foreignisation and domestication may presume the linguistic nativism, monolingualism, and nationalism of different readerships. But the terms can be recuperated, I argue, to clarify the role of the reading self and the self-in-the-world in practices of reading postcolonial literature. Translation is a form of reading, Venuti argues. But in conceiving of his own practice

---

[19] See Allan, "Reading with One Eye, Speaking with One Tongue," pp. 2–3.
[20] Venuti, *The Translator's Invisibility*, p. 29.
[21] Venuti, *The Translator's Invisibility*, p. 312.

of symptomatic reading as a practice of foreignising domestication, and of domesticating foreignisation, he also articulates reading as a form of translation. In the conceptualisation of reading as translation, different practices of reading become visible.

If, as I have argued in the Introduction, the role of the reading self is to flexibly assimilate the text's discursive protocols in an ethics of reading, its cultural activity closely resembles foreignisation. It pays attention to the "linguistic and cultural difference of the foreign text, sending the reader abroad."[22] It translates, or transforms, the reader through the register of the text. Similarly, if the role of the self-in-the-world is to make inferences about the text based on its existing affective, interpretative, and evaluative resources in a politics of reading, its cultural labour can be described as domestication. It "bring[s] back a cultural other as the same, the recognisable, even the familiar," engaging in "an appropriation of foreign cultures for domestic agendas, cultural, economic, political."[23] It translates, or transforms, the text in the register of the reader. By defining the cultural work performed by the reading self and the self-in-the-world as foreignisation and domestication respectively, I mean to suggest that practices of reading are intrinsically hybrid. Reading involves acts of self-representation and the re-inscription of cultural difference at the same time as it entails the forfeiture of self-authority and the recalibration of existing procedures of cultural differentiation. These processes of domestication and foreignisation are imbricated and co-productive during reading. The self-in-the-world brings expectations and assumptions of the self to bear on the text, domesticating its meaning in advance. The reading self takes on these domestic priorities, but suspends them where the text fails to cohere with a meaning or register already given by the self. It foreignises the cultural horizon of the self, and compels the self-in-the-world to query and revise its expectations. Put simply, reading progresses through a recursive process of domestication and foreignisation.

This conceptualisation of reading as a process of translation helps to disentangle the question of address from the question of reading. Reading is structured by, but separate from, any prior process of translation, and any production of a textual address. In the same way, it helps to distinguish between the abstract national and linguistic audiences delimited by publishers, translators and writers, and a text's actual readerships. The notion of a 'Western' reader, and of a domestic or native readership, for

---

[22] Venuti, *The Translator's Invisibility*, p. 20.
[23] Venuti, *The Translator's Invisibility*, pp. 18–19.

instance, belong to the register of literary production, rather than to that of literary reception. Decoupling the question of reading from the question of address is important because their conflation underserves non-professional readers. It is their discursive practices, and not those of professional critics, that are established as monocultural, monolingual, nativist, and nationalist. Yet, as Wendy Waring has shown in her analysis of the paratextual devices used to sell postcolonial and Aboriginal fiction, there is a significant difference between the 'market reader' for postcolonial and world literature, and actual readers, the "heterogeneity" of which "professional readers [...] should pay heed."[24] Constructed by literary producers, the domesticating 'market reader' helps to produce the value of professional literary criticism. As Sarah Brouillette has argued, "the figure of the cosmopolitan reader," or the 'market reader,' "is the shadow self of the academic critic, acting to protect him from his own proximity to the kinds of reading practices he sets aside for others."[25] Put another way, academic critics derive the value of professional reading from the (para) textual address, rather than any observable practices of non-professional reading.

A Concise Chinese-English Dictionary for Lovers may address "a more 'knowing' reader," to recall Sneja Gunew's analysis of the novel with which I opened this section, and the nature of this knowledge might be linguistic, even nativist. The novel may employ paratextual devices and the structure of the implied reader to compel future readers to enact the aesthetic, ethical, and political protocols of this audience. But by whom is the text actually read, and how? How does an engagement with actual practices of reading the novel dispute the abstraction of 'Western' readers, invested in the reproduction of cultural difference, and of 'native readers,' whose proprietary linguistic competence is rewarded by translational, English-language fiction? How does an appreciation for the heterogeneity of 'Western' and English-language readerships challenge dominant assumptions about non-professional reading practices?

---

[24] Wendy Waring, "Is This Your Book? Wrapping Postcolonial Fiction for the Global Market," *Canadian Review of Comparative Literature/ Revue Canadienne de Littérature Comparée*, 22.3-4 (1995), pp. 455–66 (p. 462). See also Graham Huggan's account of 'market readers,' in which he draws on Waring's essay: Graham Huggan, *The Postcolonial Exotic* (London: Routledge, 2001), pp. 164–76.

[25] Sarah Brouillette, *Postcolonial Writers in the Global Literary Marketplace* (Basingstoke: Palgrave Macmillan, 2011), p. 21.

On Identification

One of the most striking things about non-professional practices of reading *A Concise Chinese-English Dictionary for Lovers* is the frequency with which readers identify themselves culturally and geographically. While theories of literary consumption in world and postcolonial literary studies might presume the existence of a 'Western,' or 'native' readership, whose generalisable reading practices domesticate Guo's work, actual readers of the novel conceive of themselves and their reading practices in more specific terms. For example, in their review of the book on Amazon UK, one reader says that "As an Englishwoman it was interesting to see our society and morals from an outsider's—let alone a country Chinese woman's—viewpoint". This reader credits neither an abstract connection to the 'West' nor linguistic nativity with influence over their practice of reading, instead specifying the way that her Englishness, gender identity and implicit metropolitanism mediate her appreciation of the protagonist's perspective, which is in turn perceived as that of "a country Chinese woman." In a review of the book on Goodreads, another reader shares how their experience as a non-migrant, former resident of London shapes their comprehension of the novel. "For a former Londoner like myself," they write, "it gives a new insight into how the city must feel and look to the multitude of people who arrive from overseas for the first time, no matter the duration of their stay". For this reader, the novel's first-person narrative provides access to an affective and sensory register that is shared by migrants to the capital. The protagonist's gender and Chinese nationality is less important here than her status as a migrant to the city, which becomes a source of both cultural differentiation and empathy. A third reader engages in a similar reading practice. Only implicitly identifying as a non-migrant reader, they write in their review on Goodreads: "I was [...] struck by the bravery of anyone who travels alone to a country with a very different language that they hardly know. [...] I'm not sure that I could ever be that brave". This reader identifies migration as a source of difference between themselves and the protagonist, but one that promotes connection and admiration. Reading is intrinsically social in its contexts and its practice.[26] And, to different extents, Goodreads and Amazon reward performances of identity. As Lisa Nakamura has argued, Goodreads serves as an online social networking platform that "encourage[s] [readers]

---

[26] See Elizabeth Long, *Book Clubs: Women and the Uses of Reading in Everyday Life* (Chicago: Chicago University Press, 2003), pp. 8–11.

to perform their identities as readers in a public and networked forum."[27] Amazon, meanwhile, has "fostered new kinds of community around [its] products, and book reviewers on [its] sit[e] often engage in dialog with other reviews, creating spaces where users can form micro-communities around particular products."[28] But the specificity with which readers relate to the novel and its protagonist is significant here in the way it refutes the abstract categories into which foreign readerships are typically classified.

It is not simply that non-professional readers of *A Concise-Chinese English Dictionary for Lovers* conceive of themselves more specifically than current theories of reception in postcolonial and world literary studies, but that they also self-identify more diversely. Some readers identify as Chinese; for example, one reader begins their Amazon review in the following way: "As a Chinese living in London, I'm really fascinated by the main character's thinking of western world and its culture with her own eastern cultural background". Another on Goodreads writes: "As a Chinese girl who has dated a white man and lived in London, I don't find this book interesting— pretty boring, to be honest. Cultural shock experienced by every Asian girl entering a foreign, western country". While both of these Chinese readers to some extent identify with the protagonist, the first finds pleasure in the comparison, while the second finds it a source of tedium. The latter implies that the novel narrates a story so familiar that it needn't be written, or certainly needn't be read by Chinese women who have migrated to 'Western' countries. Several readers describe themselves as (former) international students. "I am into cross-culture and all, myself being an international student coming to England for the first time," writes one reader in their Amazon customer review, who goes on to criticise the protagonist and the infidelity of the novel's narrative voice. A second reader writes on Amazon that the book was "[v]ery appreciated by a foreign student that also spent a long time alone in London and felt equally lonely".

Others identify themselves as migrant readers. In their Goodreads review, one admits simply that their own experience of migration informs the pleasure they take in reading about other migrants: "As someone who immigrated from Canada to Malta, and had to learn how a culture works from language (which I still haven't fully grasped, totally my fault) to attitudes, I enjoy reading books about the immigrant experience". Others self-identify as migrants, and compare their experience of migration to that

[27] Lisa Nakamura, "'Words with Friends': Socially Networked Reading on *Goodreads*," *PMLA*, 128.1 (2013), pp. 239–43 (p. 240).
[28] Ed Finn, "The Social Lives of Books," (PhD dissertation, Stanford University, 2011), p. 29.

of the protagonist Z. In their Amazon review, one reader connects their enjoyment of the novel to its relatability as the story of a migrant who finds love in England. "I absolutely adored this book," they write. "Maybe because my English was not perfect when I first came to England? And in the first few weeks, I sometimes had trouble understanding my then boyfriend (now my husband of 21 years)". A second reader agrees that the pleasure of reading the novel was intensified by their identification with Z as a migrant. Recalling their experience of reading the episode titled 'alien,' in which Z narrates her arrival in Heathrow Airport, London, they write "I found it funny because I nearly had the same thoughts about that word alien when I was pretty young and flying over to England for the first time". This reader enjoys Z's narrative perspective in an almost nostalgic way, recognising a younger version of themselves in the protagonist. Another reader suggests that their ability to comprehend and empathise with Z was enriched by their own experience of migration. "I just loved the way she described the English world through Chinese eyes," they write. "I could understand her struggling with the culture clash—having myself moved from Austria to England for one year". Their shared experience of migration to England is, for this reader, a valuable resource for reading the text. A different migrant reader, reviewing the novel on Goodreads, is less quick to overlook the differences between their own migration and that of Z. As part of their review of the novel, they write:

> I'm an immigrant, but I was lucky enough to know the language of the country I had immigrated to. I never had to feel self-conscious about the way my tongue could not mould around words properly, or feel like my thoughts could never be understood when I translated them into speech.

This reader experiences the protagonist's migration as a source of both connection and differentiation. They recognise that, while they share the experience of moving to a foreign country, they did not have to engage in second language learning, nor face linguistic discrimination.

For all their differences, self-identified and not, these readers have in common that they self-identify in relation to the novel's protagonist. It is not just that they compare themselves to Z, identifying differences and similarities, but that they appear moved toward different models of self-identification and relation. The first-person narrative of Z—a young Chinese woman from a rural, peasant background, who moves to London to study English for a year—guides readers to appreciate the way that their own cultural belonging, linguistic competence, cosmopolitanism, and gender shape their self-expression. Put simply, readers become English or Chinese, migrant or non-migrant, Londoner or urbanite through their encounter with the protagonist of the text. Their reading selves are compelled to assimilate the text's patterns of identity construction and cultural differentiation so that linguistic and cultural naturalisation, for instance, are prioritised as constitutive of identity over social class or housing security. They engage in a process of foreignisation, exchanging any pre-existing protocols of identity performance for those presented in the text. This is an ethics of reading, in which readers suspend their assumptions and expectations. Their selves-in-the-world mediate this ethics of reading using their pre-existing knowledge and experience of identity formation and differentiation, including their self-knowledge (that is, their awareness that the self is not that of Z in the text, nor any real counterpart she may represent). The self-in-the-world recalibrates the singularity of Z's model of identity construction according to the domestic resources of the self. Her novel way of self-representation is transformed into something useful, valuable, or enjoyable for the way it clarifies aspects of the self and its horizon. In this politics of reading, the self-in-the-world and its mode of knowledge production is not necessarily affirmed, but is rather brought into play in the translation of that which is unfamiliar or not of the self. We can see this at work in the frequency which readers report having learned something about themselves from the text. They may articulate their practices of reading without the language and authority associated with the formal institutions of literary culture, but these non-professional readers clearly participate in processes of self-scrutiny and self-reconstitution.

By identifying themselves in ways more specific and more diverse than is presumed by dominant approaches in world and postcolonial literary studies, non-professional readers query the relationship between the question of address and the question of reading. Their retrospective descriptions of the text also serve to differentiate them from the British narratees within the text. For instance, in their book reviews on Amazon UK and Goodreads, several readers persistently call the protagonist her given name Zhuang rather than Z, the name she adopts because people in London don't attempt to pronounce her name. In the episode titled 'full english breakfast,' which takes place within the first three days of her residency in London, the protagonist tells us, "Nobody know my name here. Even they read the spelling of my name: *Zhuang Xiao Qiao*, they have no idea how saying it. When they see my name starts from 'Z', stop trying. I unpronounceable Ms Z".[29] Of the

---

[29] Xiaolu Guo, *A Concise Chinese-English Dictionary for Lovers* (London: Vintage, 2008), p. 18.

fifty-four Goodreads reviews that mention 'Zhuang,' thirty-four (almost two thirds) only use the name Zhuang to refer to the protagonist, except in cases where they differentiate it from 'Z,' the name she takes in England for ease. By referring to her as Zhuang throughout their reviews, such readers not only disidentify with the intratextual, unnamed Londoners who refuse to attempt the pronunciation of her name, but also the extratextual English-speaking audience that they signify. These readers protest the assumption that they resemble and behave like an addressed audience of English-speaking readers, ignorant of Chinese. While the primary aim of non-professional readers appears to be to distinguish themselves from the text's English narratees, and a corresponding domesticating 'market' readership, their practice of naming the protagonist is interesting in the way that it distinguishes them from professional readers of *A Concise Chinese-English Dictionary for Lovers*, who scarcely refer to the protagonist by her full name. Not one critical essay on the novel only refers the protagonist by Zhuang, or by her full name Zhuang Xiao Qiao.[30] Rachael Gilmour, Annalisa Oboe, Angelia Poon, and Ania Spyra each choose to call the protagonist by her full name just once, before referring to her as Z for the remainder of their essays.[31] In each of her three essays on the novel, Fiona Doloughan refers to the protagonist as Z only.[32] Eunju Hwang also only calls the protagonist by her adopted name Z.[33]

Why do professional and non-professional readers exhibit such different practices of naming the protagonist? Certainly, performances of reading and interpretation in communal spaces are subject to processes of conventionalisation. The fact that early essays on *A Concise Chinese-English Dictionary for Lovers* adopt a particular practice of naming the protagonist Z, for instance, likely shapes the interpretative and discursive practices of later scholars.[34] Through reading and citation, naming the protagonist Z

---

[30] As far as I am aware, this was accurate in May 2023.
[31] Gilmour, "Living between Languages"; Gilmour, *Bad English*; Oboe, "Language, Eros and Culture in Xiaolu Guo's *A Concise Chinese-English Dictionary for Lovers*"; Poon, "Becoming a Global Subject"; Spyra, "On Labors of Love and Language Learning."
[32] Doloughan, "Text Design and Acts of Translation"; Doloughan, "The Construction of Space in Contemporary Narrative"; Doloughan, "Translation as a Motor of Critique and Invention in Contemporary Literature."
[33] Eunju Hwang, "Love and Shame: Transcultural Communication and Its Failure in Xiaolu Guo's *A Concise Chinese-English Dictionary for Lovers*," ariel: A Review of International English Literature, 43.4 (2013), pp. 69–95.
[34] The first essay published on *A Concise Chinese-English Dictionary for Lovers*, for instance, introduces the protagonist as 'Zhuang Xiaoqiao,' and recounts her adoption of the name 'Z', before using the name 'Z' for the rest of the essay.

becomes conventionalised as a professional protocol. Similarly, and as DeNel Rehberg Sedo has shown, online discussion forums are governed often inexplicit practices of moderation, which create a level of discursive and ideological conformity among public contributions that is not necessarily present among contributors. The real or perceived cultural authority of some amateur reviewers, Sedo finds, guides other readers to replicate their interpretative performance, or risk facing the exclusion of other reviewers.[35] When readers replicate the language or interpretations of other readers, it may be unconscious: as James Procter and Bethan Benwell have shown of book groups, sometimes readers "consciously or not, modify, revise and re-read the text" in light of other readers' responses.[36]

Forces of conventionalisation might therefore explain the uniformity exhibited by both professional readers in published essays and non-professional readers on public social reading platforms. But they cannot account for the divergent discursive procedures adopted by these different interpretative communities in the first place. The difference, I think, has to be located in the different objects of attention and attachment that these readerships tend to take. The foremost object of attention and attachment for professional readers is the text. "[T]he text," Elizabeth Long argues, is the "primary imperative of literary analysis."[37] The historic prioritisation of the text and the attendant deprioritisation of character bespeaks the codification of what Toril Moi calls a "'modernist-formalist' ethos [which] encouraged literary critics to privilege form over subject matter."[38] The primacy awarded to the text and to a modernist-formalist aesthetic is especially visible in the field

---

Wenche Ommundsen, "From China with Love: Chick Lit and The New Crossover Fiction," in *China Fictions/English Language: Literary Essays in Diaspora, Memory, Story*, ed. by A. Robert Lee (Amsterdam: Rodolpi, 2008), pp. 327–45.

[35] DeNel Rehberg Sedo, "'I Used to Read Anything That Caught My Eye, But...': Cultural Authority and Intermediaries in a Virtual Young Adult Book Club," *Reading Communities from Salons to Cyberspace*, ed. by DeNel Rehberg Sedo (Basingstoke: Palgrave Macmillan, 2011), pp. 101–23. Elizabeth Long makes a similar argument in her study of North American book discussion groups, suggesting that "informal processes of social control can be extremely effective in silencing or stigmatizing members so as to enforce conformity." See Long, *Book Clubs*, p. 187.

[36] James Procter and Bethan Benwell, *Reading Across Worlds: Transnational Book Groups and the Reception of Difference* (Basingstoke: Palgrave Macmillan, 2015), p. 48.

[37] Long, *Book Clubs*, p. 145.

[38] Toril Moi, "Rethinking Character," in *Character: Three Inquiries in Literary Studies*, ed. by Amanda Anderson, Rita Felski, and Toril Moi (Chicago: University of Chicago Press, 2019), p. 30.

of postcolonial studies. During the process of defining the discipline, Chris Bongie argues, "the primary emphasis [...] came to be placed on the *text*, a text that could take any material form [...] but that had to be *read*, and read in a certain 'time-lagged' way, a *modernist* way."[39] In calling the protagonist Z, professional readers can be seen to sustain a kind of attention and obligation to the text's own naming procedures, which purposefully and self-reflectively misrepresent the protagonist in order to articulate the absence of her cultural belonging and self-authority in England. These professional practices of reading pursue the modernist aesthetic that Bongie describes in that they sustain a kind of fidelity to the text's qualities of 'aesthetic resistance' and 'political resistance.'[40]

Non-professional readers, by contrast, have fewer reservations about expressing their attention and attachment to character. As Long notes in her study of North American book clubs, "consideration of characters often dominates reading group discussions" with "readers respond[ing] to fictional characters almost as if they were real people, analysing their emotional responses to them and associating outward from aspects of their own lives or those of kin and friends."[41] In their study of the international reception of diasporic and postcolonial literatures, Procter and Benwell similarly find that non-professional readers frequently treat characters as real people in a manner that "may seem hopelessly naïve from an academic perspective."[42] Non-professional readers, they suggest, observe an orientation to character that does not obtain in literary-professional contexts, evaluating the 'realism' of characters and the 'faithfulness' of their authors as creators. In their study, Charles Dickens was adopted as a frame of comparison more frequently than any other writer.[43] We can see something similar in the reception of *A Concise Chinese-English Dictionary for Lovers*. In their Amazon review, one non-professional reader bemoans the lover's anonymity and Zhuang's denial of her name as "modernist clever business" and complains that "both Z and her lover [...] came across as a bit insubstantial." "Guo has recently criticized Dickens for being unreadable" they conclude, "but she could do with more of his storytelling skills!" Modernist form is here not only relegated in importance, but viewed as an explicit barrier to connection and empathy. In the naming protocols adopted by professional and non-professional readers

---

[39] Chris Bongie, *Friends and Enemies: The Scribal Politics of Post/Colonial Literature* (Liverpool: Liverpool University Press, 2008), p. 289; original emphasis.
[40] Bongie, *Friends and Enemies*, p. 65.
[41] Long, *Book Clubs*, pp. 152–53.
[42] Procter and Benwell, *Reading Across Worlds*, p. 114.
[43] Procter and Benwell, *Reading Across Worlds*, p. 109.

of *A Concise Chinese-English Dictionary for Lovers*, then, we can see how forces of conventionalisation entrench pre-existing differences between how interpretative communities read and value literature, and the different objects of their attention.

In this context, the tendency of non-professional readers to use the protagonist's full name can be seen as a realist aesthetic that facilitates recognition and identification. It intervenes in the text's formal delimitation of her agency and self-expression. In the way that they name and relate to the novel's protagonist, these non-professional readers can be seen to assimilate the character's foreignness, and to contravene the text's own distancing devices. They deploy the interpretative and affective repertoire of their selves-in-the-world to sustain processes of identification and recognition, where the text would deny them the opportunity to do so. In making the protagonist 'real,' these readers simultaneously make the narrative 'realist,' and so diminish its aesthetic difficulty and its resistance to a liberal, cosmopolitan address. They locate the meaning and value of the novel in its realist representation of a Chinese migrant's experiences in Britain and their correspondence to real experiences of migration. In the pursuit of identification and recognition, then, these non-professional readers can be said to appropriate the text in a practice of domestication. Yet, has postcolonial studies too quickly dismissed the ethical and political value of domestication? As Procter and Benwell ask in their analysis of the realist modes of reading frequently adopted by non-professional readers:

> What might it mean in this context to pause over domestication and appropriation as *inevitable and necessary* dimensions of reading, as more than problematic (e.g. exoticising), but also as potentially productive and useful? [...] Arguably, without *any* domestication of the literary text there could be no 'positive' connection or engagement with otherness. Postcolonial critics have developed a rich set of reading strategies for de-familiarising difference, but have hardly anything to say about what might be at stake when readers familiarise themselves with it. We would argue in this context for the need to re-open reading practices to the dangers of domestication, the political outcomes of which are not inevitably conservative, that is to say, reactionary rather than resistant.[44]

For Procter and Benwell, the value of domesticating reading practices lies precisely in the way that they overcome otherness, and make difference

---

[44] Procter and Benwell, *Reading Across Worlds*, p. 116; original emphasis.

familiar. Domestication is here understood as a form of ethical and empathetic engagement, which can train readers in the expression of liberal-democratic political action. In part because the resolve to name and relate to the protagonist as Zhuang depends on a process of foreignisation, through which the reading self implicitly or explicitly registers the text's own aesthetic and political othering of the protagonist, domestication in this context can constitute a reparative reading practice that intervenes in the text's construction of the character and its narrow conception of the audience for her story. It can be viewed as the purposeful adoption of a realist practice of reading that responds to, but ultimately repairs the aesthetic and political limits imposed by the text.

A realist aesthetic, and the process of domestication it serves, therefore "allows [readers] to actively *imagine*, emotionally invest in and engage with others, forge creative attachments and connections in crossing cultural differences or coming to terms with ideological differences."[45] But how does the operation of domestication, in transforming the novel into a realist narrative, rub up against formally or politically challenging aspects of the text, or that which cannot be domesticated? What of those readers who don't or can't relate to the protagonist, and whose realist aesthetic therefore fails to translate cultural or ideological connections?

Realist Aesthetics, Domestication, and Disidentification

While some non-professional readers successfully pursue identification by engaging a realist aesthetic that eliminates formal barriers to proximity and relation, others experience disidentification through the application of realist practices of reading. They express frustration at their inability to identify with the protagonist. One reader on Amazon UK says simply: "You don't really identify with the main character. An interesting read, not compelling". Others offer more detailed criticisms of the character and her lack of relatability. For instance, in their review on Goodreads, a non-professional reader suggests that they expected to identify with the protagonist because of their shared migrant background. "Z was also frustrating to identify with," they write, "even with my background as an immigrant". This reader finds the protagonist's behaviour contradictory and, at times, repulsive. They continue:

> I finished the book feeling quite empty and disconnected. It's not because I expect every culture shock story to be about self discovery

---

[45] Procter and Benwell, *Reading Across Worlds*, p. 116; original emphasis.

and hope and cross-cultural romance / yearning, yet I can't help but wonder—what was the point really?

Though they disavow expectations that the narrative should fulfil certain generic and thematic conditions, they appear to project these desires onto the text in a domesticating practice of reading that produces indifference toward the protagonist, where they hoped to experience connection. They draw attention to the persistence of their expectations both in their description of the text as a "culture shock story," and in their concluding criticism of the book on account that the protagonist "didn't change in any way fundamentally through the experience [of migration]." It is implied that they anticipated that the protagonist would undergo a process of transformation through her experience, and that the novel would represent migration in this way. This reader can therefore be said to only momentarily undertake a practice of foreignisation through which the protagonist is produced as singular and unfamiliar, in relation to the existing affective and epistemic repertoire of their migrant self-in-the-world, before her singularity is domesticated by a prior moral code that conceives of her as unrelatable, and by pre-existing aesthetic desires that render the narrative disappointing. Here, we can see how a realist aesthetic, and the process of domestication it serves, can produce disidentification and indifference.

Other readers find that she is insufficiently real to compel a realist aesthetic through which they, as selves-in-the-world, empathise with her. They locate the protagonist's fraudulence in the artifice of the narrative voice. One reader on Amazon, for instance, writes: "The novel is written in the style of a diary, so the English is deliberately fragmented (although the spelling is perfect, except in cases where Z's accent would create a different word, which rather undermines the conceit)". For this reader, the inauthenticity of the protagonist's staged non-fluency draws attention to the text's own artifice. They conclude by disclosing their affective ambivalence toward the protagonist. "[W]hile I felt vaguely sorry for Z," they write, "I never cared that much." A second reader shares a similar view. "I found the faux-naif style in which this was written enormously irritating as well as entirely unconvincing", they write. "There was scope for this to be a much better book but as it is, it's artificial and contrived and that is a problem because it means you don't really care about the artificial and contrived characters". This reader makes an explicit connection between the artifice of the protagonist, and the inability to imagine and invest in her and other characters. The text's "contrived" form compels a realist aesthetic that is abortive in that it fails to produce identification, attachment, or empathy. A third reader on Amazon UK criticises the artificiality of the narrative voice through an appeal to cultural authority. "Sorry, for me it just doesn't ring true. [...] 'Z' speak[s] a form of Chinglish that I have never heard a Chinese person use in real life (and I know many)", they write. This reader performs their cultural knowledge of real Chinese people to authorise their reception of the protagonist's linguistic practice as fake. They proceed to interrogate the authenticity of her beliefs and practices in relation to the purported beliefs and practices of real Chinese people: "[S]he also professes to think that the action of squatting (as in sitting on one's heels) would be painful and uncomfortable, whereas in real life squatting comes /far/ more naturally to the Chinese (and adjacent races, such as the Vietnamese) than it does to we spoiled Westerners who are never far from our comfortable chairs". As this excerpt shows, this reader's claim to possess the cultural authority to speak of real Chinese people may be dubious, but they nonetheless assert that the novel is unbelievable according to their pre-existing ideas about Chinese life. Perhaps more explicitly than the first and second readers, this reader engages in a process of domestication that reaffirms their existing understanding of Chinese people. Domestication here oversees a practice of disidentification, rather than identification, where the protagonist's singularity is appropriated to signify her fraudulent representation of Chinese life.

Some non-professional readers locate their frustration to identify with the protagonist less in the protagonist herself than in the writing. In a 2,250-word review of the novel on Goodreads, for instance, one reader justifies their one-star rating in an expletive way. "[T]he characters FUCKING SUCK!" they write. They chastise Guo for her apparent "laziness" in not adequately explaining the reason for the protagonist's migration to England until the very end of the novel. The character of the unnamed lover, and the protagonist's passive infatuation with him moreover leads them to complain that the novel is poorly constructed. They write:

> The love interest in this particular novel is totally toxic, and, from the moment he shows up, he absolutely dominates the story which should have been about Z. [...] [A]lmost every single damned paragraph from page 30 onwards involves some variation of "I think of you"; "I wish I could understand you"; "I wonder about your thoughts". It's like Z literally lives for this man, and the novel absolutely lets the ball drop to Hades regarding character development: Z doesn't even have a single friend, or any storyline that doesn't involve this man, or even a part-time job to keep her entertained while he isn't around.

This reader criticises the priority awarded to the unnamed lover through the narrative focalisation of the novel's protagonist. They explicitly challenge the novel's representation of the protagonist, or lack thereof, and imply that a better novel could have emerged from her story. According to this reading practice, the protagonist has been underserved by the novel, which renders her superficially, and has her enter passively into an unequal relationship with an undesirable love interest. This reader concludes their review by redeeming the author as having the potential to write better novels, but says of *A Concise Chinese-English Dictionary for Lovers:* "all of that sexism, as well as some racism, made it an impossible read for me. [...] [It] could be called 'A Book about a Chinese Girl with no Will-Power getting into an Abusive Relationship and Becoming Addicted to Sex.'" The thematic content of the novel prompts a visceral reaction in this reader, who implicitly signals their desire that its characters reproduce their own norms and behaviours: the protagonist ought to be more independent, self-disciplined, and modest; the male characters ought not to sexually harass and assault her; the unnamed lover ought not ridicule her linguistic performance and subject her to cultural and racial stereotypes.

While the reader above makes a relatively restrained criticism of Xiaolu Guo for the novel's reproduction of sexual and racial discrimination, preferring to lodge their complaint with the text itself, others offer more sustained critiques of the author. One Goodreads reader, for example, praises the opening sections of the book, which narrate the protagonist's arrival in London and her early experiences in the city. "The start," they write, "had me questioning and thinking about Chinese immigration. It actually prompted me to go talk to my mum honestly about her experiences, how much I admired her, and how I came to the realisation [...] that I'm too selfish to ever make the same choice". The text here inspires prosocial action, compelling this reader to revisit their understanding of Chinese migration, and to seek to learn and exchange more about migration with their mother (who, it is implied, is also a [Chinese] migrant). Through a process of foreignisation, the reading self assimilates the text's representation of Chinese migration, which is subsequently domesticated by the self-in-the-world and put to work as a way of retroactively understanding the migration of their mother. For this same reader, the formal representation of the protagonist's language development thwarts proximity and relation. What initially "seemed quaint and honest soon felt grating and gimmicky" and "her 'skill' in English developed too quickly to seem realistic." Yet, their principal issue with the novel lies in its representation of the protagonist's travels around Europe on a Schengen Visa. Here, I quote in full:

Then Z travels around Europe. -- I think I have a longing for stories about solo female travellers. I want adventures. I want discovery, and excitement, and empowerment. I want a woman to be able to see the world in the way that men have been writing their travel memoirs for-fucking-ever. *Where is my female Teju Cole?* And, inevitably, I get instead awful narratives of women being abused. Women miserable and lonely. The undertones always: stay home. The world is too dangerous for you.

Z gets raped. That's what it is. I cannot stand it that the author thought that's what she deserved. Worse, that it was her fault and that she further needed punishment for how badly it was her fault. At this point, I no longer felt I could feel anything warm towards this book. A shame, because otherwise that ending suits my preferences.

I think... I think this was a book built on a premise first: *wouldn't it be great to write a story about a Chinese immigrant as if you were reading the worlds of a Chinese immigrant?* Rather than a story that is bursting with the life of its characters. I'll say it for a third time: It felt like a gimmick. Artificial. A ploy. And so to a larger extent, it then made Z's Chinese female identity feel just like a ploy. If being Chinese did not feel authentic -- what was the point of this book?

A desire and expectation that literature represents a specific kind of female empowerment, indexed by emotional and sexual independence, compels this reader to exhibit a particularly affective response when *A Concise Chinese-English Dictionary for Lovers* represents the rape of the protagonist while abroad in Faro, Portugal. Guo is accused of reproducing the misogynistic norms that mediate the sexual harassment and assault of women, as well as the cultural representation of women as victims. The author is implicitly understood as callous toward her protagonist for not only depicting her as a victim of rape, but also for making her partly responsible for the violence committed against her. This reader looks to the Nigerian-American writer Teju Cole as a standard for the representation of international travel. Curiously, they evaluate the novel unfavourably not in relation to Cole's literary models, but his autobiographical writing: the original Goodreads review includes a hyperlink to Teju Cole's 2015 essay for the *New York Times Magazine* about his experience of travelling in Switzerland after receiving a residential fellowship from Literaturhaus

Zürich.[46] Their realist aesthetic is therefore informed by the discursive protocols and thematic parameters of autobiography, rather than literary realism; hence their ongoing search for empowering "travel memoirs" by women, and their concluding criticism that the novel is "artificial" and inauthentic. And so, this reader domesticates the text as a cultural narrative that affirms, rather than challenges violence against women and the structural discrimination of women writers. Their desire for attachment to the protagonist causes them to disidentify with the author, who is constructed as disingenuous and "gimmicky."

While the reader above's primary quarrel with Guo is that she misled them, both in the sense of courting expectations of female discovery and adventure, and in the artifice of her formal representation of language learning, they also implicitly question to whom the book is addressed. Their final question "what was the point of this book?" raises another: "Who is this book for?" If the book poses as the diary, autobiography, or travel memoir of a real Chinese migrant, but does not satisfactorily overcome its own artifice, they insinuate that it can neither realistically represent the experience of migration, nor solicit realist practices of reading that empathise with the protagonist as if she is real. By inhibiting this particular reader's realist aesthetic, *A Concise Chinese-English Dictionary for Lovers* deprives them of the pleasure they usually take in reading—an idiosyncratic pleasure, whose dissatisfaction leads them to derive the book's failure.

Other readers implicitly raise similar questions about the limits of the text's address, suggesting that it rewards literary-professional rather than non-professional reading practices. In their Amazon UK review of the novel, one reader, for instance, expressly states that the book was a required purchase for a university class, rather than something they chose to read for pleasure: "Univerity [sic] class made me buy book. I no recommend you person read this book for the fun". Throughout their review, they mimic the voice of the protagonist to draw attention to the author's duplicity. They write: "Book written by lady who speak good English, but pretend she not. I write review same way. All book written like this. Book more annoying than nice for me to read". This reader imitates the protagonist's narrative voice to criticise the ease with which the author stages a 'non-standard' voice that is not her own. They implicitly demand that the fictional narrator observe fidelity to its author's linguistic competence—an unusual request, if not for the novel's own paratextual devices, which carefully and deliberately make a connection

---

[46] See Teju Cole, "Far Away from Here," *The New York Times Magazine*, 23 Sept 2015 <https://www.nytimes.com/2015/09/27/magazine/far-away-from-here.html> [accessed 28 February 2024].

between the author's own experience of migration and the novel. Xiaolu Guo herself has admitted that "[a]ll [her] novels are really quite autobiographical," and *A Concise Chinese-English Dictionary for Lovers* "was based on [her] diary in the year 2002 to 2003 when [she] came here [to Britain], the first year."[47] In any case, this reader's reference to the institutionalisation of the text serves to situate it within a professional scene of reading, and to warn unwitting non-professional readers that it defies the ordinary pleasures of reading. A second reader, this time on Goodreads, similarly argues that the book addresses a literary-professional audience. I quote their review in full:

> What was good about this book? I struggled with this book as the protagonist struggled with her English, and it wasn't the Chinglish. Indeed, that was the easy part. No, it was the annoying and shallow characters, the fact that nothing worth reading happens, the terrible coincidences, the feeling that a lot of potential had been wasted, the frustration, and the horrible icky feeling of reading a book where you feel the author has decided they will write about lots and lots of meaningless sex because sex sells, right?
>
> I thought this book couldn't be that bad. It had a quirky premise and it was shortlisted for the Orange Prize for fiction. Ugh, you can't trust judges/shortlisters of book awards. What did they see in this book? Possibly the "I wrote using this special Chinglish style" or "I used themes of racial conflict and LGBTQI as well as vegetarianism so it must be good because that's so woke?" or "I wrote this in the second person, how challenging and clever of me". Surely having compelling storyline and compelling characters is important in a book - alas, many people don't seem to care about that nowadays, not in "judging/assessing literature".

This reader criticises Guo for cynically representing sex to sell copies of the book. But their primary complaint is reserved for the literary-professional audience who, in awarding the novel the Orange Prize, secured its circulation among a non-professional readership invested in the legitimacy of literary prizes. They identify as a member of this readership, suggesting that the text's receipt of the Orange Prize, alongside its "quirky premise," caused them to believe that it "couldn't be that bad." But, upon reading the novel, their initial

---

[47] Xiaolu Guo, quoted in OpenLearn, "Writing Across Cultures," *Medium*, 9 July 2017 <https://openlearn.medium.com/writing-across-cultures-fd191d0c0a33> [accessed 12 June 2023].

belief in the authority of literary prizes and their judges turns to distrust. Guo is understood as a writer who cynically "uses" formally and thematically challenging material to address a professional-critical class, who, in turn, is understood to fulfil the terms of its address in rewarding fiction that is difficult rather than compelling. This reader's interrogation of the consecration of *A Concise Chinese-English Dictionary for Lovers* should not surprise us, for as James Procter and Bethan Benwell found in their study of transnational book groups, non-professional readers "appear far more savvy and self-aware consumers than academic accounts have tended to give them credit for": they do not take for granted the relationship between literary quality and literary prizing, but instead "spend a significant amount of time raising questions around the consecration, public notoriety and fame of authors, [and] the awards they've received."[48] But this reader's denunciation of the literary prize industry is an important reminder that non-professional readers are aware of a professional-literary industry and of professional practices of reading, and not necessarily interested in the cultural capital that they offer their practitioners.

The text compels disidentification among some non-professional readers, then, where it fails to reward a realist aesthetic, and where its formal and thematic difficulty is seen to address a professional audience. Such non-professional readers have few anxieties about their exclusion from the text's address. They portray the text's investment in a professional address as cynical. And they express no desire to relinquish their aesthetic sensibilities and assimilate those of an approximated literary-professional public in order to be addressed by the text. In calling attention to *A Concise-Chinese-English Dictionary for Lovers'* implicitly professional address, these readers illuminate an understudied aspect of the question of address in postcolonial and world literature studies. That is, while scholars have drawn attention to the ways that texts address different linguistic and national audiences (including, at its simplest, through their language of publication and distribution patterns), they have not substantially interrogated the ways that texts address different socio-institutional groups, including through canonisation and the awarding of literary prizes.

Conclusion

While *A Concise Chinese-English Dictionary for Lovers* may address an English-speaking audience, 'native' readers, or a 'Western' readership, its actual readership is far more diverse. We have seen non-professional readers

---

[48] Procter and Benwell, *Reading Across Worlds*, p. 150.

undertake practices of foreignisation through which they reconstitute their sense of self and expression of self-identity in relation to the protagonist and her singular performance of identity. We have also observed non-professional readers refuse to relate to the novel's English narratees and the English-speaking audience they indirectly signify, through a reparative reading practice that insists on the use of the protagonist's full name, Zhuang. We have furthermore seen non-professional readers interrogate the text's address in a politics of reading that appropriates their perception of professional criticism to comprehend the novel's critical acclaim. Non-professional readers, this chapter has shown, may sometimes pursue identification in a manner that distinguishes their practice as non-professional. They may articulate their practices of reading without the language and authority of professional literary criticism. And, at times, they adopt a realist aesthetic, and relate to and pass moral judgement over characters. But, in an important way, such realist practices of reading enable readers to differentiate themselves from narratees and addressees that are, at best, dismissive of Chinese names, and, at worst, racist. Such practices are not strictly domestication, then, for they respond to the text's own imaginative construction of its implied audience. This is not to idealise either the adoption of a realist aesthetic or non-professional practices of reading. We have seen instances where, in struggling or failing to relate to the protagonist as real, non-professional readers engage in sometimes naïve critiques of the novel as either bad fiction or failed memoir. It is instead to recognise that non-professional readers perform complicated and sometimes sophisticated practices of reading, and that their desires for attachment can animate powerful critiques of both postcolonial writing and the literary-professional industry that rewards it. These readers are explicitly not the addressed audience of Guo's novel. And yet, they read the novel anyway. The difference between reading and address needs to be heeded in postcolonial studies, not just because actual readerships are more diverse and complex than the addressed audiences defined by publishers, translators, and writers, but also because actual readerships notice, negotiate, and resist textual address during reading. In this sense, professional and non-professional practices of reading are more alike than has tended to be acknowledged in postcolonial studies.

CHAPTER 3

Reading and Non-Understanding

The opening chapter of *The Maestro, the Magistrate and the Mathematician* (2014) by Zimbabwean writer Tendai Huchu features a scene of reading. The Magistrate's daughter, fifteen-year-old Chenai, picks up a copy of *Harare North* from the coffee table after her uncle Alfonso unceremoniously changes the television channel, interrupting her enjoyment of a music video. Skimming the first page, she is almost instantly dismissive:

> "Dad, if this guy cannae be bovvered to learn proper English, why did he write a novel?" Chenai slapped Harare North back on the table. The Magistrate didn't have an answer. He'd seen the book in Waterstone's in Cameron Toll, whilst perusing legal texts, and had bought it on a whim. He couldn't get into it either. It appeared to have been written to deliberately turn the English language inside out.[1]

Chenai finds *Harare North* difficult. She believes that its use of language is incompatible with the novel form. There is a certain irony in her advocacy on behalf of 'proper English,' for Chenai does not herself speak 'proper English,' but has rather lived in Edinburgh long enough that she has acquired "a slight Scottish inflexion."[2] But while Chenai's Scottishness distinguishes her from her Shona father, the Magistrate, he at least privately shares her difficulty with the novel. It is implied that he never finished reading it ("he couldn't get into it"), and that his purchase was ill-informed (the book happened to

---

[1] Tendai Huchu, *The Maestro, the Magistrate and the Mathematician* (Bulawayo: 'amaBooks, 2014), p. 4. I am not the first to note that Huchu's novel stages a scene of reading *Harare North*. see Isaac Ndlovu, "Writing and Reading Zimbabwe in the Global Literary Market: A Case of Four Novelists," *Journal of Postcolonial Writing*, 57.1 (2021), pp. 106–20 (p. 114).

[2] Huchu, *The Maestro, the Magistrate and the Mathematician*, p. 3.

be on display when he visited the bookstore of a large Edinburgh shopping centre to read legal texts).

I begin with this fictional representation of practices of reading *Harare North*, for it stages many of the issues raised in this chapter, chiefly: the difficulty of the novel's narrative voice; its address of non-Zimbabwean audiences; and the inability of non-professional readers to understand the book, and sometimes their refusal to finish reading it. Through an examination of the reception of *Harare North*, this chapter makes the case that we need to rethink difficulty and non-understanding in postcolonial studies. I explore explicit confessions of difficulty and non-understanding in practices of reading the novel, together with implicit experiences of difficulty and non-understanding, with the aim of interrogating the professional consensus in the discipline that difficulty and non-understanding represent symptoms of reading failure. I start by exploring how professional and non-professional readers discuss the difficulty of the text's narrative voice. Far from being a mere expression of interpretative inadequacy, the description of the narrative voice's 'difficulty,' I show, functions as a practice of identity work, enabling readers to articulate their proximity to the perceived cultural and linguistic context of the novel. This is difficulty as distinction. And this particular practice of distinction is shared by professional and non-professional readers alike. This does not mean that audiences read the narrative voice, or indeed the novel, in the same way.

From an analysis of competing interpretations and judgements of the narrative voice's difficulty, I proceed to clarify the different ways that readers comprehend the plot of *Harare North*. I identify three dominant approaches to reading the novel's plot, which cut across professional and non-professional audiences: realist reading, diagnostic reading, and revelatory reading. My aim is not to adjudicate on this interpretative disagreement. It is instead to suggest that, in their partiality and mutual incompatibility, these different approaches to understanding the novel's narrative plot exemplify the unacknowledged role of non-understanding in practices of reading postcolonial literature. Non-understanding can be seen as an important interpretative departure point from which to make postcolonial literature meaningful and valuable. Motivated by one non-professional reader's explicit confession of non-understanding, I move to evaluate the efficacy of non-understanding as a practice of reading postcolonial literature. Self-acknowledged non-understanding, I argue, defies textualist and materialist interpretation as reading failure. Sometimes, avowed non-understanding signifies the recognition of the limits of the self and its horizon, and the refusal to calibrate textual difference by any existing pattern of differentiation. The potential ethical and political value of non-understanding in the reception of postcolonial literature, I conclude, should compel us to interrogate the value and authority that we as professional readers invest in practices of reading that draw strength from mastery, vigilance, and self-possession. The dominance of such reading practices in the discipline not only conceals the role of non-understanding in our own interpretative performances, but risks entrenching assumptions about the ignorance or disinterest of non-professional readers that don't obtain among actual audiences in any generalisable way.

A Difficult Read

Published in 2009 by Johnathan Cape, an imprint of Random House, *Harare North* is Zimbabwean-born author Brian Chikwava's first novel. The text is narrated by an unnamed protagonist from Harare, Zimbabwe, who arrives in London. The narrator lies to enter the country as an asylum seeker, telling the immigration officers at Gatwick Airport a "story [...] tighter than thief's anus" that he is an opposition party supporter, and therefore faces government persecution in Zimbabwe.[3] Early in the narrative, readers learn that the narrator is actually a former Green Bomber, a member of the National Youth Service, a youth training programme set up in 2001 by the ruling political party, the Zimbabwean African National Union Patriotic Front (ZANU-PF) under President Robert Mugabe. Though the Zimbabwean government insisted that the programme was concerned with supporting internal security, the Green Bombers, named for their green uniforms and appetite for violence, were "notorious for beating up, torturing, dispersing and killing opposition supporters."[4] The narrator of *Harare North* travels to London, not with the intention of seeking asylum, then, but rather with the aim of raising five thousand US dollars: a thousand to repay his uncle for his plane ticket to London, and four thousand to bribe the police back in

---

[3] Brian Chikwava, *Harare North* (London: Vintage, 2010), p. 4.
[4] Fidelis Peter Thomas Duri, "'Green Bombers,' Torture and Terror: Political Security and the Nazi Legacy in Zimbabwe, 2001-2009," in *Development Naivety and Emergent Insecurities in a Monopolised World: The Politics and Sociology of Development in Contemporary Africa*, ed. by Munyaradzi Mawere (Bamenda: Langaa RPCIG, 2018), pp. 35–76 (p. 38). As Duri continues, "ZANU-PF was politically insecure owing to its waning legitimacy within the country and the rising popularity of the MDC [...] This largely explains the emergence of the Green Bombers as a paramilitary force whose major preoccupation was to orchestrate terror on opposition apologists so as to guarantee ZANU-PF's perennial stay in power" (p. 41).

Zimbabwe to lose the docket that details his murder of an opposition party supporter named Goromonzi. On his arrival in London, the narrator first stays with his cousin Paul and Paul's wife Sekai in east London. Unwanted and fearing that Sekai will inform immigration enforcement that he is working illegally, he soon moves in with Shingi to a house rented out by live-in landlord Aleck. There, he meets Shingi's fellow tenants: seventeen-year-old Tsitsi, who has fled her aunt and rents out her baby to other women so that they can fraudulently apply for council housing as single mothers; and Farayi, a former teacher of religious education at a mission school. Shortly after revealing to Shingi, Tsitsi, Farayi, and Aleck that he was a Green Bomber, and that Aleck has been illegally charging them rent on a squat, Aleck and Farayi leave the house, and are replaced by Dave and Jenny, a homeless couple that Shingi has befriended. It is at this point that the narrator's relationship with Shingi begins to break down, and the novel uses symmetrical imagery to complicate its distinction between the two characters.

Harare North decisively addresses an international, English-speaking audience. In an interview with Marianne Dutrion, Chikwava explains that he decided to write the novel in English for the "simple" reason that "the world of literature in English is bigger than that of Shona/Ndebele literature. I just chose to go to the biggest soirée that I could get into. No use going to the smallest."[5] The targeting of an English-language audience can be seen in the way that the text italicises and glosses the few instances of chiShona and isiNdebele in the text. For instance, *mamhepo* is glossed as "the winds—someone can raise them against you and your family if you kill they innocent relative"; *mudzimu* as "the spirits", *umbuyiso* as a "ceremony to bring your spirit back home so it can leave with other ancestor spirits", and *umgodoyi* as "the homeless dog that roam them villages scavenging until brave villager relieve it of its misery by hit its head with rock."[6] The novel's use of English is yet linguistically 'non-standard.' The author describes the narrative voice as "a mixture of Shona/Ndebele idiom translated into English, Zimbabwean contemporary street language/slang and Creole from the Afro-Caribbean."[7] The narrator communicates by way of creative aphorisms, euphemisms, and idioms, whose meaning must be inferred contextually. My own deductive reading produces "spin them smooth jazz numbers" as 'lie' (p. 4); "yari yari

---

[5] Brian Chikwava, quoted in Marianne Dutrion, "A propos d'*Harare North*. Une conversation avec Brian Chikwawa," *Malfini*, 4 October 2012 <http://malfini.ens-lyon.fr/document.php?id=170> [accessed 8 July 2019].
[6] Chikwava, *Harare North*, pp. 47, 44, 16, 226.
[7] Chikwava, quoted in Dutrion, "A propos d'*Harare North*."

yari" as 'prattle' (p. 8); "boys of the jackal breed" as 'Green Bombers' (p. 18); and "Mars bars" as money (p. 24, p. 34).

Several professional readers of the text have praised the originality of its narrative voice for the way that it forestalls easy cultural, ethnic, or political identification. For Gugulethu Siziba, the anonymity of the protagonist, together with his use of both chiShona and isiNbebele, thwarts the determination of his ethnic identity, and so prevents readers from discerning his association with the ruling party ZANU-PF.[8] Madhu Krishnan argues that the narrator's linguistic creativity allows him to "continually evad[e] mastery and aver[t] fossilization in a voice which foregrounds partial becomings over totalizing beings."[9] In her thoughtful reading of the novel, she suggests that the narrator's linguistic ingenuity compels particular practices of reading. She writes:

> [T]he use of language destabilizes any singular attempt at reading or unitary work of readerly identification. The reading public which the novel fabricates is thus forced, through this linguistic play, into a heterogeneous self-reflection, identified through difference. Put rather bluntly, it is not possible to simply read the novel and construct a single version of the story; instead, the reader of *Harare North* is left in a continual process of comprehension and revision, leading to a perpetual slippage in signification. [...] The narrator can neither be seen as a cipher for national allegory, nor can his relationships be taken as a microcosm of a wider Zimbabwean community because the narrative remains forcibly contingent, both reflecting upon the political while engaging the aesthetic to resist an ethical collapse.[10]

---

[8] Gugulethu Siziba, "Reading Zimbabwe's Structural and Political Violence through the Trope of the Unnameable and Unnamed in Brian Chikwava's *Harare North*," *Literator*, 38.1 (2017), pp. 1–9 (p. 3). Following independence in 1979 and the first democratic elections in 1980, Robert Mugabe's ZANU-PF led Zimbabwe as a Shona 'ethnocracy.' "The triumph of ZANU-PF in the 1980 elections," Ndlovu-Gatsheni argues, "temporarily united Shona-oriented groups through ruling group identity whereas the Gukurahundi violence of the 1980s [the genocide of an estimated 20,000 Ndebele] united the Ndebele-oriented groups through fostering a victimhood identity." Sabelo J. Ndlovu-Gatsheni, *Coloniality of Power in Postcolonial Africa: Myths of Decolonization* (Dakar: Council for the Development of Social Science Research in Africa, 2013), p. 210 and p. 224.

[9] Madhu Krishnan, *Contemporary African Literature in English: Global Locations, Postcolonial Identifications* (Basingstoke: Palgrave Macmillan, 2014), p. 143.

[10] Krishnan, *Contemporary African Literature in English*, p. 52.

The heterogeneity and direct address of the narrative voice, Krishnan suggests, defers readerly identification, compelling readers to undertake a temporary, dissociative, and self-othering performance of the self, akin to that practised by the narrator. By rendering identity contingent and iterative, she continues, the text inhibits an allegorical reading of the protagonist as a symptom of Zimbabwean malaise.

To simplify, then, for both Siziba and Krishnan, the particular ingenuity of the narrative voice demands a (con)textualist practice of reading through which the narrator is met on his own terms, rather than produced from without in a politics of reading that precomprehends his national-allegorical function. Isaac Ndlovu has similarly refuted the Zimbabweanness of the narrative voice. He argues that the "hyperbolic brokenness" of the narrator's English "reflects the prejudiced perceptions and expectations of the novel's potential Western readership."[11] During reading, the novel's actual readership is invited to participate in the ridicule of the narrator's linguistic competence, he continues, but "is in turn lightly teased for his or her laughing—for the condescending attitude, and the attribution to the African of the role of exotic 'other', that this laughing arguably cannot entirely avoid."[12] For Ndlovu, then, it is not so much that the narrative voice is culturally, ethnically, or linguistically indeterminate, but rather that it courts and interrogates readers' preconceptions about the linguistic practices of African speakers. To have faith in the narrator as a representative Zimbabwean English speaker is, by implication, to reveal the self-in-the-world's ignorance of the politics of language in Africa. To quote Ndlovu once more, it is to fail to recognise that "[t]he exoticized broken English of *Harare North* is itself the product of a high-level mastery of the English language".[13]

Non-professional readers of *Harare North* yet regularly identify the narrator as Zimbabwean or Shona. They frequently describe the text as 'difficult,' and locate its difficulty in the writing's proximity to the linguistic performance of Zimbabwean speakers. For example, in their review of the novel on Goodreads, one reader states: "The text is written with Zimbabwe dialect which at times makes sense and at others lost me. [...] I was happy to finish it as it is quite difficult read". In their review on Amazon, another reader agrees, writing: "I found this book quite difficult to read as it is written in 'pidgin' Shona/English". A further three readers describe the novel's 'pidgin' English as a barrier to their enjoyment. On Goodreads, one reader

---

[11] Isaac Ndlovu, "Language and Audience in Brian Chikwava's *Harare North* (2009)," *English Academy Review*, 33.2 (2016), pp. 29–42 (p. 31).
[12] Ndlovu, "Language and Audience," p. 31.
[13] Ndlovu, "Language and Audience," p. 31.

says that "[t]he pidgin English thing was distracting", while another says simply "am not sure I enjoyed the pigeon/pidgin English." A reader with an otherwise positive view of the novel admits on Amazon UK that the "pigeon English [...] can be a bit tricksy but it is still a very good book once you get into it." It is implied here that, as 'pidgin,' the language of the novel inhibits the immersion and pleasure of non-African readers, and must, in some sense, be overcome. Each of these readers comprehends the difficulty of the text by perceiving it as written in a 'non-standard,' 'non-native' form of English spoken in Zimbabwe. Implicitly identifying themselves as non-Zimbabwean readers, they find the novel difficult because they experience the writing style as (too) Zimbabwean.

Such practices of reading clearly conflict with those idealised by Siziba and Krishnan, and described by Ndlovu, in the way that they identify and allegorise the narrator as Zimbabwean. Yet they cohere with the both the narrator's own self-identification as Zimbabwean, and the marketing and packaging of the text as the allegorical story of an African migrant. Chikwava was awarded the Caine Prize for African Writing in 2004 for his short story "Seventh Street Alchemy." His receipt of Africa's foremost literary prize features in the author biography inside all editions of the book, and in all major booksellers' descriptions of the book. The promotion of Chikwava as a Caine Prize winner produces the author as an African writer, and necessarily informs the reception of his work as African writing. As Pucherová puts it, "the Caine Prize markets certain authors as authentic representatives of something called "Africa," providing authentic access to the "African experience."[14] This is the case even though the Caine Prize's vision of 'Africanness' is highly particular: it typically rewards stories of and by African emigrants,[15] a cultural priority that *Harare North* satisfies.[16] The book's jacket, furthermore, solicits allegorical practices of reading, through which the narrator's story is understood as representative of the

---

[14] Dobrota Pucherová, "'A Continent Learns to Tell its Story at Last': Notes on the Caine Prize," *Journal of Postcolonial Writing*, 48.1 (2012), pp. 13–25 (p. 14).

[15] Ashleigh Harris, "Awkward Form and Writing the African Present," *The Salon*, 7 (2014), pp. 3–8 (p. 3).

[16] The Caine Prize also participates in the economic dispossession of Africa. Its primary sponsors are based in the UK and the US. See Pucherová, "'A Continent Learns to Tell its Story at Last'," p. 13. In addition, "[the prize's] major funding comes from the Oppenheimer Memorial Trust, which was founded on Ernest Oppenheimer's money, much of which came from gold and diamond mining" in South Africa and former Rhodesia. See Sarah Brouillette, "On the African Literary Hustle," *Blind Field*, 14 Aug 2017 <https://blindfieldjournal.com/2017/08/14/on-the-african-literary-hustle/> [accessed 16 April 2019].

real story of Zimbabwean migrants to Britain. "[O]ur narrator [...] battl[es] with the weight of what he has left behind in strife-torn Zimbabwe," the blurb reads. "This is the story of a stranger in a strange land—one of the thousands of illegal immigrants seeking a better life in England". The blurb encourages readers to make a connection between the fictional narrator and the many real migrants to England, in such a way as to produce the protagonist's material resonance outside of the text as a Zimbabwean illegal immigrant. Reviewers of the text reproduce this allegorical reading: an endorsement from the *Scotsman* featured on the back cover of the book describes it as "an unsentimental view of the African immigrant experience in London's Brixton." The tendency of non-African, non-professional readers to account for the difficulty of the text through an understanding of its narrative voice as Zimbabwean, or as 'pidgin,' then, does not necessarily represent the appropriation of the narrator's linguistic performance in an extratextual, domestic register. Rather, it signifies an ethics of reading that is responsive to both the intratextual and paratextual construction of the narrator as an allegory for the experience of real Zimbabwean migrants. These readers' politics of reading is defined by its absence of relevant knowledge: readers' selves-in-the-world lack the knowledge or experience of actual Zimbabwean linguistic practices to distinguish the text's narrative voice as an invented linguistic performance, and so depend upon their reading selves' partial assimilation of the text's own protocols of cultural and linguistic authorisation.

While an absence of cultural knowledge and authority leads non-African, non-professional readers to conclude that the text's difficulty lies in its Zimbabweanness, some non-professional readers leverage their cultural and linguistic fluency to identify themselves as ideal readers of *Harare North*. For example, one reader, whose Goodreads handle suggests that they are based in Cape Town, South Africa, states in their review of the novel: "at times I found the Zimbo-lingo (read pidgin English) irritating. However, it all makes sense if you read it as an African listening to an African". This reader draws on their (South) African identity to authenticate the text's imitation of Zimbabwean English, using the second person to present themselves as an authoritative guide to understanding the text, and address a future African readership of the novel. In their review on Amazon UK, another reader suggests that, in its formal style and thematic references, *Harare North* addresses a Zimbabwean readership. "I thoroughly enjoyed this book," they write, "but I would imagine that if you're not from Zimbabwe it may be difficult to understand a lot of the references" and the novel's "very different style." This reader implicitly identifies as Zimbabwean through their professed enjoyment of the novel, and their belief that non-Zimbabweans are likely to find it difficult. Another reader suggests that the narrator's linguistic performance is one that they recognise, and whose existence is linked to the history of 'global English.' In their Goodreads review, in which they append a hyperlink to a longer review of the book on their personal blog, they describe the protagonist as someone "who is not versed in the English syntax because it is not his first language; or even if it were, [...] [who] has adopted and adapted it to suit his daily needs." They authenticate the narrator as a non-native speaker, who communicates in "the layman's English as it is spoken and understood by the majority of non-English speaking folks whose formal education was cut short before they could imbibe the whole grammatical rules." For them, the narrator does not speak in a 'pidgin' particular to Zimbabwe, but in a 'broken English' that is familiar to non-native speakers compelled to learn English imperfectly at school (for instance, by way of English as a medium of instruction). The particularity of the narrative voice, they conclude, makes the character "not only believable in his actions but also in his speech and thought" because it evokes the real linguistic performances of non-native English speakers.

The reader above leverages their cultural identity, non-native English competence, and knowledge of English as a medium of instruction in Africa to authenticate the narrative voice as African. In this way, their practice of reading resembles that of professional, African readers. In a short essay for *Wasafiri*, writer and literary critic Koye Oyedeji suggests that Chikwava provides the narrator with "an authentic provincial Zimbabwean voice by having him speak in a broken pidgin English that is both sharp and biting in places."[17] "The broken English", he continues, "is a legacy of the imperial influence, a hybrid, which Chikwava brings back to its 'roots' in order to engage in a cultural conversation".[18] Like the non-professional African reader above, Oyedeji substantiates the authenticity of *Harare North*'s narrative voice by evoking his knowledge of the history of colonial education. In an article for *Journal of the African Literature Association*, Zimbabwean critic Yuleth Chigwedere deploys her knowledge of Zimbabwean linguistic practices, and her competence in chiShona, isiNdebele, and English to authenticate the 'Zimbabweanness' of the narrative voice. She suggests that the narrator combines chiShona and isiNdebele lexis, syntax, and morphology in a "Zimbabwean-flavoured English" that "is easily recognizable by the native

---

[17] Koye Oyedeji, "Out of the Frying Pan... (Literary London Still Has a Colonial Welcome for its Postcolonial Migrants)," *Wasafiri*, 28.4 (2013), pp. 47–52 (p. 49).
[18] Oyedeji, "Out of the Frying Pan...," p. 49.

speakers of Zimbabwe."[19] In her recognition of the narrator's 'Zimbabwean English,' Chigwedere both identifies herself as Zimbabwean and corroborates the text's depiction of Zimbabwean linguistic practices. In much the same way as non-professional African readers, Chigwedere anticipates that certain audiences outside of Zimbabwe will find the narrative voice difficult to comprehend. Some aspects of the narrative such as the 'me I' subject form, she argues, "may make for some heavy reading on the part of the non-native Shona speaker, as the narrative may be difficult to comprehend and require a lot of concentration."[20] African readers' experience of the narrative voice as Zimbabwean troubles critical accounts like Ndlovu's, in which it is implied that only a 'Western' audience would mistake the narrator's linguistic creativity for the actual linguistic practices of an African English speaker. The professional and non-professional African readers above can hardly be dismissed as members of a "neoliberal and neo-colonial readership."[21] Such African professional and non-professional practices of reading demonstrate that is possible to read the narrative voice as Zimbabwean without necessarily mastering the text, or engaging in a deterministic politics of reading that reads the protagonist as merely national allegory. In their claims about the narrative voice as Zimbabwean, such readers distinguish the narrator as linguistically representative rather than culturally or politically paradigmatic.

On this particular point, it is important to note that several non-professional readers disagree entirely that *Harare North* portrays Zimbabwean ways of communicating in its use of language. However, they make very different claims than Krishnan, Siziba, or Ndlovu about their experience of reading the narrative voice. In their practices of reading, such readers claim cultural and interpretative authority through their associations with Zimbabwe or their acquaintance with Zimbabwean English speakers, and criticise the text for depicting Zimbabwean linguistic practices in an unrealistic, and even discriminatory, manner. The novel is difficult, these readers suggest, because its narrative voice is unfamiliar and deceptive. "The language used by the author was painful if not annoying," one reader writes in their Goodreads review. "I have never heard of this language in Zimbabwe or outside. This really put me off as the portrayal I feel is not representative of how Zimbabweans speak". Another on Goodreads also describes the book as "painful to read." They write: "As a person who was born and grew up in Harare I was thrilled to stumble

---

[19] Yuleth Chigwedere, "The Wretched of the Diaspora: Traumatic Dislocation in Brian Chikwava's *Harare North*," *Journal of the African Literature Association*, 11.2 (2017), pp. 169–82 (pp. 171–72).

[20] Chigwedere, "The Wretched of the Diaspora," p. 172.

[21] Ndlovu, "Language and Audience," p. 30.

upon this book because who doesn't love a book written by one of their own right? Much to my dismay I found the author's writing style painful to read". This reader expresses cultural affinity with Chikwava as a fellow Zimbabwean, but is frustrated by the book's narrative voice.

Two non-Zimbabwean readers make representations on behalf of the linguistic competence of Zimbabweans, and contest the novel's circulation of misinformation about the way that Zimbabweans speak. Describing the text as "[q]uite a hard read," one reader on Goodreads writes: "no one speaks English like that in Zimbabwe. Zimbabweans may not speak the best English nor do they have to but no one speaks it like that so it didn't feel authentic". A second, again on Goodreads, makes stronger representations on behalf of the linguistic practices of Zimbabweans in the criticism of the novel's narrative voice. "I am no Zimbabwean," they write, "But most every Zimbabwean I know speaks and writes the Queens English better than Brits. Which is a gross over generalisation, but one that coloured my preconceived notions enough to really detest reading this book written in a lazy pidgin". On Amazon, one reader explicitly asks who the text seeks to address with its unrealistic narrative voice. They write:

> I waited for the publication of this novel with great excitement but was disappointed when I read it. First, it was very difficult to read the ungrammatical English the author insisted on using throughout the story. The story unfolds mostly in a stream of consciousness from the protagononist [sic]. If he was semi literate, as portrayed, then surely this internal dialogue would have been in Shona (translated into grammatical English by the author since the novel is in English)and not the painful ungrammatical English which noone [sic] in real life would use to think when they have their own first language to use to speak to themselves? This is so unrealistic it is quite annoying. Who is Brian writing for anyway because even in Zimbabwe, those who would buy this book are fluent in English and would find it difficult to read this one. Certainly, those learning to be fluent in English would regress after reading it! If he is writing for a non Zimbabwean audience elsewhere, then he has given the wrong impression of the competence of Zimbabweans in the diaspora to use English, in speech or thought, grammatically, which is a false impression as most Zimbabweans are very fluent in English, our national second language.

Harare North, this reader argues, fails to either address or serve Zimbabwean readers in its representation of Zimbabwean English competence as 'non-standard,' or, as they put it, 'ungrammatical.' Identifying themselves as Zimbabwean through an avowed ownership of English as "*our* national second language," they perform a realist aesthetic through which the novel's protagonist is deemed "unrealistic," and its representation of Zimbabwean linguistic practices is evaluated as inauthentic. Like non-professional readers of *A Concise Chinese-English Dictionary for Lovers*, this reader's realist practice of reading leads them to query the text's intended audience and purpose (see Chapter 2, pp. 94–97). They fear that non-Zimbabwean readers will mistake the narrator's linguistic competence for that of Zimbabweans, and thereby derive a "false impression" of Zimbabwean linguistic practices. By suggesting that reading the novel might cause English as an Additional Language (EAL) learners to "regress," they exhibit their utilitarian view of novels as instruments for learning and consolidating English competence.[22] Thirteen fellow Amazon customers have upvoted this reader's review of *Harare North*, indicating that they found it 'helpful.'

'Difficulty' in the reception of *Harare North* therefore signifies different qualities of reading the novel. However, what professional and non-professional readers have in common is their use of 'difficulty' as a practice of identity performance. Non-professional, non-African readers use 'difficulty' to name the cultural and linguistic difference of the text and its narrator. Professional and non-professional African readers define the narrative voice as 'difficult' to distinguish themselves as ideal readers of the text, and perform their linguistic and cultural intimacy with its perceived contexts. And some non-professional Zimbabwean readers use 'difficult' interchangeably with 'painful' to criticise the narrative voice as fabricated, and to promote the 'standard' English competence of Zimbabweans like themselves. African and Zimbabwean readers frequently chart a relationship between their cultural-linguistic identities and their reading practices with the aim of legitimising their interpretations. In this way, their practices exemplify the tendency of readers to seek to derive interpretative authority

---

[22] Several scholars have argued that a utilitarian belief that fiction-reading improves language skills is dominant in African countries that have adopted English as an official language. On *Harare North* and utilitarian reading practices, see Ndlovu, "Language and Audience," p. 31. On utilitarian reading practices in African countries more generally, see Irene Staunton, "'Sorry: No Free Reading,'" *African Research and Documentation*, 69 (1995), pp. 17–22; and Stephanie Newell, *West African Literatures: Ways of Reading* (Oxford: Oxford University Press, 2006). On the relationship between reading and cultural-economic location, see Jenni Ramone, *Postcolonial Literatures in the Local Literary Marketplace* (London: Palgrave Macmillan, 2020).

through proximity to the 'local' context.[23] But the diversity of their reading practices, and the identity work that they serve, demonstrates the ways that readers develop what Benwell, Procter, and Robinson have called 'reading identities,' which are "not mappable or subsumed by sociological categories such as gender, ethnicity or nationality," but "interact in relevant ways with notions of location."[24] The non-professional Zimbabwean reader's critique of the novel's staged linguistic non-fluency, for instance, successfully galvanises the support of other readers and elevates their social capital as a reader and as a consecrator of literary value, at the same time as it secures their cultural authority to speak as a Zimbabwean on behalf of Zimbabweans.

While an examination of 'difficulty' in the reception of the novel's narrative voice reveals the different, complex kinds of identity work performed by reading, it also draws attention to the multiple and conflicting ways that the narrative voice has been read. Some readers, such as Krishnan and Siziba, commit to an ethics of reading, through which their reading selves' obligation to the singularity of the narrative voice is ultimately appropriated in a politics of reading that registers, and even wards off, the production of Zimbabweans as national-ethnic subjects. Some, including many non-professional readers, practise an ethics of reading that, upon encountering the singularity of the narrative voice, transforms into a politics of reading that produces the narrator as a national other and the book itself as culturally and linguistically distant. Some, such as Oyedeji and Chigwedere, and several non-professional readers, engage in a politics of reading that projects their familiarity with colonial and postcolonial language policy and Zimbabwean linguistic practices into the text to produce the narrative voice as authentic. And some readers practise a politics of reading that, precisely by evaluating the text against their existing beliefs about Zimbabwean linguistic practices and their aesthetic priorities, affirms that the narrative voice is insufficiently realistic, disparaging, and even linguistically deleterious, and that the novel must therefore address a non-Zimbabwean audience of first-language English speakers. In this way, readers demonstrate the partiality of reading, where interpretation is a selective realisation, or non-understanding, of the text. What does it mean for non-understanding to be a condition of reading

[23] Bethan Benwell, James Procter, and Gemma Robinson, "'That May Be Where I Come from but That's Not How I Read': Diaspora, Location and Reading Identities," in *Postcolonial Audiences: Readers, Viewers and Reception*, ed. by Bethan Benwell, James Procter, and Gemma Robinson (London: Routledge, 2012), pp. 43–56 (p. 45).

[24] Benwell, Procter, and Robinson, "'That May Be Where I Come from but That's Not How I Read,'" p. 50.

postcolonial texts like *Harare North*? How else does non-understanding manifest in the reception of the novel? How do professional and non-professional readers negotiate non-understanding differently?

Losing the Plot

If we look carefully at the different claims that readers make about *Harare North*, it becomes clear that professional and non-professional readers understand the novel's plot differently. That is to say, readers do not only perceive the narrative voice difficult to understand, and apply different practices of reading in order to manage its difficulty. Rather, they also appear to find the novel's plot difficult or complicated, and accordingly prioritise and deprioritise the significance of different events in the narrative to develop an interpretative horizon from which to decode the text, if not necessarily appreciate or enjoy it. It is not that readers explicitly admit that they find the narrative plot challenging to follow, but that their diverse and mutually conflicting accounts of the novel's story attest to the partiality of their practices of reading. The process of clarifying how readers interpret the novel's plot is difficult. In published articles and books, professional readers often reveal very little about how they perceive the plot of given texts. Likewise, in their online book reviews, non-professional readers tend not to provide detailed descriptions of their understanding of a book's plot. The social function of reading in professional and non-professional contexts, together with the different formal conventions and affective norms of those contexts, somewhat obscures readers' specific understanding of narrative plot.

Professional reading has the social function of labour, and takes place within an institutional and disciplinary economy concerned with distinguishing between its value in relation to an outside characterised by pleasurable consumption (see Introduction, pp. 3–6). As John Guillory suggests, professional reading, as "a kind of *work*," is "a *disciplinary* activity, that is governed by conventions of interpretation and protocols of research."[25] Its affective orientation tends to be *"vigilant"*: "it stands back from the experience of pleasure in reading, not in order to cancel out this pleasure, but in order necessarily to be wary of it."[26] Professional reading's disciplinary

---

[25] John Guillory, "The Ethical Practice of Modernity," in *The Turn to Ethics*, ed. by Marjorie Garber, Beatrice Hanssen, and Rebecca L. Walkowitz (New York: Routledge, 2000), pp. 29–46 (p. 31; original emphasis).

[26] John Guillory, "The Ethical Practice of Modernity," p. 31; original emphasis.

conventions, together with its affective self-discipline, tend to foreclose long and thoughtful interpretations of narrative plot, which might mimic the pleasures and difficulties of actual reading. Instead, professional reading takes place in a kind of belated register that eliminates elements of the text that are inconsistent or incoherent to make claims on behalf of texts—claims, which, in their apparent transparency, function at the same time as claims about the authority of professional readers. Affective management and the reproduction of disciplinary norms takes on a particular appearance in the subdiscipline of postcolonial studies, so that what is made transparent is postcolonial literature's political commitments, or else its shortcomings. Hence, professional readers of *Harare North* have praised the novel in distinctly professional-postcolonial terms for its depiction of the "systemic exploitation of migrants"[27] and the 'planned violence' of London,[28] for "highlighting the contingency of racial becomings,"[29] for bearing witness to a traumatised "diasporic consciousness,"[30] and for withholding a diagnosis of either dissociation or spirit possession.[31] The ease with which professional readers read *Harare North*—as political critique, ethical aperture, or epistemological enquiry—becomes as an endorsement of the reader as critic, as much as it serves to apprize the text.

Non-professional reading, as it takes place on online book-reviewing platforms, has its own formal, social, and affective conventions. Users of both Amazon UK and Goodreads can write freely about any given book provided that reviews are relevant, and that they do not engage in hate speech, libel, or self-promotion.[32] Amazon UK permits customers to review the seller and delivery process as well as the product in a way that complicates attempts to decipher non-professional readers' particular understandings of a text and its plot. (One reader of *Harare North* on Amazon appraises the delivery process rather than the product). Moreover, because sites like Goodreads, and to a

---

[27] Fiona McCann, "Uncommonly Other in Belfast, London and Harare: AlieNation in Robert McLiam Wilson's *Ripley Bogle* and Brian Chikwava's *Harare North*," *Commonwealth Essays and Studies*, 37.1 (2014), pp. 67–78 (p. 75).
[28] Elleke Boehmer and Dominic Davies, "Literature, Planning and Infrastructure: Investigating the Southern City through Postcolonial Texts," *Journal of Postcolonial Writing*, 51.4 (2015): pp. 395–409 (p. 397).
[29] Krishnan, *Contemporary African Literature in English*, p. 46.
[30] Chigwedere, "The Wretched of the Diaspora," p. 170.
[31] Dave Gunning, "Dissociation, Spirit Possession and the Languages of Trauma in Some Recent African-British Novels," *Research in African Literatures*, 46.4 (2015), pp. 119–32.
[32] Full terms and conditions of reviews are available on Goodreads.com ("Review Guidelines"), and Amazon.co.uk ("Customer Reviews").

lesser extent Amazon UK, operate as social media platforms in which users can "perform their identities as readers in a public and networked forum"[33] and secure cultural capital, non-professional reviewers can sometimes be motivated less by a desire to convey their understanding or beliefs about a given book, than by a desire to meet social goals, including the establishment of belonging and expertise as well as making friends. As such, their reviews are sometimes a form of position taking, at the same time as they are a performance of reading.

Notwithstanding the relatively unformalised character of non-professional reading's social venues, amateur digital book-reviewing culture also tends toward certain formal and affective norms that limit its explanatory qualities. As Simone Murray has argued, non-professional online book reviews are characteristically "personal, intimate, conversational, resounding and unembarrassedly *affective*."[34] Goodreads distinguishes its reviews as 'authentic,' she continues, by contrast with "university-generated literary criticism [which] has virtually expunged emotion from authorized literary responses".[35] The tendency of non-professional readers towards emotional evaluation rather than dispassionate description makes their book reviews qualitatively different than published, professional reading practices, but nonetheless ensures that their interpretations of narrative plot are unclear or absent entirely. "Reviewers' most valued qualities, in fiction especially," may include "relatability of the plot," as Murray suggests.[36] But, by remarking on their identification or disidentification with a text's plot, non-professional reviewers sometimes disclose very little about their actual comprehension of a given plot.

While the conventions of professional and non-professional reading tend to impede the study of readers' interpretations of narrative plot, it remains possible to describe readers' comprehension of *Harare North*'s plot through the identification and analysis of claims that readers make about the novel's meaning. And, although we might expect that ongoing processes of formal and informal conventionalisation in professional and non-professional venues produce a certain level of uniformity within, if not between, professional and non-professional practices of reading the novel's narrative plot (see Chapter 2, 86–87), readers in fact present diverse and mutually incompatible

---

[33] Lisa Nakamura, "'Words with Friends': Socially Networked Reading on *Goodreads*," *PMLA*, 128.1 (2013), pp. 239–43 (p. 240).

[34] Simone Murray, *The Digital Literary Sphere: Reading, Writing, and Selling Books in an Internet Era* (Baltimore: John Hopkins University Press, 2018), p. 125; original emphasis.

[35] Murray, *The Digital Literary Sphere*, p. 125.

[36] Murray, *The Digital Literary Sphere*, p. 125.

interpretations of its plot. A provisional taxonomy of the novel's reception reveals three dominant practices of reading the novel's plot, which cut across professional and non-professional distinctions:

> *Realist*: the narrator and Shingi are different characters who suffer in different ways the systematic exploitation faced by migrants.
>
> *Diagnostic*: the narrator becomes mentally ill, or possessed, and ultimately transforms into Shingi, or vice versa.
>
> *Revelatory*: the narrator and Shingi are two embodiments of a single traumatised self, whose existence is only explicitly revealed at the end of the novel.

In the selective and partial character of these practices of reading plot, professional and non-professional readers of *Harare North* can be seen to make the text significant and valuable through non-understanding.

Realist practices of reading

Realist practices of reading produce the narrator and Shingi as different characters, whose stories reflect the hardships of migration. In this way, realist practices of reading *Harare North* also represent allegorical readings, in that they make a connection between the narrated experiences of the text's fictional characters and lives of real refugees, asylum seekers, and migrants. In realist practices of reading, the reading self pays ethical attention to the narrator's unlawful asylum claim, the overcrowded and unsanitary squat in which the main characters live, and their degrading search for employment and food. The self-in-the-world is compelled to produce the characters' experiences materially, so that they realistically and allegorically signify illegal migration and work-related offences, and the insecurity and precarity of undocumented migrants in Britain. This doesn't mean that realist approaches always involve an ethics of reading, whose approximate identification with the narrator is subsequently translated into an empathetic politics of reading, and a critique of the British state's dehumanising immigration policies. But realist practices of reading *Harare North* at least tend to elicit empathy for the suffering endured by refugees, asylum seekers, and migrants.

In their essays on the novel, both Muchemwa and Siziba, for instance, maintain a distinction between the narrator and Shingi, arguing that the narrator's theft of Shingi's identity (in the form of his passport, national insurance number and mobile phone) is a survival strategy among those who are deprived of legal recognition.[37] These realist readings principally activate a politics of reading, whereby the text becomes an interface through which to recognise the precarity of Zimbabwean migrants (Siziba), and what is lost and gained during migration (Muchemwa). Patricia Noxolo offers a similar realist reading of the novel's plot. In her essay on the representation of embodied security in *Harare North*, she suggests that the narrator illustrates the ways that asylum seekers function as a site of articulation for securitisation. To this end, she reads the narrator and Shingi as two separate characters, with the narrator sending money to Shingi's relatives and Shingi suffering from drug addiction. The novel's closing chapters, for Noxolo, represent a "dual crisis" in that they mark the breakdown of the narrator's "relatively stable household" and the assault of his friend Shingi by a homeless person.[38] To sustain this realist reading of the characters as different signifiers of the embodied precarity of asylum, she reads the protagonist's recognition of himself as Shingi in a reflective puddle metaphorically, writing: "[The narrator] loses a sense of self."[39] Notwithstanding her engagement with the text's form, the unreliability of the narrator, and the politics of representation, Noxolo concludes that the novel exemplifies the ways that border control and immigration legislation curtail the material, corporeal, and emotional agencies of asylum seekers. Her self-in-the-world produces the text's characters as real, material signifiers, and translates her reading self's ethical comprehension of their formal singularity into a political question related to the narratability of asylum.

Non-professional readers regularly engage in realist practices of reading *Harare North*'s plot. One reader on Goodreads makes the claim that "[t]his book is about a Zimbabwean man who claims asylum in London. He lives in abject poverty and struggles to earn a living". They add that the text "manages to underline how vulnerable asylum seekers are in the U.K. while also keeping a sense of humour." Another on Goodreads describes *Harare North* as "a novel that will introduce many readers to a new world of illegal immigration, hand-to-mouth living and the unseen trauma many who arrive

---

[37] Kizito Z. Muchemwa, "Old and New Fictions: Rearranging the Geographies of Urban Space and Identities in Post-2006 Zimbabwean Fiction," *English Academy Review*, 27.2 (2010), pp. 134–45 (p. 142); Siziba, "Reading Zimbabwe's Structural and Political Violence," pp. 6–7.

[38] Patricia Noxolo, "Towards an Embodied Securityscape: Brian Chikwava's *Harare North* and the Asylum Seeking Body as Site of Articulation," *Social & Cultural Geography*, 15.3 (2014), pp. 291–312 (p. 303).

[39] Noxolo, "Towards an embodied securityscape," p. 303.

in Britain bring with them from pervious [sic] experiences." A third reader on Goodreads suggests that "[t]he novel Harare North exposes the unheroic harsh realities of life as an Immigrant in London through the precarious lifestyle of his unnamed [sic] and his best friend Shingi. This is a novel that boldly touches on the struggle for identity when living in a diaspora". These non-professional readers' deployment of realist reading practices transforms the text into a realist narrative, which narrates the experience of asylum and immigration. The process of reading seems to generate empathy in these readers, because, motivated by intratextual references to London and the UK, their selves-in-the-world produce *Harare North* as a realistic account of migrants' real hardships in Britain. If the second of these non-professionals explicitly calls attention to the text's potential to teach readers something unknown or unfamiliar about migration by suggesting that it "will introduce many readers to a new world of illegal immigration," the language of 'exposure' in the third non-professional's review implicitly suggests that the text reveals aspects of life as a migrant that are scarcely contemplated, or experienced by the novel's readership.

In their realist practices of reading the novel, two non-professional readers specifically reflect on their relationship to the protagonist as a Zimbabwean migrant to London. In their Goodreads review, one writes:

> This book is so powerful. I grew up white and middle-class (and British) in London and it was heart-breaking and fascinating to see my hometown through completely different eyes. I'd highly recommend this book, and if you're very familiar with London I'd recommend it even more.

The experience of reading *Harare North* compels this reader to identify themselves in relation to the protagonist, distinguishing themselves as racially, materially, and politically privileged. Their practice of reading can be described as realist in the way it negatively defines the protagonist as not white, not middle class, not British, and not from London (i.e., a Black asylum seeker), whose first-person narrative perspective allows them to "see [their] hometown through completely different eyes." This realist reading may represent a kind of anthropological reading in its comprehension of the text as a transparent vehicle for the articulation of Zimbabwe migration to London. But it facilitates a process of self-reflection and self-reconstitution, elicits empathy, and secures the political urgency of migrant narratives. Hence, they conclude by imploring others, especially fellow Londoners, to read the book.

A second reader similarly relates to the novel's London setting, but differentiates their knowledge and experience of the city from that of the text's characters. In their Goodreads review, they describe the novel's plot in the following way:

> Set in Brixton in areas I know, lived a group of African illiegal [sic] immigrants. Two were from Zimbabwe another was a woman with a baby. All lived in an awful, rat infested squat and tried to make a life together. It gave a good insight into the struggles of finding 'graft' and living hand to mouth. The discovery of the food bin behind Marks and Spencers led to violence. [...] Overall at [sic] interesting enough insight into another world in Brixton and the harsh realities of surviving in an alien world, in territory I am familar [sic] with.

This non-professional reader explicitly describes the narrator and Shingi as different characters ("[t]wo [...] from Zimbabwe"). In suggesting that the experience of reading offered them "insight into [...] the harsh realities of surviving in an alien world, in territory I am familar [sic] with," they can be seen to undertake a realist practice of reading that treats the narrator's perspective as a realistic account of the experiences of illegal immigrants in Brixton. Their self-in-the-world projects their intimate knowledge of Brixton into the text, but their reading self is obliged to the narrator's perspective and unfamiliar experience of south London. Their reading self and self-in-the-world together authenticate the narrative as a different, but nonetheless real account of living in Brixton, with the effect of producing the experience of reading as defamiliarising.

Diagnostic practices of reading

Diagnostic practices of reading comprehend that the text portrays the narrator's transformation into Shingi, or, less frequently, Shingi's transformation into the narrator. Some readers apply different explanatory models to understand this transformation, including mental illness and spirit possession. Some identify symptoms and seek to locate traumatic causes. Some readers simply register the narrator's transformation as central to the plot. For example, in their Goodreads review of the novel, one non-professional reader describes *Harare North* as the "[s]tory of a Zimbabwean migrant in Britain who tries to hide his past and in so doing morphs his identity". For them, the narrator's becoming Shingi allegorises the difficulty of "building a new life within political constraints." For another non-professional reader on Goodreads, the novel is "very good on [the] disturbing life of migrant whose identity eventually slips into his compatriot." This reader withholds any explicit reflections on the cause or significance of the narrator's inhabitation of Shingi, and instead simply conveys their interpretation that the text follows the narrator's transformation into Shingi.

While diagnostic practices of reading are neither especially common nor particularly revealing among non-professional readers, they are prevalent and detailed among professional readers. A greater number of professional readers than non-professional readers engage in diagnostic practices of reading *Harare North*, perhaps in part because such practices are characterised by vigilance, the dominant affective orientation of professional literary criticism.[40] Compared with their non-professional counterparts, their elaborate reading practices are also more revealing about the characteristics of diagnostic practices of reading. As we will see in the following professional practices of reading *Harare North*, in diagnostic practices of reading, the reading self pays attention to the text's formal and thematic concern with the narrator and Shingi's reciprocity, including the narrator's recognition of Shingi's reflection staring back at him in the puddle at the novel's end. What is crucial in such diagnostic practices is that readers refuse the aestheticisation of this slippage between the characters: the reading self does not produce the narrator and Shingi's apparent mutuality as merely singular—unusual perhaps, from the perspective of ordinary experience, but coherent within the internal logic of the literary text. Instead, it recruits the help of the self-in-the-world in making the narrator and Shingi's doubled identity meaningful in relation to something else outside the text. The reading self enlists the self-in-the-world in a politicisation of the ethics of reading, so that the aesthetic and interpretative experience of the narrator's transformation into Shingi, or Shingi's transformation into the narrator, comes to signify the politics of stateless personhood, or the psychical trauma and alienation endured by asylum seekers.

In their essays on the novel, Zoë Wicomb and Dobrota Pucherová describe the narrator as undergoing an "ontological crisis,"[41] and treat his transformation into Shingi symptomatically. For Wicomb, the novel's "unreliable narration does not make it clear at what stage his identity merges with

---

[40] Guillory, "The Ethical Practice of Modernity," p. 31.
[41] Zoë Wicomb, "Heterotopia and Placelessness in Brian Chikwava's *Harare North*," in *The Globalization of Space*, ed. by Mariangela Palladino and John Miller (Abingdon: Routledge, 2016), pp. 49–64 (p. 52); Dobrota Pucherová, "Forms of Resistance against the African Postcolony in Brian Chikwava's *Harare North*," *Brno Studies in English*, 41.1 (2015), pp. 157–73 (p. 166).

Shingi's."⁴² She explores the significance of formal features, such as the 'me I' subject form, the use of the second person, and the figurative language used to describe the house as Shingi's head, in establishing the doubleness of the narrator and Shingi over the course of the narrative that is finally confirmed when the narrator recognises Shingi's reflection in the puddle at the end of the novel. "[T]he narrator does not name/rename himself," Wicomb admits, but, motivated by the text's formal and thematic doubling, "the reader [...] finally attaches the name of Shingi to him."⁴³ This doubleness, she argues, through an engagement with Michel Foucault's concept of 'heterotopia,' communicates the disturbing character of heterotopic spaces, and helps to establish the illusory nature of London among migrants. Pucherová attaches greater significance to the novel's ending in depicting the narrator's transformation into Shingi. She suggests that "the story ends with [the narrator] being fully split between his own self and his alter-ego, Shingi, who lies in a coma."⁴⁴ She writes, "the protagonist's ludic engagement with multiple identities turns against him as he no longer knows who he is, losing any touch with reality."⁴⁵ Pucherová reads the narrator's loss of identity as a symptom of "the brutalized postcolonial subject who never had any identity in the first place."⁴⁶ Both Wicomb and Pucherová therefore politicise the ethics of reading to produce the narrator's apparent transformation into Shingi as either an allegory for the experience of asylum seekers or a literalisation of postcolonial subjectivity respectively.

While Pucherová only indirectly medicalises the narrator's condition through references to a 'split' identity, some professional readers explicitly adopt medical frameworks to comprehend the narrator's transformation into Shingi. For instance, Yuleth Chigwedere applies the psychoanalytic theories of Freud and Laing, together with trauma theory, to diagnose the narrator's insecurity and self-dispossession. She locates their traumatic cause in repressed memories of "his participation in the murder of an opposition party member, and the violence of his rape in prison" as well as "his present sense of alienation and displacement."⁴⁷ Isaac Ndlovu draws on the explanatory models of schizophrenia, possession, and haunting interchangeably to comprehend the narrator's transformation into Shingi. He summarises *Harare North*'s plot in the following way:

---

[42] Wicomb, "Heterotopia and Placelessness," p. 52.
[43] Wicomb, "Heterotopia and Placelessness," p. 52.
[44] Pucherová, "Forms of Resistance against the African Postcolony," p. 166.
[45] Pucherová, "Forms of Resistance against the African Postcolony," p. 166.
[46] Pucherová, "Forms of Resistance against the African Postcolony," p. 167.
[47] Chigwedere, "The Wretched of the Diaspora," p. 177.

the idea that his mother's spirit is restlessly wandering because proper burial rituals have not been performed haunts the narrator until he becomes schizophrenic. The notion that the narrator is haunted is introduced early in the novel, when Sekai indicates that he is possessed by some spirits.[48]

By suggesting that the narrator's failure to perform the Ndebele tradition of *umbuyiso* haunts him, Ndlovu can be seen to engage in a textualist reading through which his reading self assimilates the narrator's fear that his mother's spirit has yet to be lain to rest with the ancestors. Yet his self-in-the-world proceeds to rearticulate the haunting of the narrator in a medical diagnosis of schizophrenia, so that the Ndebele belief in spirits is fictionalised as a symptom of psychosis. Structured by the self-in-the-world's projected diagnosis of schizophrenia, his reading self proceeds to conceive of descriptions of the narrator's possession as allusions to his haunting, and therefore implicitly as early indicators of his schizophrenia. In this way, Ndlovu's diagnostic practice of reading subtly diminishes the explanatory power of Shona and Ndebele spiritual belief systems, rendering them symptomatic of the traumatic dislocation of migration. His self-in-the-world produces *mamhepo* as a symptom rather than a cause. Spirit possession is produced as a non-worldly experience that can be explained by contrastively 'material' phenomena like schizophrenia.

By interrogating the interpretative logic of Ndlovu's diagnostic practice of reading, my point is not necessarily to delegitimise his pathology in favour of the application of local or intratextual explanatory models, but to draw attention to the way that he seeks to eliminate the text's indeterminacies and overcome non-understanding. Ndlovu's appeal to understanding is at the same time a performance of cultural proximity and authority. In his wariness to diagnose *mamhepo*, for instance, he seeks to distinguish himself from a foreign cosmopolitan audience, for he perceives that *mamhepo* functions only an "ethnographic" reference intended to appeal to the exotic aesthetic preferences of "a more affluent British and North American audience."[49] Yet, by participating in the clinical diagnosis of the narrator, Ndlovu differentiates himself from this imagined English-speaking audience, only to risk resemblance to the intratextual character of Jenny, whose amateur diagnosis of dissociative identity disorder (DID) anticipates and interrogates medical interpretations of the narrator's condition. Jenny is loathsome: she wields a righteous politics in the service of animal rights, while taking advantage

---

[48] Ndlovu, "Language and Audience," p. 40.
[49] Ndlovu, "Language and Audience," p. 35.

of Shingi and the others at the Brixton squat, despite being electively homeless. In this context, her diagnosis can appear misguided, perhaps even opportunistic, for it enables her to undermine the narrator and continue to live a parasitic existence eating the group's food and smoking their cannabis. In fact, while diagnostic practices of reading originate with an ethical obligation to the textual representation of the narrator and Shingi that is subsequently politicised, made representative, the character of Jenny reveals that such interpretative practices presuppose a politics of reading. The self-in-the-world may not be invested in clinical models; we have seen examples of non-clinical diagnosis, after all. But it must be invested in the authority of symptomatic reading, which entails a belief in a particular relationship between fiction and the world that can be uncovered by certain forms of reading. Diagnostic reading practices are therefore partial in the sense that they produce a particular and limited ethical engagement with *Harare North*'s plot, wherein the indeterminacy of the relationship between the narrator and Shingi is resolved by the projection of the self-in-the-world's knowledge of the politics of migration and displacement or psychiatric disorders. But they are also partial in the sense that they are premised on the self-in-the-world's particular relationship to literature as symptom, or literature as allegory, which is not necessarily common among non-professional readers.

Revelatory practices of reading

Revelatory practices of reading perceive the narrator and Shingi as the same person, whose mutuality is only made explicit at the end of the novel. By defining them as 'revelatory,' I mean to capture the way that such practices experience the narrator's recognition of Shingi's reflection in the puddle at the end of the novel as a revelation—a surprise that compels them to retrospectively reinterpret the *Harare North*'s plot. In this sense, revelatory practices of reading emerge from other practices of reading, including realist and diagnostic modes, which are subsequently understood as misinterpretations.

Koye Oyedeji exemplifies a revelatory practice of reading. He suggests that, "by the end of the novel, we are to believe that our protagonist and his friend Shingi are one and the same person, two spirits occupying the same body—a split personality, if you will."[50] The novel's ending inspires Oyedeji to return to the prologue wherein the narrator self-identifies as "illegal" and uses Shingi's passport, and to use his new knowledge that the narrator is

---

[50] Oyedeji, "Out of the Frying Pan...," p. 49.

Shingi to comprehend that the narrator represses Shingi because Shingi's documented status does not express the struggles he faces as a migrant in London. Speaking of the narrator's disposal of documents that signify his legal citizenship, Oyedeji argues that "[the narrator] needs to take his legitimate ownership of them away in order to better understand his place in London."[51] The novel's concluding pages guide Oyedeji's reading self to co-produce the narrator and Shingi's personhood in a way that conflicts with his self-in-the-world's archived, realist interpretation of the two characters as representative of the experiences of undocumented and documented migrants respectively. His self-in-the-world revises its application of material referents and epistemic schemata that have to do with migration and its challenges, modifying them with reference to models of psychological repression, spirit possession, and dissociative identity disorder. It projects this revised interpretative framework onto his reading self, which now concludes that the narrator represses his embodiment as Shingi, itself a result of possession and/or dissociative identity disorder, because his experience of migration does not feel legal. The self-in-the-world supports this reading by calling forth once more an awareness of the material inequalities that characterise contemporary British immigration.

Some non-professional readers also engage in revelatory practices of reading, through which they disclose their surprise at the text's ending. In their Goodreads review, one writes that *Harare North* is "[a] truly brilliant and thought-provoking read but the ending totally caught me off guard!!" They continue: "I think I would have given it 5 stars if the huge plot twist had been more than a few lines long. Would have made it easier to understand/digest". This reader doesn't disclose the "plot twist," the cause of their surprise, likely so as not to spoil the book for others.[52] However, it appears highly likely that they are articulating their revelatory practice of reading here, given that the ending can only be understood as a "plot twist" if it is produced as the revelation that the narrator has, until then, disavowed his identity as Shingi. Paying ethical attention to the text's language of 'doubles,' the narrator's corporealisation as Shingi, and the narrative shift to the second person, their reading self produces the narrator and Shingi as the same person. By recognising their difficulty understanding the novel's ending, this reader at the same time engages in a politics of reading that alludes to the

---

[51] Oyedeji, "Out of the Frying Pan...," p. 49.
[52] Goodreads introduced spoiler tags in 2011 in response to community feedback. Users can now hide portions of their text that contain important plot points in both group discussion and review contexts. Many users nevertheless continue to simply omit reference to key story developments in their online posts.

expectations of their self-in-the-world, and measures the novel's value against an existing archive of aesthetic experiences and tastes. Consequently, their practice of reading embeds the potential, if not the realisation, of a process of self-recognition and self-critique.

In this way, their revelatory practice of reading differs from that of another non-professional reader, who lambastes *Harare North* for its surprising ending. Awarding the novel a rating of just one star on Goodreads, they complain: "The only semi-likable character apparently doesn't even..... / No. / Just no. / My copy is for sale". Again, this reader does not make their reading of the plot explicit; they do not reveal which "semi-likeable" character "doesn't even [exist]." However, it is likely that they are referring to Shingi, whose innocence and politeness contrasts with the narrator's deviousness and vulgarity, and with the duplicity of Aleck, who illegitimately charges the squatters rent, Tsitsi, who facilitates benefits fraud, and Dave and Jenny, who exploit Shingi. When their reading self perceives that the narrator is Shingi, and that therefore Shingi doesn't exist in the way that they imagined, this reader seems to resent having been misled to sympathise with Shingi, and consequently seeks to register their dissatisfaction by distancing themselves from *Harare North* as a material object. Their ethical obligation to the structural doubling of the text's final episode can be seen to foster a reactionary politics of reading through which they deploy their aesthetic judgement to disavow the text and the time they spent reading it. They forfeit the opportunity to politically interrogate their preference for Shingi, and the strength of their displeasure at having been deceived.

Chapter 2 showed that the social spaces in which professional and non-professional practices of reading take place can ensure the reproduction of formal and informal conventions, and can lead to a certain uniformity among, but not between, professional practices and non-practices (see pp. 86–89). The reception of *Harare North* is interesting in the way it demonstrates both the abiding diversity of practices of reading postcolonial literature, and the latent non-understanding that drives both professional and non-professional practices of reading postcolonial literature. By paying close attention to the claims that readers make about the experience of reading the novel, we can see that they have developed distinctive and mutually incompatible practices of reading its plot. Realist, diagnostic, and revelatory practices of reading the novel are each in their own ways limited readings. They prioritise different aspects of the text and deprioritise or eliminate others in order to achieve partial understanding. And the partial understanding they offer is different: they produce the text's meaning and value differently. Yet, these partial practices of reading also enable processes of ethical self-work and political self-recognition. In this way, non-understanding can be seen as an essential feature of reading postcolonial literature.

Reading Postcolonial Literature as Non-Understanding?

While non-understanding is implicit in the practices of reading that we have so far considered, one non-professional reader of *Harare North* explicitly confesses their non-understanding. In their Goodreads review, they write:

> I really enjoyed the use of dialect and the compromised unreliable narrator. Phrases like "giving forgiveness" stuck in the mind. This must be one of the most promising debut novels I've read in a while. I'm looking forward to what he does next. I didn't quite understand the ending though.

This non-professional's practice of reading cannot easily be taxonomised as realist, diagnostic, or revelatory, for it neither discloses any particular understanding of the narrator and Shingi, nor lends the text's ending coherence. By referring to the novel's "unreliable narrator," and directly quoting from his unreliable, idiomatic register, they display the ethical character of their practice of reading—its attention to the productive work of language, without the intervention of any moral framework or political imperative that would judge, and therefore recode, the narrator. But they also exhibit the political disposition of their practice, by defining the text as a "debut novel" that excites them about Chikwava's potential, and therefore revealing themselves as a regular reader, familiar with aesthetic judgement. But what interpretative practice does their avowed non-understanding of the novel's ending signify? How should we read self-acknowledged non-understanding as a response to postcolonial literature? What does this non-professional reader's confession of non-understanding reveal, if anything, about dominant approaches to reading in postcolonial studies?

A textualist examination of non-understanding would likely define it as reading failure. Recall that the textualist tradition of reading postcolonial literature, responsible for the development of critical reading strategies, derives its authority and legitimacy in distinction to 'lay' reading practices, and from its perceived proximity to the cultural context and political horizon of postcolonial texts (see Introduction, pp. 7–8 on Attridge and Boehmer). It inherits the "vigilance" of the dominant form of professional reading,[53] or what Eve Kosofsky Sedgwick has described as "the present paranoid consensus" in literary and cultural studies,[54] observing an "anxious paranoid determination that no horror, however apparently unthinkable, shall ever come to the reader *as new*."[55] In textualist practices of reading postcolonial literature, vigilance, or paranoia, takes a particular form, where professional readers ward off the pleasure of reading until the nature of the pleasure can be appropriately checked for cultural and political biases, and the reproduction of colonial-imperial epistemic and ideological formations. The "belated" temporality of professional reading facilitates the performance of this vigilance, enabling readers to perform culturally, politically, and interpretatively authoritative practices of reading with the benefit of hindsight.[56] We can observe this vigilance in the critical reception of *Harare North*. In his comparative essay on the treatment of trauma in British-African fiction, Dave Gunning speaks of 'Western' trauma models, and the "imperial logic behind much of the internationalisation of trauma theory."[57] His reflex is to oppose clinical interpretations of trauma as colonial, even though he concludes that the novel is interesting for the way it questions the authority of *both* medical and spiritual frameworks used to understand trauma and dissociation. Gunning, Chigwedere, and Musanga each also read the novel through the lens of *ngozi* (meaning avenging spirit), despite no mention of the word in the text, and the text's own use of *mamhepo* and *mudzimu* to describe spirit possession.[58] From a textualist perspective, then, non-understanding not only signifies disinterest and ignorance, which can take on cultural and political significance as an exoticist or othering aesthetic mode. It also represents an investment in the pleasures and difficulties of actual reading that doesn't obtain in textualist approaches.

Materialist postcolonial critics would likely sympathise with self-acknowledged non-understanding, and conclude that it draws attention to the fact that non-professional readers do not possess the same time and opportunity to engage with literature that professional readers enjoy.

---

[53] Guillory, "The Ethical Practice of Modernity," p. 31.
[54] Eve Kosofsky Sedgwick, *Touching Feeling: Affect, Pedagogy, Performativity* (Durham: Duke University Press, 2002), p. 144.
[55] Sedgwick *Touching Feeling*, p. 146; original emphasis.
[56] Guillory, "The Ethical Practice of Modernity," p. 31.
[57] Gunning, "Dissociation, Spirit Possession and the Languages of Trauma," p. 124.
[58] See Gunning, "Dissociation, Spirit Possession and the Languages of Trauma"; Chigwedere, "The Wretched of the Diaspora"; and Terrence Musanga, "'Ngozi' (Avenging Spirit), Zimbabwean Transnational Migration, and Restorative Justice in Brian Chikwava's *Harare North* (2009)," *Journal of Black Studies*, 48.8 (2017), pp. 775–90.

In support of their perspective, they might look to the frequency with which non-professional readers of *Harare North* explicitly refer to the time management required to perform reading. In their Goodreads review, one reader describes the novel as "[a] bit complicated for the level of attention I gave it. Grim too". They find the text difficult, and either too time-consuming or unworthy of their attention. Less critical of the book, but also short on time, another reader on Goodreads writes: "I am so excited to have found this book and now catching snippets of reading in between a hundred other things to do—brilliant". For this non-professional reader, reading takes place between activities deemed more urgent or important. They nonetheless implicitly conceptualise reading as important, itself a form of labour alongside the "hundred other things *to do*". Recalling Sarah Brouillette's search for more ethical forms of consumption (see Introduction, pp. 12–13), materialist criticism might reward such readers for undertaking practices of explicit self-critique, which implicate them in the discursive construction of reading postcolonial literature as a laborious process. Conversely, they might be concerned by the apparently guilt-free non-understanding confessed by this non-professional reader of *Harare North*. Though this kind of materialist analysis of non-understanding usefully comprehends the precipitating material conditions of non-professional reading compared with professional reading, it stops short of analysing the effectiveness of non-understanding as a response in its own terms. As such, it can run the risk of implying that non-professionals would read, and would read better, if they had the leisure afforded to professionals through employment, and the self-consciousness to register the ways that their aesthetic desires are mediated by the global culture industry. In this way, a materialist approach continues to hold up professional reading as a standard, even if it understands how and why that standard will never be met.

In different ways, then, textualist and materialist approaches comprehend non-understanding as a symptom of reading failure. By a textualist logic, non-understanding represents a failure to replicate the interpretative and discursive protocols of professional reading, especially the vigilance to proactively and retrospectively eliminate indeterminacies. By a materialist logic, non-understanding signifies a failure of the necessary time and opportunity to read, and read well, and a failure to interrogate this failure as a symptom of the desires and pleasures we pursue in reading because of capitalist appropriations of culture and labour. I want to suggest that non-understanding is not simply reading failure, but can be a viable reading of postcolonial literature in and of itself. This is not just because non-understanding testifies to an act of reading having taken place, but because, at least in the instance above, it appears to entail an ethics and politics of reading. The reading self produces the ending as inconsistent with the rest of the novel as it has been assimilated by the reading self and the self-in-the-world working in cooperation. The ending's indeterminacy motivates the reading self to return to the self-in-the-world to help to overcome the text's opacity. The self-in-the-word supplies different referents, as well as any cultural knowledge and aesthetic experience it possesses, but the reading self continues to find itself unable to reconcile the text's ending with either its archived comprehension of the text so far or any extraneous schema provided by the self-in-the-world. This feedback loop may occur several times, but eventually the reading self and the self-in-the-world consent to non-understanding. The reading self is therefore engaged in an ethics of reading. It is reading from without the self, and is open to constituting the self through the othering horizon of the text. It also engages the self-in-the-world in a politics of reading, exposing the self-in-the-world to its partiality, its inability to know everything as its own. The-self-in-the-world withholds the desire to assimilate the indeterminacy of the text by any pre-existing conception of difference. It is guided to suspend any ideal of mastery or authority. Self-acknowledged non-understanding expresses no will to know better—no belief that, on a second, or third, reading, greater understanding would be possible. This suspension of authority represents a refusal to 'colonise' the text, for it retains the liminal space and the incalculable difference of the textual object.[59] Understood in this way, non-understanding represents a form of unregulated cultural- and self-critique.

Non-understanding can therefore be an apposite practice of reading postcolonial literature. It prevents pernicious forms of empathetic engagement and desires for mastery, ceding some of the authority of self-representation to the text. It is also acutely self-conscious in the way it names the limits of the self: hence, "I didn't quite understand the ending though". The advantages of self-acknowledged non-understanding raise questions about the dominance of professional practices of reading postcolonial literature, which in different ways exert self-authority and prize understanding. That is not to say that non-understanding, self-acknowledged or otherwise, cannot sometimes harbour retrograde impulses. Readers may elect non-understanding as a practice of reading postcolonial literature to express the frustration or humiliation of unrealised desires for mastery, to differentiate their social and cultural identity from that of the text's actual or implied audience (for

---

[59] See Wolfgang Iser, *The Range of Interpretation* (New York: Columbia University Press, 2000), p. 151.

instance, see Chapter 1's discussion of non-readers of *The Satanic Verses*, pp. 42–44 and 54–55), and to perform disengagement with that which is outside the self and its horizon. But this particular non-professional reader's avowal of non-understanding in their practice of reading *Harare North* suggests that we as critics should remain sensitive to the potential efficacy of non-understanding as a practice of reading postcolonial literature.

Conclusion

My examination of the reception of *Harare North* has uncovered its difficulty among both professional and non-professional readers. It has clarified the different ways that readers manage difficulty, including by confessing difficulty and non-understanding, but also by imputing national, ethnic, or cultural difference, and by eliminating or denying qualities of aesthetic resistance. In the process, it has developed the work of Procter and Benwell (2014), by disentangling cultural identity from cultural authority. Though several readers leverage their African or Zimbabwean identity in their interpretations and evaluations of the text, the heterogeneity of their readings illustrates the complex relationship between reading and sociological categories such as location and nationality. While this chapter has principally been concerned with the persistence of difficulty and non-understanding among both professional and non-professional readers, it has also drawn attention to self-acknowledged non-understanding as a uniquely non-professional practice of reading postcolonial literature.

Avowed non-understanding may be produced by the conditions of non-professionality, including the social function of reading as a leisure activity rather than a labour activity, and the unavailability of socio-institutionally privileged forms of cultural evaluation. And it can be appropriated as a case for the professionalisation of reading postcolonial literature. But non-understanding is more than just reading failure. Thinking about non-understanding as an effective practice of reading postcolonial literature, I have suggested, raises questions about the dominance of a limited interpretative and discursive repertoire in postcolonial studies. Because postcolonial literature is "frequently written *against* the very (Western) audience for which it is largely marketed,"[60] the appearance of reading with ease—with full understanding—has social and cultural value. It enables readers to evade interpellation as 'market readers,' and to distinguish themselves by

---

[60] Graham Huggan, *Interdisciplinary Measures* (Liverpool: Liverpool University Press, 2008), p. 101 (original emphasis).

their possession and application of the appropriate cultural knowledge and aesthetic experience to read comprehensively. Yet, relinquishing authority seems to be an essential feature of reading postcolonial literature. Whether unrecognised or disavowed, non-understanding mediates the reading self's surrender of the self and the self-in-the-world's struggle to define the object of its attention in relation to itself. The confidence with which non-professional readers articulate their difficulty reading postcolonial literature, or their limited understanding, reminds us of this, and clarifies the socially mediated character of our self-authorising practices of distinction.

CHAPTER 4

Popular Reading and Popular Texts

In Chapter 30 of *Noughts & Crosses* by Malorie Blackman, one of the protagonists, Callum McGregor, gets into an argument with his history teacher, Mr Jason. Callum raises his hand to insist on the contribution of noughts to human history, offering the example of Robert Peary. Peary was a real white American explorer, who, alongside Black explorer Matthew Henson, is credited with first reaching the geographic North Pole.

> "How come I've never heard of him then?" Mr Jason challenged. "Because all the history books are written by Crosses and you never write about anyone else except your own. Noughts have done lots of significant things, but I bet no-one in this class knows."[1]

In this episode, Blackman inverts the history of white supremacy and its institutionalisation in practices of history telling and formal education to satirise the underrepresentation of Black scientists, artists, and explorers, as well as abiding stereotypes of Black people as belonging to "backward civilizations" in need of moving "onwards."[2] The novel as a whole inverts events, motifs, and strategies of racial oppression from different historical formations to create a dystopian alternate history in which dark-skinned 'Crosses' hold power over light-skinned 'noughts.' Its narration alternates between the protagonists, nought Callum McGregor and Cross Sephy Hadley, as they attempt to sustain their friendship and love while growing in social and political consciousness. From his argument with Mr Jason in this episode, Callum concludes that greater representation of nought history will only arrive if noughts have access to the means of knowledge production. "[U]s noughts aren't in any of the history books," he complains to Mrs Paxton, a

---

[1] Malorie Blackman, *Noughts & Crosses* (London: Corgi, 2002), p. 139.
[2] Blackman, *Noughts & Crosses*, p. 138.

kind teacher who supports racial integration, "and we never will be unless we write them ourselves."[3]

Callum here analogises Malorie Blackman's own experiences at school. In an "Author's Note" included at the end of *Noughts & Crosses*, she recalls learning about white people like Robert Peary as the protagonists of history. She confesses that she wishes she had learned about the African-American inventors and explorers discussed in Callum's history class, but suggests that "if we had, maybe I wouldn't have written this book".[4] Blackman has since spoken candidly about the dominance of white voices and perspectives when she was growing up, and has admitted that she didn't read a book featuring a black protagonist until she was in her twenties.[5] Born in south London in 1962, Malorie Blackman completed compulsory education before the publication of the Swann Report, officially known as *Education for All: Report of the Committee of Inquiry into the Education of Children from Ethnic Minority Groups* (1985). The Swann Report principally recommended the implementation of multiculturalism in the professional teaching workforce.[6] But, as Roger Bromley has argued, it also "gave official recognition to the existence of racism in schools and at all levels of society," and therefore helped to justify the introduction of African, Black British, Caribbean and Asian writing to school curricula.[7] If Blackman was part of a generation of Black Britons who were failed by the UK education system, she was also excluded by the publishing industry—at least initially. She received more than eighty rejection letters from publishers, before finally publishing her first short story collection *Not So Stupid! Incredible Short Stories* with The Women's Press in 1990. And she continued to find the publishing industry

---

[3] Blackman, *Noughts & Crosses*, p. 143.

[4] Blackman, *Noughts & Crosses*, p. 446.

[5] Annabel Nugent, "Malorie Blackman: 'I Didn't Read a Book That Featured a Black Protagonist Until I was 21,'" *Independent*, 6 December 2020 <https://www.independent.co.uk/arts-entertainment/books/features/malorie-blackman-interview-noughts-and-crosses-b1765578.html>. See also Alison Flood, "Malorie Blackman: Developing Negatives," *The Guardian*, 10 November 2008 <https://www.theguardian.com/books/2008/nov/10/malorie-blackman-doublecross-noughts-crosses>.

[6] For a critique of multicultural approaches to racial inclusion, and a broader history of racism in educational policymaking in the UK, see Hazel V. Carby, "Schooling in Babylon," in *The Empire Strikes Back: Race and Racism in 70s Britain*, ed. by the Centre for Contemporary Cultural Studies (London: Routledge, 1982), pp. 181–209.

[7] Roger Bromley, "Reading the 'Black' in the 'Union Jack': Institutionalising Black and Asian British Writing," in *The Cambridge History of Black and Asian British Writing*, ed. by S. Nasta and M. Stein (pp. 417–32) (Cambridge: Cambridge University Press, 2020), p. 425.

either unreceptive, tokenistic, or hostile toward her as a Black author writing about Black characters.[8] Blackman's experience tracks trends in the publishing industry. In a 2019 report for BookTrust, Melanie Ramdarshan Bold found that, between 2007 and 2017, just 8.62% of children's book creators were people of colour, with 1.96% of children's book creators British people of colour.[9] Ramdarshan Bold's 2022 report celebrated the growing awareness of racial inequalities in the sector and the increased visibility of creators of colour, but noted that the proportion of creators of colour remains below the proportional population of people of colour in the UK, and is significantly lower than the proportion of school-age students from a minority ethnic background in England.[10]

Today, Malorie Blackman is one of the most decorated and bestselling living Black British authors. The British state awarded her an OBE for services to children's literature in 2008, and she held the title of Children's Laureate from 2013 to 2015. Published in 2001, *Noughts & Crosses* is the first in a series of novels, which concluded with the publication of the sixth instalment *Endgame* in 2021. Over two million copies of the book series have been sold worldwide.[11] The text has been productively studied from the perspectives of children's literature and young adult fiction,[12] education and learning,[13] and the adaptation

[8] Georgina Lawton, "Malorie Blackman: 'Don't Apologise to Anyone for Living, or Being'," *gal-dem*, 19 August 2019 <https://web.archive.org/web/20240415052053/https://gal-dem.com/malorie-blackman-dont-apologise-to-anyone-for-living-or-being/>.
[9] Melanie Ramdarshan Bold, "Representations of People of Colour among Children's Book Authors and Illustrators" (BookTrust, 2019), p. 21.
[10] Melanie Ramdarshan Bold, "Representations of People of Colour among Children's Book Creators in the UK (2020–2021)" (BookTrust, 2022), pp. 18–19.
[11] "*Endgame* Publishes 20 Years after *Noughts & Crosses*," *The Agency*, n.d. <https://theagency.co.uk/childrens-books/endgame-publishes-20-years-after-malorie-blackmans-noughts-crosses> [accessed 19 December 2023].
[12] See, for example, Christine Wilkie-Stibbs, "The 'Other' Country: Memory, Voices, and Experiences of Colonized Childhoods," *Children's Literature Association Quarterly*, 31.3 (2006), pp. 237–59; Clare Bradford, "Race, Ethnicity and Colonialism," in *The Routledge Companion to Children's Literature*, ed. by David Rudd (Abingdon, Oxon: Routledge, 2010), pp. 39–50; and Catherine Butler, "Counterfactual Historical Fiction for Children and Young Adults," in *The Edinburgh Companion to Children's Literature*, ed. by Clémentine Beauvais and Maria Nikolajeva (Edinburgh: Edinburgh University Press, 2017), pp. 179–93.
[13] Marit Elise Lyngstad, "Integrating Competence and *Bildung* through Dystopian Literature: Teaching Malorie Blackman's *Noughts & Crosses* and Democracy and Citizenship in the English Subject," *Utbildning & Lärande*, 15.2 (2021), pp. 11–26; and Ghazal Kazim Syed and others, "Developing UK and Norwegian Undergraduate Students' Conceptions of Personal Social Issues in Young Adult

economy.[14] However, it has not received the same attention in postcolonial literary studies. Why has *Noughts & Crosses* not been studied as postcolonial literature? How have non-professional readers, including writers, directors, and educational organisations responsible for adapting and remediating the novel read the text and secured its popularity? How does the reception of the text question persistent beliefs in the discipline of postcolonial studies that popular culture is aesthetically, culturally, and politically debased?

This chapter looks at the circulation and reception of *Noughts & Crosses* to explore postcolonial studies' anxious relationship to popular culture. It discusses the discipline's founding suspicion of political and aesthetic conformity, and the field's renewed scepticism of the cultural, political, and economic forces that mediate the circulation of culture. The implied audience for popular culture comes to be understood as ideologically corrupted or corruptible. By extending Stuart Hall's work on popular culture, I argue for an understanding of popularity as an effect of reading. Cultural forms become popular not just because of how much they are read, but *how* they are read, and by whom. The reception of *Noughts & Crosses* offers useful insights into popularity as a process of circulation and reception because it has been a site for struggles between competing popularities. In its reception, the character of the novel's popularity has been interrogated, and its perceived educational value has been continually redefined. What this chapter attempts to show is that popularity is not just achieved, but also queried by audiences. Popular cultural forms may at times trade aesthetic engagement for profit, reproduce cultural biases, or else manufacture consent for dominant political-economic forms and structures like the state, the individual, and wage labour. In this sense, popular culture may at first glance seem inimical to the goals and interests of postcolonial studies. Yet audiences of popular culture are not passive vessels for this content, but people with interests, tastes, and values of their own, who engage with popular culture critically and passionately. An engagement with popular culture offers us the opportunity to refine our understanding of its audiences as consecrators of cultural value and popularity, and to appreciate the affinities between non-professional readers' reservations about popular culture and our own. In the wider context of this book, then, the study of popular texts like *Noughts & Crosses* offers a way to foreground reading, and further demystify the connections between professional and non-professional practices of reading postcolonial literature.

Fiction through Transnational Reflective Exchange," *English in Education*, 55.1 (2021), pp. 53–69.

[14] Christopher Hogg, *Adapting Television Drama: Theory and Industry* (London: Palgrave, 2021), pp. 21–29.

Popular Literature, Popular Reading

Popular culture has received relatively little attention in postcolonial studies. The discipline was founded on a privileging of formally experimental literature. This orientation was premised on an aesthetic, or way or reading, that connected discursive representation and political representation. As John McLeod recalls,

> postcolonial writing that seemed especially innovative, experimental, or irreverent now came to appear ideologically radical, not just aesthetically fresh: "counter-discursive" and resistant to colonialist representation. A postcolonial text deemed to be "disobedient" at the level of form seemed automatically to be ideologically defiant: texts which functioned to disrupt discursive norms acquired the glamour of political critique, even if no declared political or ideological standpoint could be readily identified at the level of content or theme.[15]

This particular vision of literature, and of formal 'disobedience' as political critique, had the effect that cultural forms other than literature, and especially those that were more formally conventional, not only fell outside of the discipline's purview, but were reprehended for their ideological complicity with colonialism.

The discipline's prizing of 'difficult' literature had important implications for its understanding of reading. For Chris Bongie, the discipline's investment in formally challenging literature as a vehicle for political critique repurposed a distinctly 'modernist' set of evaluative criteria that prized "aesthetic resistance (promoting stylistic difficulty) and political resistance (promoting radical change)."[16] These criteria in turn idealised particular readerships. "[T]he dual directives of modernism," Bongie writes, "legitimized two very different but related types of ideal audience—on the one hand, the estranged intellectual still capable of appreciating highbrow texts in the wasteland of degraded 'mass' culture [...] and, on the other, the 'people' capable of resisting the threat of massification and answering the clarion call of either the ancestral past or the revolutionary future".[17] Put another way, in adopting the 'modernist' fetishisation of resistance, postcolonial studies produced professional readers and an ill-defined proletariat or subaltern class as its ideal audiences. These audiences were idealised for

---

[15] McLeod, "Postcolonial Studies and the Ethics of the Quarrel," p. 458.
[16] Bongie, *Friends and Enemies*, p. 289.
[17] Bongie, *Friends and Enemies*, p. 291.

their apparent distance from the corrupted cultural, political, and economic logics of the marketplace. This perceived distance or opposition to 'mass' culture gifted professional intellectuals with aesthetic taste, and subalterns cultural and political legitimacy. The consumption of popular culture, by implication, was associated with aesthetic vulgarity, cultural vacuity, and political compromise.

In its implicit suspicion of commercially popular culture, postcolonial studies reproduced abiding biases in cultural studies. Scholarship in cultural studies, as Nadia Atia and Kate Houlden have argued, sought to challenge cultural elitism "most often from a position that defended working-class and subcultural heritages" but which "did not always do away with the idea that the vast majority of culture consumed en masse was, at best, to be dismissed as vacuous."[18] That is, some cultural studies work reified a distinction between 'authentically' popular culture (the 'real,' local cultures of disenfranchised classes) and 'inauthentically' popular culture (the 'mass' culture churned out for profit by multinational corporations).[19] In doing so, it endowed the cultural practices of working and subaltern classes with historical agency, and distinguished them from global cultural industries and their undiscerning 'mass' consumers.

Today, these practices of distinction between 'authentic' popularity and 'inauthentic' popularity, and between the 'people' and the consuming 'masses,' do not obtain in any explicit way in postcolonial studies. Yet, the discipline continues to neglect commercially popular cultural forms. Even the blockbuster superhero movie *Black Panther* (2018), based on the Marvel comics of the same name, has received relatively scant critical attention in the discipline, to say that it grossed almost 1.5 billion dollars. Are we to presume that the film's alternate future of an uncolonised African country, its engagement with resource politics and extractive histories, and its reflections on the traumatic legacies of colonialism and the transatlantic slave trade through the character of Erik Killmonger are in some way diminished by its popularity? "[I]n its unstated reliance on a high/middlebrow vision of literature and its reluctance to take 'inauthentic'-popularity seriously into account," Bongie writes, postcolonial literary studies "perpetuates a watered-down version of canonical thinking and only bothers to give a

---

[18] Nadia Atia and Kate Houlden, eds, "Introduction," in *Popular Postcolonialisms: Discourses of Empire and Popular Culture* (New York: Routledge, 2019), pp. 1–23 (pp. 3–4).

[19] I'm drawing here on Chris Bongie's distinction between 'authentic popularity' and 'inauthentic popularity.' See Bongie, *Friends and Enemies*, pp. 280–321.

voice to the 'people' when they say, do, and consume the 'right' thing".[20] In other words, by refusing to assimilate 'lowbrow' culture as a viable and valuable object of study, postcolonial studies tacitly maintains a sense of what constitutes 'good' culture and worthwhile cultural experiences, as well as a hostility toward popular and non-academic audiences.

Postcolonial studies' "anxiously under-theorized relation to the empirical question of popularity"[21] is therefore integral in the history of the discipline's institutionalisation, and has secured the status and relative success of postcolonial literary fiction and the distinction of its professional readers. One of the consequences of the discipline's historic lack of engagement with popular culture is that, when it does engage with popular cultural forms, it tends to nourish a somewhat celebratory attitude toward local cultural forms as 'authentic,' vernacular cultures. At times, scholars consecrate popular culture as the occasion of everyday life, and thereby "risk fetishizing the cultural phenomena they claim to be explaining, and [...] arguably supplant one form of elitism—the Arnoldian connoisseurship of 'high' culture—with another".[22] Postcolonial approaches to popular culture can end up defining local popular cultures as the 'real' site of sociopolitical energy in a way that disavows their relationship to 'high' culture, global market forces, and liberal politics. The characterisation of the local cultural forms and practices of post-colonial nations as culturally and politically 'authentic,' when taken to its limits, can moreover represent the uncritical endorsement of illiberal politics. As Simon Featherstone has shown in his discussion of Jamaican scholarship on dancehall, the scholarly treatment of Buju Banton's homophobic lyrics as a form of national popular resistance "situates such localizing argument at a dangerous political crux."[23] "[T]he return of music to the national popular consciousness [...] exposes a politics which [...] is defined not by nationalist optimism but by a reactionary positioning that colludes with the very forces it purports to resist".[24] That is to say, homophobic incitements to violence are not only repulsive to a liberal political imaginary, but also legitimise heterosexuality in a way that complements the global dominance of heterosexuality. 'Local resistance' is, in this case, exactly in step with global

---

[20] Bongie, *Friends and Enemies*, p. 291.
[21] Bongie, *Friends and Enemies*, p. 283.
[22] Graham Huggan, *Interdisciplinary Measures* (Liverpool: Liverpool University Press, 2008), p. 38.
[23] Simon Featherstone, "Postcolonialism and Popular Cultures," in *The Oxford Handbook of Postcolonial Studies*, ed. by Graham Huggan (Oxford: Oxford University Press, 2015), pp. 380–95 (p. 392).
[24] Featherstone, "Postcolonialism and Popular Cultures," p. 392.

politics. But, more importantly for our interests in this chapter, postcolonial studies' historic neglect of popular culture has produced a mostly dismissive consensus about commercially popular cultural forms and their audiences.

Where postcolonial scholars have studied the production and reception of commercially popular culture, they have tended to affirm its circumscription by the values of producers in the global culture industry. In their essay on the film *Black Panther*, Ainehi Edoro and Bhakti Shringarpure ultimately conclude that "Africans are imagined in the most Western way possible in this film".[25] Edoro and Shringarpure blame the film's 'Western' imagination on the Americanness of the film's director Ryan Coogler and the established aesthetics of Hollywood. But some responsibility likely lies with the specific tastes and target audiences of the film's producer Marvel Studios and distributor Disney. In this sense, to what extent is *Black Panther* more 'Western,' or more complicit with the global culture industry, than a work of literary fiction like *Americanah* by Chimamanda Ngozi Adichie? The novel was published by American publishing house Alfred A. Knopf, part of American publisher Penguin Random House, which is owned by German media conglomerate Bertelsmann, while Ivy League-educated Adichie now spends most of her time in the US. *Americanah* itself follows protagonist Ifemelu, who migrates to the US and forges a successful career as a race blogger. At least at the level of the central story, then, the novel affirms a distinctly neoliberal brand of feminism.[26] Neither the novel's production history nor its neoliberal politics have impeded *Americanah*'s canonisation in postcolonial studies and African studies. As Amber Lascelles notes, "*Americanah* [...] has generated a vast range of critical material, becoming widely included in university syllabuses."[27]

My point here is not that both *Black Panther* and *Americanah* are complicit, but that cultural forms like *Black Panther* are treated with greater suspicion for their cooperation with 'Western' and capitalist forces than 'highbrow' culture, even where there are unmistakable similarities in their production processes. In her essay on the 'postcolonial middlebrow,' Hannah Pardey similarly critiques the 'Western' and neocolonial interpretative and

---

[25] Ainehi Edoro and Bhakti Shringarpure, "Why is the Cultural Life of *Black Panther* so Derivative?" *Africa Is a Country*, 26 February 2018 <https://africasacountry.com/2018/02/africa-is-a-country-in-wakanda> [accessed 22 December 2023].

[26] Amber Lascelles, "We Should All be *Radical* Feminists: A Review of Chimamanda Ngozi Adichie's Contribution to Literature and Feminism," *Journal of Postcolonial Writing*, 57.6 (2021), pp. 893–99 (pp. 896–97).

[27] Amber Lascelles, "Black Feminism in a Neoliberal World: Resistance in Contemporary Black Women's Fiction" (PhD thesis, University of Leeds, 2020), p. 91.

aesthetic practices of producers and consumers of popular culture. She argues that "the middlebrow online encounters between authors, distributors and readers function to disseminate neocolonial ideologies and perpetuate colonial power structures that bear on the continued Western control over the international book market and its consumers' approach to reading."[28] Participation in middlebrow or popular consumption is here understood as the reproduction of colonial, capitalist, or 'Western' patterns of exploitation, assimilation, and domination. In both Pardey's and Edoro and Shringarpure's analyses, the critique of the 'West,' and the coeval romanticisation and essentialisation of 'non-Western' cultural production and consumption participates in what Caroline Koegler calls the anti-capitalist branding narrative of postcolonial studies. In this branding narrative, Koegler explains, "(big) business is represented as an exclusively 'western' practice" despite "the economic success [and increasing influence] of *non*-western businesses of all sizes, as well as the involvement of non-western governments in this success."[29] And so, popular culture and its consumption not only comes to be associated with capitalist cooperation, or commodification, but also with the reproduction of 'Western' cultural and political values.

Several scholars have helpfully intervened in the characterisation of popular culture as complicit with neoliberal capitalism, and therefore involved in the perpetuation of cultural, political, and economic inequality. In their introduction to a 2011 special issue of *Continuum*, Vijay Devadas and Chris Prentice, for instance, contend that "postcolonial popular cultural forms and practices challenge structures of power," even if they "are sometimes complicit with the very institutions and operations postcolonial studies seeks to challenge."[30] Nadia Atia and Kate Houlden have similarly argued that "popular and profitable forms are not only shaped by market demands but themselves reflect or subvert the dominant capitalist modes of the societies in which they circulate so widely."[31] However, where such work has tended to locate the capacity for resistance in the formal or thematic composition of popular cultural forms, it is perhaps more useful to locate the political ambivalence of popular postcolonial culture in the tensions

[28] Hannah Pardey, "Middlebrow 2.0: The Digital Affect and the New Nigerian Novel," in *Imperial Middlebrow*, ed. by Christopher Ehland and Jana Gohrisch (Leiden: Brill, 2020), pp. 218–39 (p. 222).
[29] Caroline Koegler, *Critical Branding*, p. 186.
[30] Vijay Devadas and Chris Prentice, "Introduction: Postcolonial Popular Cultures," *Continuum: Journal of Media & Cultural Studies*, 25.5 (2011), pp. 687–93 (p. 688).
[31] Atia and Houlden, introduction, p. 10. See also Pamela Butler and Jigna Desai, "Manolos, Marriage, and Mantras: Chick-Lit Criticism and Transnational Feminism," *Meridians*, 8.2 (2008), pp. 1–31.

between its production, circulation, and reception. That is to say, even if we maintain that some popular cultural forms are designed to reproduce the dominance of 'Western' cultural values or to naturalise capitalism's abstractions of life and work, readers and other cultural consumers are not passive vessels for cultural and ideological content. As Stuart Hall has persuasively demonstrated in "Notes on Deconstructing 'the Popular,'" to understand participation in commercially popular culture as "purely manipulative and debased," is, by extension, to assume that consumers of this culture are "debased by these activities or else living in a permanent state of 'false consciousness.'"[32]

In this way, the refusal to participate in popular culture, or the critique of popular culture, functions as a practice of distinction. It produces the inexpertise and naivety of participants in popular culture. A belief in the corrupting force of popular culture and in the ignorance of its consumers might shore up our own self-esteem and "self-satisf[action]" as conscious cultural intermediaries, capable of rejecting the products of the "capitalist cultural industries," but it neither adequately comprehends our cultural relationships nor the ambivalence that characterises popular engagement.[33] What I am seeking to highlight here is that cultural forms do not possess any inherent value, including popularity, but rather acquire value through their reception. Hall cautions against "self-enclosed approaches to popular culture which [...] analyse popular cultural forms as if they contained within themselves, from their moment of origin, some fixed and unchanging meaning or value."[34] In simple terms, the meaning and value of culture is mediated by its reception—who engages with it, and how. Recall my insistence in the Introduction, following Iser, that reading is a practice of producing meaning, rather than deciphering meaning (see p. 16).

And so, popular culture ought not be dismissed as if it were capable of nefariously capturing, reorganising, and re-educating the people in the service of the liberal capitalist state and its organisation of society, nor idealised as if it contained the values of the people. For Hall, popular culture is best understood as a struggle, where the process of definition is integral to that struggle. "[W]hat is essential to the definition of popular culture is the relations which define 'popular culture' in a continuing tension (relationship, influence and antagonism) to the dominant culture. [...] Its main focus of attention is the relation between

---

[32] Stuart Hall, "Notes on Deconstructing the Popular," in *Cultural Resistance Reader*, ed. by Stephen Duncombe (London: Verso, 2002), pp. 185–92 (p. 186).
[33] Hall, "Notes on Deconstructing the Popular," p. 186.
[34] Hall, "Notes on Deconstructing the Popular," p. 190.

culture and questions of hegemony".³⁵ In other words, there is nothing essential about popularity. Any cultural form can be popular; any popular cultural form can be transformed, or commodified. Popularity is the effect of socioeconomic processes, and the aesthetic, ideological, and affective uses to which a given cultural form is put to work. Or, as Hall puts it, "[t]he meaning of a cultural symbol is given in part by the social field into which it is incorporated, and practices with which it articulates and is made to resonate".³⁶ Reading is a key part of this social struggle over meaning and definition. "[T]he centrality of audience to the establishment of power, as well as the struggle over and renegotiation of power"³⁷ lends readers particular importance as participants in popularisation.

The reception of *Noughts & Crosses* by Malorie Blackman proves particularly fertile ground for exploring questions about popularity, and for exploding dominant assumptions about popular texts in postcolonial studies. This is because it is a site of competing popularities, in which struggles over its popular definition are highly visible. *Noughts & Crosses* is animated by a contest between national popularity, mass popularity, state popularity—a struggle which has only been intensified by the release of the 2020 television adaptation of novel. How did the novel's commercial success negate its national popularity and its explicit critique of institutional racism in Britain? How did the subsequent appropriation of *Noughts & Crosses* by (para)governmental agencies and educational organisations formalise the reception of the text? In the absence of professional responses to the novel in postcolonial studies, what practices of reading have been valued by non-professionals, including state actors?

From National Popularity to Mass Popularity to State Popularity

Noughts & Crosses was the first of Malorie Blackman's novel to treat racism explicitly. While, for years, she had written about Black protagonists, and insisted that they be reflected in the packaging of her books, she had deliberately evaded the subjects of race and racism for fear of being

---

[35] Hall, "Notes on Deconstructing the Popular," p. 189.
[36] Hall, "Notes on Deconstructing the Popular," p. 190.
[37] Bethan Benwell, James Procter, and Gemma Robinson, eds, "Introduction," in *Postcolonial Audiences: Readers, Viewers and Reception* (London: Routledge, 2012), pp. 1–26 (p. 6).

"labelled"[38] or "boxed."[39] Yet, she changed her mind after the publication of the Macpherson report in February 1999. The Macpherson report was the outcome of "The Inquiry into the Matters Arising from the Death of Stephen Lawrence," commissioned by the newly formed Labour government's then-Home Secretary Jack Straw on 31 July 1997, and conducted by Sir William Macpherson.[40] It condemned the Metropolitan Police's mishandling of the murder of Stephen Lawrence, and denounced the force as institutionally racist. Blackman felt compelled by the Report's conclusions to write explicitly about racism for the first time.[41] In this sense, *Noughts & Crosses* might be understood as a form of national-popular expression, aimed at both representing and galvanising a national-popular, anti-racist consciousness. At least retrospectively, Blackman defined the novel in antagonistic relationship to the state and its repressive apparatus. But, while Blackman named the case of Stephen Lawrence as the impetus for writing *Noughts & Crosses*, the novel is not explicitly concerned with the circumstances of the teenager's murder, but instead draws inspiration from the profound culture of institutional racism that it exposed, including that which she had experienced growing up in London.

In reading the events of the murder and subsequent inquiry into its failed investigation as a kind of spectacular anamnesis, Blackman was not alone. As Janelle Reinelt argues, the murder of Stephen Lawrence, together with its failed investigation, and the resultant Macpherson report was "theatricalized as a mode of aesthetic and social enquiry."[42] As well as possessing protagonists, antagonists and a plot, the case raised questions about the state of the nation, national identity, individual autonomy, and garnered significant public attention. It was "perceived by the public as the symbolic staging of other, recognizable, features of their national or local lives—to embody a certain kind of analogical critique of their ways of living."[43] By avowing the Stephen Lawrence case as a catalyst for her writing, Blackman therefore

---

[38] Alison Flood, "Malorie Blackman: Developing Negatives," *The Guardian*, 10 November 2008 <https://www.theguardian.com/books/2008/nov/10/malorie-blackman-double-cross-noughts-crosses>.
[39] Lawton, "Malorie Blackman."
[40] William Macpherson, *Inquiry into the Matters Arising from the Death of Stephen Lawrence on 22 April 1993 to Date, Order Particularly to Identify the Lessons to be Learned for the Investigation and Prosecution of Racially Motivated Crimes* (London: Home Office, 1998).
[41] Flood, "Malorie Blackman."
[42] Janelle Reinelt, "Toward a Poetics of Theatre and Public Events: In the Case of Stephen Lawrence," *The Drama Review*, 50.3 (2006), pp. 69–87 (p. 74).
[43] Reinelt, "Toward a Poetics of Theatre and Public Events," p. 74.

establishes her belonging to the national public and her share in its popular consciousness. This is not simply because, during the Macpherson inquiry, "it was unlikely that any 'person-on-the-street' did not know the case in detail,"[44] but because the case acts—for Blackman, as for the national public—as an interface through which to recollect, memorialise, and condemn personal experiences of racialisation, racism, and injustice in Britain. At least in Blackman's retrospective accounts of the novel's genesis, the experience of 'reading' the murder of Stephen Lawrence compels her reading self toward outrage for the injustice suffered by the Lawrence family. "I was so angry," Blackman recalls in an interview for *gal-dem*.[45] Yet the case and its spectacularisation does not remain singular and arresting for Blackman, but is materialised and politicised as part of a longer history of racism in Britain. It causes her self-in-the-world to evoke her own knowledge and experience of institutional racism. In the same interview, Blackman tells Georgina Lawton: "I was spat at when I was five, I was told to go back to where I came from, I was barged off the pavement".[46] The hybridity of this experience of 'reading' moves Blackman to perform an analogical critique of her writing career. She interrogates, and ultimately overcomes, her own reluctance to write about racism as a Black author for fear of being marketed and read as niche.

Noughts & Crosses was not just produced in response to the murder of Stephen Lawrence, but was also enabled by it. The case indirectly created an audience for Blackman's work. As Roger Bromley has suggested,

> the murder of Stephen Lawrence and the profile of the subsequent government enquiry provided the catalyst that gave rise to a public more receptive to recognising the structural inequalities across all industries and to issues of diversity, including across the publishing industry, arts, and culture.[47]

The case produced a readership for creative works about racism in Britain, and a publishing industry more willing to support the work of Black and minority ethnic authors. This is not simply because Lawrence's murder and the government inquiry into the mishandling of the case shaped a national consciousness, but because, as Asha Rogers has highlighted, the Macpherson report explicitly called for the increased incorporation of cultural diversity

---

[44] Reinelt, "Toward a Poetics of Theatre and Public Events," p. 76.
[45] Blackman, quoted in Lawton, "Malorie Blackman."
[46] Blackman, quoted in Lawton, "Malorie Blackman."
[47] Bromley, "Reading the 'Black' in the 'Union Jack'," p. 418.

in the national curriculum.[48] In doing so, the Macpherson report highlighted the role of the curriculum in the definition of the nation and its shared values. The government, as we will see, did not directly interfere with the activities of publishers, distributors, or readers to secure the promotion of cultural diversity, but rather subsidised the use of literature through different agencies and cultural policy, in keeping with what Rogers distinguishes as the British state's "arm's length approach to state patronage."[49]

While the novel's conception was severally inscribed by the national-popular case of Stephen Lawrence's murder and its theatricalised reception, its own early reception negated this relationship. Audiences incorporated the text into new social fields, recontextualising it, first by way of William Shakespeare's *Romeo and Juliet*, and second by way of international histories of colonialism, racism, sectarian violence, terrorism, and their representation. Without the epitext of the Stephen Lawrence case, many readers approached *Noughts & Crosses* as a universal love story, whose reimagining of racial hierarchies allegorised different histories of social division. This process of recontextualisation began with early reviews of novel, in which it was described as a "Romeo and Juliet-style story set in a segregated world in which blacks (known as Crosses) rule over whites (known as Noughts)," to quote *The Guardian*'s 2002 plot summary.[50] But early accounts by experts in children's literature also confirmed the text's relationship to the Shakespeare tragedy. In a 2005 book aimed at secondary school teachers, Claire Senior praised *Noughts & Crosses* for the "Romeo and Juliet quality of the story,"[51] while Karen Sands-O'Connor's 2003 essay derided the predictability of the text's "Romeo-and-Juliet plot," and the hopefulness of Sephy's pregnancy announcement at the end of the novel.[52]

Dominic Cooke's theatrical adaptation of the novel formalised the hitherto demotic reception of *Noughts & Crosses* as a retelling of *Romeo and Juliet*.

---

[48] Asha Rogers, *State-Sponsored Literature: Britain and Cultural Diversity after 1945* (Oxford: Oxford University Press, 2020), p. 178. See also Karen Sands-O'Connor, *Children's Publishing and Black Britain, 1965–2015* (New York: Palgrave Macmillan, 2017), pp. 143–44.

[49] Asha Rogers, *State-Sponsored Literature*, p. 17.

[50] "Past Lives and Present Tensions," *The Guardian*, 4 April 2002 <https://www.theguardian.com/books/2002/apr/04/buildingachildrenslibrary.booksforchildrenandteenagers1>.

[51] Claire Senior, *Getting the Buggers to Read* (London: Continuum, 2005), p. 6.

[52] Karen Sands-O'Connor, "Smashing Birds in the Wilderness: British Racial and Cultural Integration from Insider and Outsider Perspectives," *Papers: Explorations into Children's Literature*, 13.3 (2003), pp. 43–50 (p. 48).

Cooke's 2007 adaptation was produced for the Royal Shakespeare Company, a registered charity and non-profit organisation, which receives public funding through Arts Council England, an executive, non-departmental public body sponsored by the British government's Department for Culture, Media and Sport (DCMS).[53] At the same time as Cooke's adaptation established the Shakespearean tragedy as a key intertext of *Noughts & Crosses*, it overlayed the text with extratextual historical and political resonances. Speaking about the world of the novel, Cooke suggested that, for him, it evoked, "the America of the 1950s, South Africa under apartheid, and in the handling of the Liberation Militia, the IRA of the 1970s and Eighties."[54] He reflected, "It's remarkable how the story also speaks to people who have been divided on other than racial grounds".[55] Cooke was not alone in reading the novel outside of the historical experience of racism. In a 2008 interview, Malorie Blackman told *The Guardian* that Irish audiences frequently read the novel as an allegory of sectarian violence in Ireland, that some Spanish readers found analogical resemblance in the novel and Spanish separatist movements, and that, in Israel, readers thought the novel's world resonated with the conflict in Israel/Palestine.[56] But Cooke's reception of the novel was significant because it informed the theatrical adaptation of the text, and thereby legitimised a way of reading the text materially that was not related to the inquiry into the handling of Stephen Lawrence's murder.

An information pack, developed by the Royal Shakespeare Company to coincide with the premiere of Cooke's production, authorised his remarks as an objective account of *Noughts & Crosses*. In a section titled 'Some key themes,' the information pack informs us that "To make the racism in the book completely convincing Malorie Blackman includes several things in the book that have also happened in the real world".[57] It proceeds to provide brief summaries of apartheid in South Africa; sectarian conflict in twentieth-century Northern Ireland; slavery, school segregation, and civil rights campaigning in the US; and the 1996 bombing of Manchester city centre carried out by the Irish Republican Army.[58] Aimed at non-experts, these

---

[53] The Arts Council of Great Britain was devolved in 1994 to create four, separate bodies for the four nations of Great Britain. DCMS was established in 1997 to replace the Department for National Heritage.

[54] Dominic Cooke, quoted in "Noughts & Crosses," *Royal Shakespeare Company* <https://www.rsc.org.uk/noughts-and-crosses>.

[55] Cooke, quoted in "Noughts & Crosses."

[56] Flood, "Malorie Blackman."

[57] Taissa Csáky, *Noughts & Crosses* information pack (Royal Shakespeare Company, 2008), p. 8.

[58] Csáky, *Noughts & Crosses* information pack, pp. 8–9.

summaries necessarily misrepresent the complexity of the different historical formations they describe, including by overstating the religious character of The Troubles and the period leading up to them. But, more significantly, these summaries within the Royal Shakespeare Company's information pack remove *Noughts & Crosses* from the national-popular context of the Stephen Lawrence case, and identify different national histories of racism and sectarian violence as its principal historical intertexts. The extent of the information pack's engagement with racism in the UK is in fact limited to a reference to the region's "white majority," and a spurious claim that "[w]e tend to think of racism as a problem mainly experienced by non-whites and something dished out by the white majority".[59] Not only does the information pack omit to mention the failed investigation of Stephen Lawrence's murder as a context in the production of *Noughts & Crosses*, then, but it also obscures the institutional racism that the case uncovered, in favour of a representing racism as a national phenomenon, meted out by individuals. In this way, the information pack undertakes and promotes an individualist interpretation of racism that might correspond with the worldviews of the novel's child narrators, but which is queried by political structures of racial segregation in the novel, including the segregated school system, that classify and oppress noughts. My point is not that the Royal Shakespeare Company performs a 'bad' reading of *Noughts & Crosses*,[60] but rather that it engages in a selective reading of the novel that expands its international appeal and commercial potential, at the expense of its national resonance. This is perhaps unsurprising, given that the organisation was at the time under pressure to make a profit in the context of significant cuts to public subsidies for art and culture organisations.[61]

[59] Csáky, *Noughts & Crosses* information pack, pp. 8–9.
[60] Elsewhere, I've interrogated ideas about 'bad reading.' See Hayley G. Toth, "Bad Reading / Bad Gaming," *Post45 Contemporaries*, 8 April 2024 <https://post45.org/2024/04/bad-reading-bad-gaming/> [accessed 9 May 2024].
[61] Under the leadership of Adrian Noble from 1990–2003, and the presidency of then-Prince Charles, the Royal Shakespeare Company had been placed in the service of articulating a 'classical,' 'traditional' approach to Shakespeare, defined in antagonism to Shakespeare's increasing abbreviation in state education, and the critical and cultural scrutinisation of his works by literary professionals in Britain's universities. See Richard Wilson, "NATO's Pharmacy: Shakespeare by Prescription," in *Shakespeare and National Culture*, ed. by John J. Joughin (Manchester: Manchester University Press, 1997), pp. 58–80 (pp. 58–63). Noble imagined an explicitly ideological function for the theatrical experience of Shakespeare. Michael Boyd replaced Noble as artistic director, after Noble's vision for bringing the 'real' Shakespeare back to audiences with the development of a 'theatre village' on the Stratford site ultimately failed to inspire the confidence

The theatrical adaptation successfully introduced the text to new audiences and new contexts of reception. In the Royal Shakespeare Company's 2007/08 financial report, *Noughts & Crosses* was credited, alongside its production of *The Comedy of Errors*, with attracting fourteen thousand new attendees to the theatre.[62] According to Rachel Falconer, the novel already possessed the characteristics to appeal to adult audiences. Speaking of "[t]he emergence of children's literature into the cultural mainstream" in the 1990s and 2000s, she argues that "many hybrid works, incorporating two or more traditional genres, drew the attention of adult readers."[63] She cites *Noughts & Crosses* as the best example of children's literature with inherent crossover appeal: "hybridizing realism and dystopia, [*Noughts & Crosses*] was successfully adapted for national theatre, and attracted a mass adult audience."[64] Cooke's adaptation was published as a playscript in 2007, and as a playscript with additional educational information designed for 11 to 14-year-olds in 2008.[65] These playscripts facilitated *Noughts & Crosses*' formal entry into the secondary education curriculum with Cooke's adaptation now serving as one of the set texts that students can choose to be examined on as part of "Component 3: Texts in Practice" on AQA's GCSE drama.

As children's literature, or young adult fiction, *Noughts & Crosses* always possessed a potential educational or didactic function.[66] Outside

---

of investors and shareholders (including the British state), and saw Boyd inherit a deficit of around three million pounds when he took over as artistic director. Stuart Hampton-Reeves, "New Artistic Directions: An Interview with Michael Boyd," *Shakespeare*, 1.1–2 (2005), pp. 91–98 (p. 95). Through the development of education and outreach work, including the establishment of the Learning and Performance Network in 2006–17, Boyd managed to maintain a relatively high level of public funding for the RSC, but became increasingly reliant on private donors, sponsors, and grants, as well as commercial ticket sales. Siobhan Keenan, "The Royal Shakespeare Company at 50," *Shakespeare*, 8.2 (2012), pp. 195–201 (p. 197).

[62] *RSC Annual Report and Accounts, 2007/2008*, Royal Shakespeare Company, 22 September 2008 <https://www.rsc.org.uk/annual-review/previous-annual-reviews> [accessed 12 January 2024].

[63] Rachel Falconer, "Cross-reading and Crossover Books," in *Children's Literature: Approaches and Territories*, ed. by Janet Maybin and Nicola J. Watson (Basingstoke: Palgrave Macmillan in association with the Open University, 2009), pp. 366–79 (p. 372).

[64] Falconer, "Cross-reading and Crossover Books," pp. 372–73.

[65] Dominic Cooke, *Noughts & Crosses* (London: Nick Hern Books, in association with the Royal Shakespeare Company, 2007); Dominic Cooke, *Noughts & Crosses* (Oxford: Oxford University Press, 2008).

[66] See Butler, "Counterfactual," p. 182.

of GCSE drama, *Noughts & Crosses* has been enthusiastically integrated into secondary education, with teachers and pupils forming one of its most captive audiences.[67] By 2009, Phil Rigby believed that the novel had saturated the secondary English department, with *Noughts & Crosses* as one of the "standard texts that you might expect to find within departmental store cupboards."[68] The Department for Education no longer mandates the standardised testing of key stage three students, nor recommends set texts for the study of 11 to 14-year-olds.[69] Rather than being part of the national curriculum for English or a recognised English examination, *Noughts & Crosses* has therefore instead been integrated into secondary education informally. In their study of the most studied prose texts for key stage three (years seven, eight, and nine) learners in the UK, Susan Chapman and others found that Malorie Blackman is the only author of colour frequently studied by 11- to 14-year-olds at school, with *Noughts & Crosses* listed as the joint-tenth most frequently taught book to year eight pupils.[70]

The informal integration of *Noughts & Crosses* into secondary education elaborated and expanded the educational function of the novel. It has been accompanied by the development of learning resources by both publishers and secondary education teachers. These resources both respond to the prevalence of the novel in schools, and enable its further incorporation into curricula. One such resource, a *Noughts & Crosses* teacher's pack produced in 2008 by Frances Gregory for Oxford Rollercoasters, a series by Oxford

[67] In 2011, Blackman adapted the novel into a graded reader for the British multinational publishing and education company Pearson. See Malorie Blackman and Karen Holmes, *Noughts & Crosses*, Pearson Readers edn (Harlow: Pearson Education, 2011). Designed to cultivate level three reading comprehension, the Pearson graded reader facilitated the incorporation of *Noughts & Crosses* into primary education.

[68] Phil Rigby, "English Teachers and English Teaching," in *Teaching English: Developing as a Reflective Secondary Teacher*, ed. by Carol Evans and others (London: SAGE Publications, 2009), pp. 1–26 (p. 19).

[69] The growing academisation of the compulsory education sector in Britain more broadly has gifted schools with greater autonomy over curriculum design. Yet, in practice, most secondary academies continue to follow the national curriculum for most subjects. This is especially the case for the teaching of English. In a government survey of schools, 79% of primary academies and 77% of secondary academies said that they planned to follow the curriculum "to a great extent"; just one percent of primary academies and one percent of secondary academies replied that they were "not at all" planning to follow the national curriculum. Rob Cirin, "Do Academies Make Use of Their Autonomy?" (DfE, 2014), p. 33.

[70] Susan Chapman and others, "What Literature Texts Are Being Taught in Years Seven to Nine?" (United Kingdom Literacy Association, 2021).

University Press, is notable for the way that it significantly detaches *Noughts & Crosses* from the national context of Britain and its institutionalised racism. Designed to promote the study of *Noughts & Crosses* as a class reader for years seven, eight, and nine, in a context where pupils regularly study texts in excerpt, the resource principally guides students to identify how the language and structure of the text influences 'reader response.' Its understanding of reading as something that can be predicted by textual structures, and objectively catalogued by students, aligns with the assessment criteria for GCSE English language and literature study, for which key stage three English study is considered preparation.[71]

As a consequence of this goal to promote GCSE-style competency in literary reading and analysis, Gregory's *Noughts & Crosses* teacher's pack tends toward a textualist practice of reading the text, albeit one that simplifies the relationship between the reading self and the implied reader. Even as it encourages students to moralise and agonise over characters' actions and beliefs, it implores them to connect their practices of reading to intratextual features. In this sense, worksheet 9a is instructive in tabulating a direct relationship between "What the writer does" and "What effect this has on the reader."[72] But, where it encourages students to engage in a materialist practice of reading, the learning resource tends to highlight African American struggles for civil rights as the novel's main, or most illuminating, extratextual context. Lesson four, for instance, asks students to read the characters' views on violence as a mode of resistance through the lens of the struggle for civil rights in the US.[73] Students are coached to materialise Callum's brother, Jude, as a parallel for Malcolm X, for his belief in the efficacy of violence. Worksheet 4a, containing four student-facing independent research tasks,

---

[71] The Office of Qualifications and Examinations Regulation (Ofqual), a non-ministerial government department, sets the assessment objectives (AOs) for GCSE English language and GCSE English literature, and AOs are the same across all specifications and all exam boards. AO2 for GCSE English language measures students' ability to "explain, comment on and analyse how writers use language and structure to achieve effects and influence readers, using relevant subject terminology to support their views." See Department for Education, "English Language GCSE Subject Content and Assessment Objectives" (HM Government, 2013). AO2 for GCSE English Literature assesses students' ability to "Analyse the language, form and structure used by a writer to create meanings and effects, using relevant subject terminology where appropriate". See Department for Education, "English Literature GCSE Subject Content and Assessment Objectives (HM Government, 2013).

[72] Frances Gregory, *Oxford Rollercoasters: Noughts & Crosses* (Oxford: Oxford University Press, 2008), p. 28.

[73] See Gregory, *Oxford Rollercoasters: Noughts & Crosses*, p. 15.

includes a task to carry out research into the murder of Stephen Lawrence, on the basis that it inspired Blackman to write *Noughts & Crosses*.[74] But this task and its relevance to reading the novel is marginalised by the worksheet's two preceding tasks, which ask students to find out more about Martin Luther King's and Malcolm X's struggles for equality.

The early reception of *Noughts & Crosses*, including its theatrical adaptation and educational remediations, authorised particular ways of reading of text for the purpose of moral improvement and social consciousness raising. For non-professional readers, from theatre directors to educational publishers, this was a novel with the potential to teach audiences about social inequalities, especially those that obtain outside of Britain. Their practices of reading the novel were distinctive in the way that they tended to neglect the relationship between its production and historic racism in Britain in a seemingly immaterialist interpretation, only to connect its inverted depiction of racism to other 'real' histories of social division around the world, and consecrate its relationship to Shakespeare's canonical tragedy. In other words, it wasn't the case that non-professional audiences lacked the historical knowledge or desire to engage in a politics of reading. It was rather that they performed and encouraged a politics of reading that affirmed *Noughts & Crosses'* literary quality (including as a derivative version of *Romeo and Juliet*), and that, consciously or not, resemiotised its oblique critique of racism in Britain so that the text was not antagonistic toward, but assimilable by the dominant culture.

In doing so, early practices of reading *Noughts & Crosses* diminished the text's national popularity in favour of increasing its commercial or mass popularity. Importantly, this was a particular kind of commercial or mass popularity that was amenable to the state, for it minimised and, in some cases, obscured the novel's resonances with British imperialism, and its relationship to the Stephen Lawrence case and the Macpherson inquiry's conclusions about institutional racism in Britain. After all, while the Labour government had commissioned the Macpherson report (1999), and made amendments to the Race Relations Act the following year to extend its application to the police and the public functions performed by private organisations in response to the Report's findings, it later watered down its commitments to tackling institutional racism so that "the effect [of its policymaking] was almost entirely cosmetic."[75] This was also a government

---

[74] See Gregory, *Oxford Rollercoasters: Noughts & Crosses*, p. 16.
[75] David Gillborn, "Tony Blair and the Politics of Race in Education: Whiteness, *Doublethink* and New Labour," *Oxford Review of Education*, 34.6 (2008), pp. 713–25 (p. 720).

whose leader, Prime Minister Tony Blair (1997–2007), had distanced both himself and modern Britain from the Britain that presided over the transatlantic slave trade. On the bicentenary of the abolition of the slave trade, Blair wrote in the Black weekly newspaper *New Nation* that the anniversary "offers us a chance [...] to express our deep sorrow that it ever happened, that it ever could have happened and to rejoice at the different and better times we live in today."[76] By promoting the circulation of *Noughts & Crosses* as a pedagogical tool for the teaching of historic social divisions across the world, then, non-professional readers negated the novel's national popularity in the service of a mass popularity that served the state's representation of empire and racism as historic and elsewhere.

Reading *Noughts & Crosses* Again

Reviews for *Noughts & Crosses* suggest that influential actors were successful in popularising the novel. The book has received numerous reviews on digital book reviewing platforms, and has easily has the highest quantitative approval rating of any of the novels discussed in this book, having achieved an average of 4.5 out of 5 on Amazon UK and 4.19 out of 5 on Goodreads.[77] More importantly, early non-professional practices of reading and adapting the novel were instrumental in shaping its popular reception. We can see their influence on contemporary education scholarship, for instance, where scholars have affirmed *Noughts & Crosses*' international appeal, and tested the novel's ability to teach students about "social issues,"[78] or hypothesised about its value for cultivating democratic ideals and citizenship among students.[79] Yet, in addition to establishing dominant frameworks for the reception of the text as a vehicle for a liberal cultural and political education, appropriations, adaptations, and educational remediations of *Noughts & Crosses* by non-professional readers have broadened the novel's potential audience and kickstarted a process that has seen the novel become a big

---

[76] Tony Blair, "PM's Article for the *New Nation* Newspaper," *The National Archives*, 27 November 2006 <https://webarchive.nationalarchives.gov.uk/ukgwa/+/http://www.number10.gov.uk/Page10487> [accessed 14 January 2024].
[77] This was accurate in July 2024.
[78] Ghazal Kazim Syed and others, "Developing UK and Norwegian Undergraduate Students' Conceptions of Personal Social Issues in Young Adult Fiction through Transnational Reflective Exchange," *English in Education*, 55.1 (2021), pp. 53–69.
[79] Marit Elise Lyngstad, "Integrating Competence and *Bildung* through Dystopian Literature: Teaching Malorie Blackman's *Noughts & Crosses* and Democracy and Citizenship in the English Subject," *Utbildning & Lärande*, 15.2 (2021), pp. 11–26.

multimedia property, capable of being endlessly repurposed for different audiences. In 2017, the book was adapted by Ian Edington into a graphic novel, with stylised greyscale illustration by John Aggs. A second theatre adaptation—this time adapted by poet and playwright Sabrina Mahfouz, and directed by Esther Richardson for Pilot Theatre—premiered at Derby Theatre in February 2019, before touring the UK until 11 May 2019. Again, a playscript was published.[80] And, on 5 March 2020, the first series of the television adaptation *Noughts + Crosses* premiered on BBC One. The novel and associated media properties now circulate more widely than ever before. I return to book reviews on online reading platforms to ask, outside of explicitly educational or instrumental contexts, how do readers read *Noughts & Crosses*? How do non-professional practices of reading adopt or challenge the novel's dominant interpretative frameworks?

The perceived didacticism of the novel and its reception contexts made available certain kinds of critique. When we return to the social reading platform of Goodreads, and the practices of reading performed and narrated by their users outside of explicitly educational contexts, we can find readers who take issue with the didactic premise of *Noughts & Crosses*. While conservative critiques of the novel's moral and political didacticism remain available (one Goodreads reader criticises Blackman for 'lecturing' her readers, and regrets that the novel wasn't more like *To Kill a Mockingbird*), far more frequently we find that that readers complain about the didacticism of the text either because it limits their enjoyment of *Noughts & Crosses* as a novel, or because its content falls short of their social and political beliefs and aspirations. In their Goodreads review, one reader writes "DNF DNF DNF DNF. THIS WASN'T A STORY, IT WAS A FUCKING ESSAY." 'DNF,' an acronym for 'did not finish,' features in several readers' reviews on Goodreads. Here it is used to emphasise this reader's dissatisfaction with the perceived didactic, or 'essayistic' tone of the novel. They fail to find sufficient pleasure in reading the text because it thwarts their self-in-the-world's expectation and desire that the text is a story. Another reader complains that the overt didacticism of the text patronises and underestimates readers. "Instead of having faith that readers will understand the implications of the novel for themselves," they write in their Goodreads review, "the author continuously shoves her message down readers' throats". For this reader, the text possesses "[a]n extremely important message" whose "power is lost to explicitness." It is implied that *Noughts & Crosses* fails to

---

[80] Sabrina Mahfouz, *Noughts & Crosses* (London: Nick Hern Books, in association with Pilot Theatre, 2020).

promote learning and reflection because it offers readers little agency or responsibility over the production of meaning. The expository character of the text—its insistent moralising and political didacticism—minimises the role of their self-in-the-world in "understand[ing] the implications of the novel for themselves." The novel ends up foreclosing learning, because it eliminates indeterminacy, and so denies the self-in-the-world the chance to recursively learn the limits of the self and its horizon (on indeterminacy and recursion, see Introduction, pp. 16–21).

Another reader seems to agree that reading the novel prompts little reflection on racism. In a one-star review for Goodreads, one reader says of the novel that "the politics of race were treated far too simplistically." It underestimates both the knowledge and critical flexibility of their self-in-the-world. "A novel has to be more than a statement," they continue. "It's got to be a discussion. [...] [A]ll I got from this book was that racism is bad and humans are inherently prejudiced. Well Yeah. I knew that already". For this reader, the text presents a 'simple,' monological approach to racism that they already possess, and therefore the experience of reading fails to teach them anything they didn't already know. This reader implicitly expresses a desire to learn from reading novels, but perceives the simplicity and overt didacticism of *Noughts & Crosses* as a limit to its educational value. Another one-star reviewer on Goodreads, who reports reading the book with their teenage son who was studying the book at school, similarly expresses their interest in learning from reading, and thus does not refute the didactic power of novels. Yet, for them, the novel "communicates messages around racism, inequality and oppression with the subtly [sic] of a brick thrown through a window [....] Frankly, I can (and do) get my education on racial inequalities in a more varied and nuanced way without the angsty melodrama. I'm afraid this book gets a thumbs down from me". For this reader, the subject of *Noughts & Crosses*' didacticism (racial inequality) is worthy, but its delivery is too crude to be instructive. They distinguish themselves as an adult reader, with 'better' aesthetic tastes and greater political sophistication when it comes to books about racial inequalities, and thereby imply that they are perhaps not the novel's intended or addressed audience (on the relationship between reading and address, see Chapter 2).

While the reading practices described above suggest that the novel's perceived didacticism is not sufficiently enjoyable, dialogic, or subtle to possess educational potential, other readers have suggested that it inhibits the development of the text's alternate history and world. Two readers on Goodreads complain that the eponymous noughts and Crosses simply have "no culture." But several readers elaborate sophisticated critiques of the insubstantiality of *Noughts & Crosses*' text world. One reader on Goodreads has received 58 'likes' for their review, in which they articulate the novel's "poorly executed world building." They raise several questions of the text's alternate world, writing: "Why do most of the characters have English names? Why do the places have English names? That's not how conquering works. [...] [W]hy are they participating in English activites [sic] vs forcing their culture, language and customs on the people they are oppressing?"

Two further readers on Goodreads draw attention to the novel's ahistorical naming procedures. Their reviews are reproduced in excerpt below:

> I wanted to hear what the cities in Europe would be called or what the Crosses would be wearing and what the noughts would be wearing. What did I get? A pile of nothing. [...] Another problem was some shit just didn't make any fucking sense. For example, if these Africans left their content and colonized Europe, why do they all have white names? Huh, Malorie? Riddle me that.

> Why does everyone have a European name? Why are the places named the same as the locations in our world, if Africans were the colonizers? Why do they call it "Crossmas"???

These readers express frustration at *Noughts & Crosses*' historical insubstantiality, with particular emphasis on its failure to imaginatively invert cultural practices of domination. In the process, they demonstrate some knowledge of colonial onomastics, and insist upon the politics of naming.[81] The novel falls short of their expectations, for they neither enjoy nor learn from its alternate world.

Another reader goes further in interrogating the alternate history and world of *Noughts & Crosses*. In their Goodreads review, they write, "[t]he worldbuilding is so poor, it doesn't make sense. [...] The author couldn't even consider a world where 'Cafrique' invented everything?" This reader draws attention to the absurdity of an alternate world, occasioned by the expansion of the Cafrique empire, in which some of the most important inventions are produced by (African) Americans. Their criticism illuminates the incongruence of the novel's history lesson episode with which I opened this chapter, in featuring Garett Morgan's invention of a type of gas mask used by soldiers during World War I. Are we to believe that the World War

---

[81] For an account of non-professionals' recognition of the politics of naming, see Kate Spowage, "Against the Game: Sid Meier's *Civilization* and Vernacular Theories of Language," *Language in Society*, forthcoming.

I of our world also took place in the imagined, alternate world of *Noughts & Crosses*? Surely not, for elsewhere the novel suggests that the Cafrique empire has subjugated other territories for centuries. Callum tells us that "[c]enturies ago, Crosses had moved across northern and eastern Pangaea from the south, acquiring along the way the know-how to make the guns and weapons that made everyone else bow down to them".[82] The Cafrique empire moreover only "formally abolished [slavery] over half a century ago."[83] The existence of the European empires and power blocs that shaped the pursuit of war in the early twentieth century therefore seems unlikely. Another reader, who says that they thought that "[t]he premise [of *Noughts & Crosses*]—an alternate world in which black people are dominant (complete with a history of enslaving white people)—had good potential" similarly expresses their disappointment with the novel's unimaginative world. They conclude their Goodreads review in the following way:

> Sure, people are terrible, and there's nothing really inherent about people of one skin colour that makes them behave differently from others. I get that. But why bother creating an alternate history if you aren't going to do anything with it? If Africa gained access to firepower first and popped round to Europe to kidnap some white people and use them to farm loads of cassava, would we not have prosperous societies in Ghana with deep-rooted racial issues whilst Norway is a developing nation beseiged [sic] by a string of corrupt military dictatorships and power grabs? Maybe we'd listen to different music, or we'd have non-nuclear family structures. We probably wouldn't all be eating chips for dinner.

This reader's proposed alternate history may be crude. It appears to arbitrarily select Norway and Ghana in order to relocate the military dictatorships of the decolonising era to Europe, and the failed cultural integration projects of postimperial countries like Britain to Africa. And it perhaps too quickly moves from a concern with the social and political legacies of imperialism to a deceptively ahistorical account of cultural differences. But in raising questions about the social, political, and cultural insubstantiality of *Noughts & Crosses*, this reader draws on the partial knowledge of their self-in-the-world to perform a politics of reading that is disappointed by the novel's apparent vacuity. In doing so, they make a connection between their moral/political desires and aesthetic pleasures. This is a reader for

---

[82] Blackman, *Noughts & Crosses*, p. 140.
[83] Blackman, *Noughts & Crosses*, p. 140.

whom the pleasure and potency of (re)learning the novel's moral lesson that "people are terrible" is diminished by its failure to imaginatively represent an alternate world.

By highlighting the historical insubstantiality of the novel's alternate history premise, each of these readers makes a similar critique of the novel to children's literature scholar Catherine Butler, who considers the novel's failure to elaborate the consequences of "the significant events of the year 146 BC."[84] She writes:

> The 'purity' of Blackman's counterfactual historical premise is sacrificed to her local didactic needs, and to the overall project of depicting a world laterally inverted about the axis of race. In the case of *Noughts & Crosses* it seems reasonable to read the novel's counterfactual historical elements as a way of underlining that our world's recent centuries of white dominance are a contingent rather than an inevitable historical outcome.[85]

For Butler, the novel's counterfactual elements are relegated in importance, and made to serve the text's educational aspirations. The novel's lesson, she continues, is principally that white supremacy is 'contingent.' Its racial reversal can seem to imply that a Black supremacy was historically possible, and that an African state could have possessed and realised the imperial aspirations of any European empire, including through practices of colonisation and slavery. It obscures the historical specificity of racial discourse and racism as expansions of capitalist modernity.[86] Butler's professional opinion lends credibility to the view of the non-professional reader above—that *Noughts & Crosses* misses the opportunity to develop an alternate history of racism and instead principally teaches readers that "people are terrible."

The novel's representation of white supremacy and racism as historically contingent is a specific point of issue for some readers. In their responses, several readers have suggested that Blackman's use of alternate history misleads readers and therefore forfeits any didactic power. For example, in a review on Goodreads 'liked' by nine people, one reader notably frames their

---

[84] *Noughts & Crosses*, p. 73.
[85] "Counterfactual," p. 190.
[86] See Helen Scott, "Was There a Time before Race? Capitalist Modernity and the Origins of Racism," in *Marxism, Modernity and Postcolonial Studies*, ed. by Crystal Bartolovich and Neil Lazarus (Cambridge: Cambridge University Press, 2002), pp. 167–82.

response by their expectation that the novel performs a didactic function. "I'm starting to feel like my expectations are unrealistic when reading books about race relations", they write. In doing so, they define the experience of reading *Noughts & Crosses* as the act of reading for knowledge about race, and reveal something of their self-in-the-world's perception of the relationship between reading and political education (i.e., reading books about race can and should be politically informative). In these terms, they state simply that "[t]his book was really not a good one for me to spend my time on" because it "equate[s] the attitudes of the oppressed with those of the oppressors." Another reader agrees that the novel's counterfactual premise inhibits its ability to educate readers. "Clearly, the purpose of *Noughts & Crosses* is to teach about racial discrimination," they write in their Goodreads review. But "the problem with it, like all discrimination flips, is that we have to imagine a world in which the oppressed become[s] the oppressor." For this second reader, the problem not only lies in the novel's insinuation that, had an African empire existed, it would have enslaved and discriminated against white people in much the same way as Britain or the United States oppressed non-white groups at home and abroad. It is also that, in doing so, the novel cultivates an impoverished empathy with Black people that relies on a 'shared experience' of racism. In their words, *Noughts & Crosses* "encourages the reader to see things like institutionalised racism, Jim Crow and slavery as wrong but only because it is now happening to White people." In reading terms, they worry that the novel coaches readers to condemn structures of racial discrimination based on an ethics of reading that misrecognises themselves in the text. A third reader makes a similar argument, and suggests that the novel seems to address an audience that is ignorant of and unable to empathise with Black peoples' experience of racism. They write:

> I agree with another reviewer who said we don't really need a version of the Civil Rights Movement where white people are the oppressed ones. I *can* actually imagine young readers who will get something out of this, but I really didn't. (Honestly, I didn't even make it that far into the book before I couldn't take it anymore.) I kept thinking of that scene at the end of the movie *A Time to Kill* where Matthew McConaughey is giving his closing argument and ends with "now imagine she's white." Like for some people, they cannot grasp the effects of racism unless they imagine their own race being subjected to it.

This reader makes a comparison between the experience of reading *Noughts & Crosses* and of watching *A Time to Kill*, a legal drama released in 1996, based on John Grisham's 1989 novel of the same name. *A Time to Kill* is set in the 1980s in the fictional town of Clanton in Mississippi. The film follows McConaughey in the role of defence lawyer Jake Brigance as he attempts to exonerate Carl Lee Hailey (Samuel L. Jackson) for murdering the two white men who violently raped his daughter Tonya and left her for dead. When McConaughey (as Brigance) recounts the details of Tonya's brutal attack and implores the audience to "imagine she's white," he addresses the white jury and courtroom spectators whose racist prejudices stymy their empathetic imagination. For this reader to suggest that *Noughts & Crosses* reminds them of this scene from *A Time to Kill* is therefore to suggest that, like McConaughey's closing speech, the novel's alternate world capitulates to a white, racist audience that, unable to empathise with Black people, needs to be imaginatively recast as victims of racism in order to condemn racism. Its use of alternate history is understood as ethically and politically suspect.

Since the release of the first series of *Noughts + Crosses* in March 2020, several readers on Goodreads have reflected on the differences between the original novel and the television series. Many critical readers of the novel have suggested that the television series resolves the contradictions and insubstantiality of the original book's alternate world. For instance, the reader, discussed above, who received 58 'likes' on Goodreads for asking questions of the novel's cultural and political representation of colonisation, updated their review on 18 November 2022 with the following caveat: "Edited to add: I LOVED the TV show associated with this book. The show answers all of the questions I had about the book. I could not love the show more". Another reader on Goodreads advises prospective readers that "You're probably better skipping this [the novel] and watching the TV show instead". They write:

> [L]ike many have said the premise has so much potential. The TV show, for example, delves into the cultural consequences of the shift in power. The book does not. Neither the noughts nor the crosses have any culture, unless you count a weird riff on the IRA culture. The racism in this book is oversimplified and larger than life reminding me of a Disney movie meant to make anyone who's not cartoonishly racist pat themselves on the back and tell themselves they're doing a great job.

Another, who reports that they chose to read *Noughts & Crosses* after having watched the television series, says that, because the novel is narrated by two children, "there's a lot less exploration of the world and its more global issues," and that they "missed the more nuanced and expansive view of the world that was provided by the TV series."

By contrast with the novel, which makes only brief reference to the expansion of the Cafrique empire from southern Pangaea, episode one of *Noughts + Crosses* opens with a map depicting the Aprican Empire's expansion from northwest Africa, near the Gulf of Guinea, across Africa, toward Europe. The British Isles, labelled Albion on the fictional map, changes from a green pattern of noughts to a yellow and orange pattern of crosses to signify its colonisation "over 700 years ago."[87] The series' audio-visual elements embellish this story of empire, manifesting Cross political hegemony in language and naming conventions, architecture, fashion, and a pan-African soundtrack. Nought resistance, particularly that of the Liberation Militia, is depicted as a rejection of these cultural norms in favour of local, Albion cultural practices, such as the wearing of Celtic-inspired tattoos. The opening scenes of episode one depict an instance of police brutality that doesn't occur in the novel. Callum, Jude, and their friend Danny (who does not appear in the original text) are stopped by the police on suspicion of attending an illegal gathering. Furious with a Cross police officer for using the racial slur 'blanker,' and for the unlawful nature of their detention, Jude refuses to comply with the officer's orders. Danny is brutally beaten by the officer as he tries to intervene and calm Jude down. The series later makes transparent the connection between the officer's actions and the state; Home Secretary Kamal Hadley (Sephy's father) appears on the news to express public support for the officer's actions, and to suggest that he was simply defending himself.

While audiences have tended to enjoy the more elaborate alternate world of the television series *Noughts + Crosses*, especially compared with that of the original novel, some viewers have questioned the television adaptation's use of alternate history, and the audiences that it addresses and serves. In a post on Twitter (now X), one prospective viewer suggests that the trailer of *Noughts + Crosses* "romanticiz[es] the irrational fear that White people generally have that if Black people were to ever have greater/equal socioeconomic power than Whites, we'd do what they've done to us." By presenting an alternate history and world in which Black people enslaved, colonised, and culturally oppressed white populations, *Noughts + Crosses* suffers from the same problem as the novel on which it is based. As they point out, its alternate world implies that empire and racism were

---

[87] "Episode 1," *Noughts + Crosses*, dir. Julian Holmes and Koby Adom, season 1, episode 1 (BBC, 2020), 00:00:00–00:00:15.

contingent; that, in other circumstances, Black people might hold social, cultural, and political power over white people; and that, they would engage in the same practices of domination and racial discrimination. This viewer identifies as Black through the first-person plural pronouns "we" and "us," and distinguishes themselves from the series' target audience.

Another viewer similarly links their identity as a Black woman to their critical reception of *Noughts + Crosses*. While they praise the television adaptation's "really positive [...] representation of Black people," with specific reference to its casting of dark-skinned actors, and its costume design and display of natural hairstyles, they too worry that its alternate world stokes racist fears of white replacement. In their video review of the show, they tell viewers: "Keep in mind this is the type of world, right, this idea of Black supremacy, that, you know, white supremacist Nazis fear will take place". But primarily, this viewer describes the television show as ethically and politically flawed. Again and again, over the course of their video review, they return to question its use of alternate history, or what they call its "simulation":

> [F]rom episode one, this is where I was struggling right, with the concept of having to portray the world as opposite in order to express the difficulties for Black people [...] personally, that's not a method I would use. [...] everyone has a different perspective on how change can be brought about and [...] there's different ways that we can convey messages. [...]
>
> I could not go along with the simulation. It just made me feel 'do we really have to do all of this for you to understand?' [...] I thought for a moment, and I'm like 'This is not for me, is it? This programme is not for me.' And I think that's the conclusion I came to. [...] With my politics and with 24 years' experience on this earth, I just—as a Black woman—this show just was not for me. [...]
>
> Why do we always have to do these grand things [...] to show 'oh hey guys, you know you're oppressing us, right?' [...] That whole conversation, debate, that very liberal approach to change—[...] there may be certain situations where that does work but I think for people, specifically Black women who are exhausted, [and] for our siblings, [...] they spend a lot of time having to explain, to justify [...] that there's just something that I just can't vibe with when it comes to this BBC adaption [sic] and this book.

This viewer's critique of the television adaptation is similar to that of the reader who compared the novel to *A Time to Kill*. They express frustration with the politics of the text's aesthetic premise, asking whether it's necessary, or politically desirable, to "'do all of this'"—to represent an alternate world in which white people are racially oppressed—to cultivate white audiences' understanding of racism. I say 'white audiences,' for this viewer's interrogative interjections explicitly castigate an imagined white audience—a "you" that is not "we"—that requires the ethical interface that the television adaptation and the original novel provide. For them, the show's ethical premise, that white audiences must imaginatively inhabit the role of the racialised minority in order to comprehend the racism experienced by Black people is a "very liberal approach to change." The viewer doesn't explain what they mean by a 'liberal approach,' but certainly the alternate history of both the novel and film invests implicitly in the notion that, forced to roleplay as the victims of racism, white individuals would no longer possess conscious and unconscious racist attitudes, and racism would end. For this viewer, then, the perceived didacticism of the television series and the original novel is insufficiently radical, and therefore fails Black audiences: hence, they say, "With my politics and with 24 years' experience on this earth, I just—as a Black woman—this show just was not for me".

While non-professional readers in (para)educational settings, from national portfolio organisations (NPOs) like the Royal Shakespeare Company to publishers to schools, have influentially elaborated the didacticism of *Noughts & Crosses*, non-professional readers do not necessarily assimilate the interpretative protocols established by these actors, nor have the same faith in the educational value of *Noughts & Crosses* or its associated media properties. They offer thoughtful critiques of the novel's didactic tone, its cultural and political ahistoricism, its representation of racism as contingent, and the political liberalism of the ethics of reading it compels. And though many praise the television adaptation for eschewing the overt didacticism of the novel, and for developing its alternate world in culturally and politically meaningful ways, they remain suspicious of its alternate history. The reader above in particular suggests that its racial reversal panders to white audiences. The television series and novel alike do not necessitate any solidarity on the part of their addressed white audiences, but merely ask them to recognise and condemn racism based on an ethics of reading through which they roleplay as racially oppressed. This reader may themselves underestimate white audiences, but their principal point is that the television adaptation and the original novel can only teach white audiences a conditional empathy, based on a faulty understanding of the historical conditions of racism.

Conclusion

My aim in focusing on the reception of *Noughts & Crosses* has been to suggest that popular culture is more complicated than postcolonial studies has tended to conclude. Reading confers popularity. Certainly, if a text is read widely, it might be said to have achieved mass popularity. But it also matters who reads, and how. In the relative absence of a professional audience, early non-professional readers obscured the national popularity of *Noughts & Crosses* (as a response to police failures in the prosecution of Stephen Lawrence's killers), and enabled its international, mass circulation. By reading and remediating the novel's associations with *Romeo and Juliet*, and with apartheid, Jim Crow, and the IRA, and by minimising its relationship to Britain and the Macpherson report's conclusions about institutional racism, these readers elaborated new educational value for reading the novel and changed its relationship to the state. Outside of didactic contexts, on online platforms, non-professional readers have interrogated the novel's apparent didacticism using their knowledge of empire and colonialism, their political beliefs, and their lived experience of racism. Precisely by reading the novel, and by watching the television adaptation, they have attempted to participate in the redefinition of these texts' popularity.

Reading popular texts may hold little value or interest for professional postcolonial critics. The novel's popularity may ensure this, for the discipline of postcolonial studies has entrenched a hierarchy of culture and cultural experience that diminishes the value of popular cultural consumption. This hierarchy is difficult to set aside, for it builds on dominant conceptions of reading, where the social value of reading depends on the restricted circulation and reception of a given literary text, or, as Bourdieu writes, "the rarity of the disposition and competence which [a work of art] demands and which determines its class distribution."[88] Yet, if we continue to associate the consumption of popular culture with aesthetic vulgarity, cultural vacuity, and political compromise, we risk perpetuating a defective understanding of popular culture's audiences, who are by no means uniformly uncritical or uneducated, neoliberal consumers.

[88] Pierre Bourdieu, *Distinction: A Social Critique of the Judgement of Taste*, trans. by Richard Nice (Cambridge, MA: Harvard University Press, 1984), p. 229.

Moreover, as Claire Squires has shown, mass-market genres by Black and minority ethnic authors have been shown to particularly appeal to Black and minority ethnic audiences.[89] To pay popular cultural forms no critical attention is therefore to risk neglecting these audiences.

[89] Claire Squires, "Too Much Rushdie, Not Enough Romance? The UK Publishing Industry and BME (Black Minority Ethnic) Readership," in *Postcolonial Audiences: Readers, Viewers and Reception*, ed. by Bethan Benwell, James Procter, and Gemma Robinson (London: Routledge, 2012), pp. 99–111 (p. 108).

Conclusion
Deprofessionalising Postcolonial Studies?

This book has argued that there is a critical consensus in postcolonial studies, sometimes overt, often inexplicit, that reading is best left to the professionals. What 'professional' means in this context can differ. We tend to use it not simply to name individuals who are trained in the protocols of literary reading, schooled in postcolonial theory, and familiar with imperial history, but to distinguish readers who apply the dominant procedures of interpretation and evaluation of institutionalised postcolonial studies from those who do not. We speak about this latter reading community more often than we speak to them, using non-professional readers and their cultural practices to articulate the value of our own disciplinary practices. This concluding chapter focuses on one of the only sites where we regularly engage with non-professional readers: the university classroom. The classroom is used to model and authorise professional practices of reading. We meet students, not as non-professionals, but as not-yet-professionals. One of the functions of teaching is to induct students into the established practices of the discipline, and the value systems that accompany them. Yet this approach to teaching perhaps misses something essential and valuable about our students as neither professional nor non-professional readers, and as mediators of professional value.

This final chapter aims to contextualise our approach to teaching the reading and reception of postcolonial literature before situating the classroom as a site of interest for further study and practical transformation. It first looks at a range of postcolonial literature courses offered by English departments in the UK to trace how they embed particular assumptions about reading it. It argues that institutional change has prompted the elaboration of new value for reading postcolonial literature, including by incentivising its professionalisation. It proceeds to suggest that, while the classroom and indeed the larger discipline of postcolonial studies would clearly benefit from a closer engagement with materialist and sociological studies of postcolonial culture, the discipline's own mediation by processes of production, circulation, and reception limits the influence of existing scholarship that critiques postcolonial studies' self-authorising relationship with reading. The anthologisation of research into postcolonial production and consumption, for instance, risks assimilating and incorporating disciplinary critique into normative disciplinary practices. That is, teachers and students are invited by anthologies of postcolonial theory and criticism to read authority into abbreviated critiques of disciplinary authority.

I conclude by calling for professional postcolonial critics and their students to read the discipline—to scrutinise postcolonial studies with the same care and attention as they pay the literature. By focusing on one of the most important roles we undertake as professional readers of postcolonial literature—that as its teachers—my aim in this chapter is to offer some specific political-economic context to the teaching of postcolonial literature in the UK and the discipline's professionalisation of reading. But it is also to invite colleagues—teachers, readers, students—to participate in the reinvention of the discipline and the transformation of its assumptions about professional and non-professional readers. While our power to effect change in the classroom is neither total nor guaranteed, there remain opportunities to intervene in the disciplinary parameters and priorities of postcolonial studies. For teachers, this includes by engaging our students differently, not as mere non-professionals in need of aesthetic and interpretative training, but as valuable interlocutors from whom we can learn something of the discipline's biases and omissions when it comes to practices of reading.

Postcolonial Studies in the Institution

Postcolonial literature has not been institutionalised for very long. Reflecting on the tenth anniversary of *Wasafiri*, Susheila Nasta recalls that, when the magazine was founded in 1984, few university English departments in the UK offered courses that reflected the cultural diversity of Britain.[1]

---

[1] *Wasafiri* was initially published by the Association for the Teaching of Caribbean, African, Asian and Associated Literatures (ATCAL), a national organisation dedicated to promoting the teaching of Black writing in secondary and further education. For a detailed contextual history of ATCAL, see Roger Bromley, "Reading the 'Black' in the 'Union Jack': Institutionalising Black and Asian British Writing," in *The Cambridge History of Black and Asian British Writing*, ed. by S. Nasta and M. Stein (Cambridge: Cambridge University Press, 2020), pp. 417–32.

> [F]or the main, there was little real acceptance or knowledge of even major writers such as Derek Walcott (recent Nobel Prize winner), Wole Soyinka, Chinua Achebe, Margaret Atwood, Anita Desai, Bessie Head and many others with similar post-colonial backgrounds. Indeed few people studying literature had heard of let alone read many of these authors and few were interested; the reading lists of many departments reflected a narrow ethnocentric approach and where courses on subjects like 'African' or 'Caribbean' or 'Asian' writing did exist, they were [...] usually run as options which tended to stress either an anthropological interest in 'other cultures'—the 'sari and samosa' approach—or alternatively left students at a loss to see how Caribbean literature for instance might bear any relationship to European modernism or their other reading however 'good' the books might be.[2]

Nasta usefully highlights here that early efforts to diversify curricula were hampered by issues of both quantity and quality. That is, few English departments were teaching works by the handful of well-known postcolonial writers, and those that did taught them optionally, and either as transparent representations of cultural difference, or as 'other' cultures entirely, distinct from those of Europe. This has in part to do with the dominance at the time of a "historicist and realist tradition" of literary criticism that assumed "a stable relation" between literary representation and historical reality.[3]

We can be grateful that, quantitatively speaking, much has changed since the 1980s. As a discipline, literary studies may have been relatively slow in taking up the political priorities and aesthetic questions raised by decolonisation.[4] However, even by 1994, Nasta noted that, at the very least, major postcolonial writers had "begun to penetrate the inner sanctums

---

[2] Susheila Nasta, "Editorial: The Scramble for New Literatures," *Wasafiri*, 10.20 (1994), pp. 3–4 (p. 4).

[3] Simon Gikandi, "Poststructuralism and Postcolonial Discourse," in *The Cambridge Companion to Postcolonial Literary Studies*, ed. by Neil Lazarus (Cambridge: Cambridge University Press, 2004), pp. 97–119 (p. 116). Gikandi is summarising Homi Bhabha's view. See Homi K. Bhabha, "Representation and the Colonial Text: A Critical Exploration of Some Forms of Mimeticism," in *The Theory of Reading*, ed. by Frank Gloversmith (Brighton: The Harvester Press; New York: Barnes and Noble, 1984), pp. 93–122.

[4] See Aijaz Ahmad, "The Politics of Literary Postcoloniality," *Race and Class*, 36.3 (1995), pp. 1–20; Neil Lazarus, "Introducing Postcolonial Studies," in *The Cambridge Companion to Postcolonial Literary Studies*, ed. by Neil Lazarus (Cambridge: Cambridge University Press, 2004), pp. 1–18; and Neil Lazarus, "Afterword," *African Identities* (Special Issue: Marxism and African Literatures: New Interventions), 18.1–2 (2020), pp. 182–92 (p. 183).

and corridors of even the most resistant academic establishments."[5] While some older universities grudgingly and belatedly embraced the teaching of postcolonial literature, the 'new' universities of the post-1992 era oversaw the growth of English departments in the UK, and the employment of research and teaching staff specialising in postcolonial studies.[6] Today, the teaching of postcolonial literature is firmly established in the UK. Of the 92 institutions who made submissions in the English language and literature unit of assessment (UoA) as part of the Research Excellence Framework 2021, almost half (42) currently offer courses designed to survey postcolonial literature. The number of English departments who offer courses pertaining to postcolonial literary studies, but which are not explicitly designed to introduce students to the theoretical parameters of the discipline, is far greater. In fact, many of those who do not offer a survey module in postcolonial literature instead offer specialist modules in African, Black British, Caribbean, Indigenous, migrant, and multi-ethnic literatures.[7]

Qualitatively speaking, change has been slower. Certainly, postcolonial literatures are no longer taught in isolation from the concerns of modernist, post-war, and contemporary literary studies. On this, we can agree with Neil Lazarus, that "courses in post-1945 'English' literature that ignore 'minority' or 'postcolonial' writers and the issues of decolonization, migration, and diaspora are simply anachronistic."[8] However, most courses focusing on postcolonial literature remain non-compulsory, and are instead offered as options in the second and final year (or honours years in Scotland). English departments take an "additive" approach to diversification and decolonisation, "retain[ing] as much as possible of the core curriculum while opening

---

[5] Nasta "Editorial," p. 4.
[6] Bromley, "Reading the 'Black' in the 'Union Jack'," p. 428.
[7] The University of Dundee offers "Multi-Ethnic American Fiction" as a level-three option. Goldsmiths' College offers "Black British Literature" and "Contemporary Indigenous Literatures" as level-two options, and "Caribbean Women Writers" as a level-three option. The University of Plymouth offers "Literatures of the Atlantic World: Race, Resistance, and Revolution" as a level-three option. Queen's University of Belfast offers "Writing Africa: The Colonial Past to Colonial Present" as a level-three option. The University of Reading offers "Black British and Asian Voices: 1948 to the Present," and "Nigerian Prose Literature: From Achebe to Adichie" as level-three options. The University of Sheffield offers "Contemporary Black British Writing" as a level-three option. The University of Southampton offers "African Freedoms and the Novel" as a level-two option. And York St John University offers "Writing the Caribbean" as a level-three option.
[8] Lazarus, "Introducing Postcolonial Studies," p. 14.

up new subject options and degree pathways."⁹ Of the 42 institutions that offer survey-style postcolonial literature courses, for instance, just four make them mandatory. Of the four, two are 'modern' (post-92) universities (the University of Gloucestershire and Leeds Beckett University), and one is a former 'plate glass' university (post-60s), which boasts the newest English department in the UK, having only accepted its first BA English cohort in 2016 (City, University of London).¹⁰ In general, then, postcolonial literature has remained a voluntary enterprise at ancient and redbrick UK universities, with new universities and English departments continuing to play a crucial (and largely unsung) role in the institutionalisation of the discipline.

The growth of postcolonial literature courses is only part of the disciplinary picture, though. If, in the 1980s, aesthetic conventions in literary studies fostered an 'anthropological' approach to postcolonial writing as a document of 'other' cultures, today extrinsic factors such as institutional priorities mediate the teaching of postcolonial literature as transparent media for cultural, historical, and political representation. In a 2010 article for the *Journal of Postcolonial Writing*, Neelam Srivastava called attention to

> the onus placed on postcolonial writing as featured in university courses: to perform more as social document than as literary text, to act as the narrative from a 'native informant', and to offer itself as a 'true' image of cultural diversity, seen as an important part of a liberal education. While in doing so the postcolonial text fulfils an important pedagogic function, such as encouraging reflection on issues dealing with oppression, colonialism, and power, at the same time it replicates its status as 'non-canonical', which is often taken as a shorthand to mean less 'literary', and more 'political'.¹¹

She makes clear that the teaching and learning of postcolonial literature has acquired institutional and political value. Treated as documentary, postcolonial literature can participate in institutional diversity work, and exemplify a university's political commitments.

---

[9] Joe Cleary, "The English Department as Imperial Commonwealth, or The Global Past and Global Future of English Studies," *boundary 2*, 48.1 (2021), pp. 139–76 (p. 166).

[10] City, University of London's BA English Programme was "designed from the outset 'for the twenty-first-century-world' and with a postcolonial/decolonial angle in mind, emphasising literatures in English, rather than English literature." Dominic Davies, personal communication, 24 October 2023.

[11] Neelam Srivastava, "Anthologizing the Nation: Literature Anthologies and the Idea of India," *Journal of Postcolonial Writing*, 46.2 (2010), pp. 151–63 (p. 153).

Srivastava's claims are borne out by the descriptions for several postcolonial literature courses offered by English departments in the UK. For instance, the course description for the level-two option "Power, Empire and Equality" at the University of Aberdeen bills the course as "a chance for students at pre-Honours to learn about the impact of global colonialism through the writings of those who experienced it and its repercussions."[12] Postcolonial literature is here valued for its capacity to depict the history of empire, and postcolonial writers are engaged as chroniclers with lived experience of colonialism. "Post-Colonial Literature," a level-three option at Birkbeck College, "[u]s[es] writing from Africa, the Caribbean, India, Canada and Australia as examples [... to] investigate how writers from countries formerly colonised by Britain and which are now politically independent have used writing to study the experience of colonialism as well as postcolonialism".[13] Postcolonial literature must necessarily be taught by way of examples, but, like Aberdeen's, this course description presumes postcolonial writers' affinity to different national contexts, and their ability to speak as 'native informants' about colonial and postcolonial life. This is particularly unusual because the course syllabi for "Post-Colonial Literature" at Birkbeck includes writing by Bernardine Evaristo, a Black British writer, and Salman Rushdie, who, as Trivedi has argued, has scarcely spent any time in India (the country of his birth) and "[i]n more strictly literary terms [...] has proved to be more of an English writer".[14] The course description for "Postcolonial Literature and Theory," a level-three option at the University of St Andrews makes similar claims on behalf of postcolonial literature's historical representativeness. The course description explains that "postcolonialism explores a world transformed by European exploration, exploitation and empire-building" and describes postcolonial literature as "literary representations of this world."[15] Presumably designed to excite prospective students, the ascription of the field of postcolonialism as a 'world,' and one that can be entered through postcolonial writing, risks eliciting an anthropological aesthetic that takes for granted the relationship between postcolonial literature and history. In this way, this course at the University

---

[12] See <https://www.abdn.ac.uk/registry/courses/undergraduate/2022-2023/english/el2018>.
[13] See <https://www.bbk.ac.uk/courses/modules/enhu/ENHU029S6>.
[14] Harish Trivedi, "Salman Rushdie and Postcolonialism," in *Salman Rushdie in Context*, ed. by Florian Stadtler (Cambridge: Cambridge University Press, 2023), pp. 293–304 (p. 295).
[15] See <https://www.st-andrews.ac.uk/subjects/modules/catalogue/?code=EN3213&academic_year=2024%2F5>.

of St Andrews shows that the politicisation of postcolonial writing as social document and its authors as 'native informants' has implications for how we understand reading. Reading postcolonial literature, in these courses, is naturalised as a practice of 'reading representatively,' where a given text is treated as national or cultural testimony; of 'reading historically,' through which representation is related to historical and political events; and of 'reading transparently,' wherein the language of postcolonial writing acts as a transparent medium for cultural expression.[16]

Recent changes to UK higher education have only increased postcolonial studies' institutional visibility. The 'decolonise' movement, which gained international attention following the Rhodes Must Fall protests of 2015, has resulted in increased scrutiny of the colonial legacies of UK universities, and galvanised and politicised the study of postcolonial studies.[17] Yet, student calls to 'decolonise' have taken place in the context of new demands placed on programmes and courses to not simply contribute to the delivery of a high-quality liberal education, but to respond to the neoliberalisation of the universities sector. The decline in state financial support for higher education since 2012 has increased universities' reliance on other sources of income.[18] The coincident relaxation of student number controls, and their

---

[16] Here, I am borrowing the language of the 'reading regimes' identified by Asha Rogers in the teaching and examination of the poem "Nothing's Changed" by Tatamkhula Afrika in UK secondary schools. See Asha Rogers, "Crossing 'Other Cultures'? Reading Tatamkhula Afrika's 'Nothing's Changed' in the NEAB Anthology," *English in Education*, 49.1 (2015), pp. 80–93 (pp. 86–89).

[17] For a good overview of the 'decolonise' movement, see Ankhi Mukherjee and Ato Quayson, eds, "Introduction," in *Decolonizing the English Literary Curriculum* (Cambridge: Cambridge University Press, 2023), pp. 1–20.

[18] In 2010, the UK government cut most direct funding for teaching, and increased the cap on tuition from around £3,000 to a maximum of £9,000 for home students. Following an unsuccessful judicial review against the fee increase, the 200% increase in the tuition fee maximum came into effect from 2012/13, and increased to £9,250 in 2017. The tuition fee increase only applied to students resident in England. Scotland, Wales, and Northern Ireland have devolved powers over higher education. The Scottish Parliament offers higher education free to students studying their first degree who are resident in Scotland, with the Students Awards Agency Scotland (SAAS) covering the costs of tuition for up to five years in total. Senedd Cymru (the Welsh Parliament) followed England in increasing fees for 2012/13 entrants to £9,000, but provided tuition fee grants of up to £5,535 to make up the difference in fee costs. The Welsh government gradually decreased the value of these tuition fee grants, before scrapping them entirely and moving to a tuition fee loan system like England from 2018/19. In Wales today, the cost of higher education for home students remains £9,000 per year, slightly less than in England. Northern Ireland initially capped tuition fees at £3,465 for home

eventual abolition in 2015, created a situation where "if applicants had the grades, they could go where they wanted and their money followed."[19] One of the commercial priorities for British universities in this increasingly privatised landscape has therefore been student enrolment. Recent rises in inflation, together with falling public subsidies, have increased universities' dependence on international student tuition fees, which are not standardised, and can be as much as three times the cost of home tuition fees at some institutions and for some programmes.[20] While this political economy places all universities and programmes under pressure to increase their market share, fresh attacks from the British government on the value of the arts and humanities have placed programmes like English squarely in the crosshairs. A proposed cap on the number of students studying on programmes with low-wage graduate outcomes (so-called 'rip-off degrees'), expected to come into force in 2024/25, implicitly targets arts and humanities degrees, whose graduates sometimes take on temporary and insecure work in the creative

---

     students who are resident in Northern Ireland, but has gradually raised the cap in line with inflation to £4,710 (for 2023/24 entry).

[19] Tony Strike, "Taking the Long View on Student Number Control," *Association of Heads of University Administration (AHUA)*, 16 April 2020 <https://www.ahua.ac.uk/taking-the-long-view-on-student-number-control/> [accessed 30 October 2023]. Strike here paraphrases the "Independent Review of Higher Education Funding and Student Finance (2009–10)," better known as the "Browne Report," which advocated for a competitive, supply-based system of higher education, and instigated the 2012 changes in state funding and tuition fees.

[20] In July 2023, *The Guardian* reported that international students were responsible for a fifth of UK higher education institutions' income in 2022, with international tuition fees making up as much as a third or more of the total income at some universities. See Carmen Aguilar García and others, "Fifth of UK Universities' Income Comes from Overseas Students, Figures Show," *The Guardian*, 14 July 2023 <https://www.theguardian.com/education/2023/jul/14/overseas-students-uk-universities-income> [accessed 30 October 2023]. The Russell Group, a self-selected association of 24 public universities in the UK, released a statement in response to the claims, insisting that member universities continued to recruit more home students than international students. It did, however, admit that, "with Government per-student funding falling," the revenue generated by international student tuition fees "is now being used to supplement both domestic teaching and publicly-funded research." Recent modelling by the Russell Group suggests that universities in England effectively make a loss on every home student admitted, with institutions on average supplementing the cost of educating home students by £2,500 per year in 2022/23. See Tim Bradshaw, "Comment on UK Student Numbers at Russell Group Universities," *Russell Group*, 24 July 2023 <https://russellgroup.ac.uk/news/comment-on-uk-student-numbers-at-russell-group-universities/> [accessed 30 October 2023].

sector, and are typically paid less than other graduates in the same full-time positions.[21]

This context creates particular institutional value in courses that instrumentalise postcolonial literature as part of a distinctly neoliberal strategy of internationalisation, both in the sense of attracting international students, and in preparing students for work in a 'global' economy.[22] The turn away from postcolonial studies and toward world and global literatures has been a symptom of this changing political economy in some UK universities. As Nadia Atia and Kate Houlden have argued, "the proliferation of labels such as 'global fiction' and 'world literature' [...] reflect the exigencies (and fashions) of pedagogical, institutional and administrative priorities."[23] That is to say, the development of world and global literatures courses is sometimes extrinsically motivated, following university managerial priorities around internationalisation, in addition to any specific pedagogical or intellectual rationale. By becoming 'world literature' or 'global literature,' postcolonial studies can be retooled as part of an English language programme for international students. As Joe Cleary has argued in his account of the relationship between 'global English' and 'world literature':

> The English department's answer to [increasing demand for basic competency in English as a second language among constituencies in non-anglophone regions] has been [...] to convert 'postcolonial studies' into 'world literature,' conceived essentially as English world literature or 'global anglophone literature.' This is essentially a strategy to elasticate the previous 'postcolonial studies' subfield [...] so that this widened net might somehow catch whatever new writers or literatures may emerge in this vastly expanded field for the twentieth century.[24]

Cleary draws attention to the way that the transformation of postcolonial literature into 'world' or 'global literature' can be something of a rebranding

---

[21] Roberta Comunian, Alessandra Faggian, and Sarah Jewell, "Embedding Arts and Humanities in the Creative Economy: The Role of Graduates in the UK," *Environment and Planning C: Government and Policy*, 32.3 (2014), pp. 426–50 (p. 446).

[22] On the neoliberal character of internationalisation in the university, see Gerardo L. Blanco and Abdulghani Muthanna, "Looking for Hope Abroad: The New Global University Beyond Neoliberalism," in *Transformation of the University: Hopeful Futures for Higher Education*, ed. by Søren S. E. Bengtsen and Ryan Evely Gildersleeve (Abingdon: Routledge, 2022), pp. 125–38 (p. 127).

[23] Atia and Houlden, introduction, p. 2.

[24] Cleary, "The English Department as Imperial Commonwealth," p. 163.

exercise, where the political commitments of postcolonial literature are exchanged for an edifying and all-encompassing geographic category. The instrumentalisation of world and global literatures in this way sometimes tracks the priorities of writers themselves, for as Kalyan Nadiminti has provocatively argued, writers of so-called global literatures "have refashioned the geopolitical anxieties of postcolonial writing in favor of an easily digestible and far less contested concept of the global."[25]

Whether the writers of world and global literatures are willingly trading political commitment for a chance at global circulation, or whether their work is being co-opted as part of neoliberal-capitalist ventures in international student recruitment by universities, or some variation of the two, is at present less consequential than the rearticulation of the study of postcolonial literature according to the priorities of globalisation. This is because courses in world and global literatures do not appear to be displacing the study of postcolonial literature in the UK. To return to the 92 institutions who made submissions in the English language and literature unit of assessment (UoA) as part of the Research Excellence Framework 2021, just thirteen only offer world or global literatures.[26] Most English departments have introduced the study of world and global literatures additively, rather than to replace the study of postcolonial literature. What we can observe, instead, is the overt narration of postcolonial and world literature courses alike as training in intercultural competencies and global citizenship. The University of Surrey's English programme, for example, incorporates "Global Literatures" (level one) and "Contemporary Postcolonial Fictions" (level two), both compulsory, into a 'global strand' of the degree. This global strand is strategically aligned with the University of Surrey's broader curriculum framework, which aims to develop graduates who possess 'Global Cultural Capabilities' (in addition to 'Employability,' 'Digital Capabilities,' 'Sustainability and Resourcefulness,' and 'Resilience').[27] The teaching of postcolonial and world literatures alike, then, is increasingly seen as a tool for enacting administrative agendas in UK universities. Reading postcolonial literature is harnessed as an exercise

---

[25] Kalyan Nadiminti, "The Global Program Era: Contemporary International Fiction in the American Creative Economy," *Novel: A Forum on Fiction*, 51.3 (2018), pp. 375–98 (p. 390).

[26] The thirteen universities which offer courses in global and/or world literatures, instead of postcolonial literature, are Bournemouth University, the University of Chichester, De Montfort University, Kingston University, the University of Leicester, Nottingham Trent University, the University of Reading, Roehampton University, the University of Southampton, the University of Ulster, the University of Warwick, the University of Winchester, and the University of York.

[27] See <https://catalogue.surrey.ac.uk/2024-5/module/ELI2048>.

in intercultural learning, valued primarily for its ability to improve 'graduate outcomes' (employment and salary).

The influence of political decision makers, university administrators, and upper management on the design and delivery of postcolonial literature courses helps us to see the difficulties of enacting change in how we understand and teach reading in postcolonial studies. My point is not so much that institutional priorities around delivering a liberal education in a neoliberal economy restrict the avowed political commitments of postcolonial literary studies, and determine possibilities for how we teach what it means to read postcolonial literature. It is rather that such extrinsic structures intensify the discipline's preoccupation with professionalising reading. In response to political-economic changes to the funding of higher education, and the Conservative Party's recent representations of the arts and humanities as a 'hobbyist' pursuit, universities and departments have defined new social and economic value for professional practices of reading postcolonial literature. These visions of reading postcolonial literature instrumentalise both the act of reading and postcolonial writing in ways we might find disagreeable, but they do not substantially challenge the discipline's own esteem for professional reading, nor its accompanying practices of distinction. They reify the discipline's own distinction between professional and non-professional readers, endowing professional readers (graduates and teachers of postcolonial literature) with new value as global intermediaries. In short, institutional rationales for studying postcolonial literature have not determined new disciplinary priorities, but have rather elaborated the discipline's intrinsic understanding of its objects of study.

The unlikely alignment between disciplinary and institutional assumptions about the value of professionalising practices of reading postcolonial literature makes it hard to imagine how we might teach students to interrogate claims made about reading in postcolonial studies, to engage with the circumstances of postcolonial literature's actual reception, or to take seriously the aesthetic and political sophistication of non-professional readers. What of reception contexts like the Rushdie affair, where the 'professionalism' of supportive readers was wielded to silence criticisms of *The Satanic Verses* and its author (see Chapter 1)? What about non-professional readers, like those of *A Concise Chinese-English Dictionary for Lovers* that don't conform with our assumptions about non-professional reading (Chapter 2), or, like those of *Harare North* who register the limitations of established, professional practices of reading postcolonial literature (Chapter 3)? What of popular texts like *Noughts & Crosses* which, notwithstanding their global appeal and influence, have received little professional attention (see Chapter 4)? In the context of institutional pressures to distinguish our reading practices, how do we teach students about the professionalisation of reading in postcolonial studies, and about those reading practices that tend to fall outside our purview, or else be written off?

The Production and Consumption of Postcolonial Theory and Criticism

Plainly, we rely on scholarship. This book has pursued a different way of thinking about reading postcolonial literature—one that registers the patterns of distinction that have characterised existing discussions about reading in the discipline, while at the same time breaking down assumptions about the differences between professional and non-professional reading practices. In this way, *Reading Postcolonial Literature* is particularly indebted to Bethan Benwell, James Procter, and Gemma Robinson, whose collaborations have clarified the role of professionalisation in the discipline's treatment of reading and reception, and developed the applied study of the reception of postcolonial literature. But the book perhaps most owes its existence to the work of Graham Huggan, whose 2001 monograph *The Postcolonial Exotic* placed the materialist study of the sociology of postcolonial studies and its objects of study on the discipline's agenda. No single work has been more influential on this book, not just because it directly informs it, but also because Huggan's work has legitimised the material-historical and sociological study of reading in the discipline. *The Postcolonial Exotic* animates the work of Benwell, Procter, and Robinson, Sarah Brouillette, and Caroline Koegler, whose own studies in turn have inspired further metacritical analysis of postcolonial studies and its intersecting cultural industries. To support the teaching of postcolonial reception studies, we need more of this work—more applied studies of postcolonial reception, as well as a broader investment in scrutinising the social, political, economic, and institutional contexts that mediate the production, circulation, and reception of postcolonial literature. To quote Simon Featherstone, we need scholarship that takes up "[o]ne of the necessary tasks of doing postcolonial studies," which is "to analyse the context and practice of that doing."[28] However, this scholarship needs the support of publishers and editors and readers if it is to find readers and ultimately be teachable.

---

[28] Simon Featherstone, *Postcolonial Cultures* (Edinburgh: Edinburgh University Press, 2005), p. 15.

Postcolonial studies has always been shaped by print availability. Simon Featherstone attributes some of the early institutional success of Edward's Said's *Orientalism* and its exposition of colonial discourse analysis to the difficulty of procuring the work of his radical, anticolonial contemporaries. "The academic classic *Orientalism*," Featherstone writes, "with its analysis of the means by which discourse constituted the practices of imperialism, was published as popular editions of the works of [Julius] Nyerere, [Kwame] Nkrumah and [Amílcar] Cabral were going out of print".[29] Of course, *Orientalism* itself only found an audience at all because of the radical, leftist vision of André Schiffrin, then-editorial director of Pantheon, at the time an autonomous imprint of Random House—and the support of Robert L. Bernstein, then-CEO of Random House, who "had long insulated Schiffrin from conglomerate pressure" and without whom "[many] writers might not have found their audience in the US."[30] That Said's work was available at all, then, is historically contingent upon the frustration of radical, anticolonial, and liberation movements in the 1960s and 1970s, and the editorial independence of an American publishing imprint that no longer exists in the same way today. That it was read as a critique of discourse—a book primarily about the constitutive power of colonial representation—moreover speaks to reception conditions at the time, i.e. the institutional dominance of a poststructuralist aesthetic. The poststructuralist reception of *Orientalism* in turn limited the circulation of its claims about the sociology of print and its mediation by colonial political economies. As Benita Parry has argued, Said's work "was appropriated by participants [in the development of postcolonial studies] to license the privileging of 'discourse' as the model of social practice, and consequently to promote an incuriosity about enabling socio-economic and political institutions."[31] *Orientalism*'s critique of academia, pursued most strongly in its introduction, faded from view.[32] The print and reception history of *Orientalism* shows us that the specific circumstances of postcolonial theory and criticism's production and consumption—who and what gets published, and when, as well as who reads works of scholarship, and

---

[29] Featherstone, *Postcolonial Cultures*, p. 20.
[30] Dan Sinkyin and Edwin Roland, "Against Conglomeration," *Journal of Cultural Analytics*, 6.2 (2021), pp. 72 –107 (p. 75).
[31] Benita Parry, "The Institutionalization of Postcolonial Studies," in *The Cambridge Companion to Postcolonial Literary Studies*, ed. by Neil Lazarus (Cambridge: Cambridge University Press, 2004), pp. 66–80 (pp. 68–69).
[32] For an account of the partial critical reception of *Orientalism*, see Huggan, *Interdisciplinary Measures*, pp. 196–209.

how—has historically made a difference in the formation of the discipline's paradigms.

Publishers and distributors continue to influence the organisation of the discipline, enabling the study of some literary and theoretical materials, and hindering the study of others. As Featherstone has argued,

> In designing a university postcolonial studies course, novels by Salman Rushdie, say, or Zadie Smith, or Ben Okri are both readily available and relatively cheap, as are now-standard theoretical materials, such as Edward Said's *Orientalism* (1978), and essays by Homi Bhabha and Gayatri Spivak, which are widely anthologised in all the discipline's most successful readers.[33]

While Featherstone's references here may have dated, his point stands: the mass availability of particular works of postcolonial literature and theory secures their authority in the discipline. This is because, in the design of curricula and syllabi, we have to think practically about how students can access primary and secondary resources. In 2008, Rushdie remained the second-most taught author on introductory postcolonial literatures courses, after Chinua Achebe.[34] Today, it remains far easier, practically speaking, to teach Rushdie, whose works are affordable and widely available, than Abdulrazak Gurnah, for instance, many of whose works were out of print when the news broke that he had won the Nobel Prize for Literature in 2021, and whose work has continued to have a relatively small audience because of "a combination of a low profile, rights issues, and the unavailability of his titles."[35] Likewise, it remains easier to teach works of postcolonial theory and criticism that have been anthologised. Anthologies and readers not only provide relatively cheap access to a range of theoretical material, but also organise and digest topics for ease of teaching and learning. With the majority of UK students in paid employment for the first time on record, and

---

[33] Featherstone, *Postcolonial Cultures*, p. 8; see also Huggan, *The Postcolonial Exotic*, p. 252.

[34] Jopi Nyman, "A Post-Colonial Canon? An Explorative Study of Post-Colonial Writing in University-Level Courses," in *Diasporic Literature and Theory—Where Now?*, ed. by Mark Shackleton (Newcastle: Cambridge Scholars Publishing, 2008), pp. 36–56 (p. 45).

[35] Paulo Lemos Horta, "'The Most Secret Memory of Men': Global South Print Culture Between Bolaño and Mbougar Sarr," in *The Bloomsbury Handbook of Postcolonial Print Cultures*, ed. by Toral Jatin Gajarawala, Neelam Srivastava, Rajeswari Sunder Rajan, and Jack Webb (London: Bloomsbury, 2023), pp. 153–65 (p. 155).

therefore tasked with managing the competing commitments of work and study, anthologies can be a way of introducing students to the theoretical and political concerns of the discipline in excerpted form.[36]

Anthologies are highly practical, then, for teachers and students. But, precisely by securing the availability of certain works of postcolonial theory and criticism, anthologies and readers demarcate the parameters of the discipline. As Graham Huggan has argued, "Anthologies and readers obviously fulfil an ideological as well as an informative function in disseminating knowledge to both students and teachers about the postcolonial field".[37] *The Post-Colonial Studies Reader* by Bill Ashcroft, Gareth Griffiths, and Helen Tiffin is one of the most popular readers in the UK. First published by Routledge in 1995, the reader was reprinted in 1995, 1997, 1999 (twice), 2001, 2003, and 2004, and was revised and republished for a second edition in 2005. Its success has eclipsed that of its contemporaries, such as Padmini Mongia's *Contemporary Postcolonial Theory: A Reader*[38] and Patrick Williams and Laura Chrisman's *Colonial Discourse and Post-Colonial Theory: A Reader*.[39] In their introduction to the reader, the editors acknowledge the uneven distribution of postcolonial theory and criticism around the world. "One purpose of this collection," Ashcroft, Griffiths, and Tiffin write, "is to make a wide range of post-colonial critical material available in a relatively accessible and inexpensive form".[40] But while the second edition of the reader features an additional three essays under the subheading 'Production and Consumption,' and maintains in the section's headnote that postcolonial production and consumption is "one of the most important and so far neglected areas of concern" in the discipline,[41] it offers a very limited introduction to the field. Three of the six essays appeared in the first edition. Four were originally published in the 1970s or 1980s. Just one, an excerpt

---

[36] On the growing number of UK students in paid employment, see Johnathan Neves and Rose Stephenson, *Students Academic Experience Survey 2023* (Higher Education Policy Institute, 2023), pp. 35–36.
[37] Graham Huggan, *The Postcolonial Exotic*, p. 252. On the ideological function of anthologies and headnotes in general, see also Vincent B. Leitch, "Ideology of Headnotes," in *On Anthologies: Politics and Pedagogy*, ed. by Jeffrey Di Leo (Lincoln: University of Nebraska Press, 2004), pp. 372–83.
[38] Padmini Mongia, *Contemporary Postcolonial Theory: A Reader* (Abingdon: Routledge, 1997).
[39] Patrick Williams and Laura Chrisman, *Colonial Discourse and Post-Colonial Theory: A Reader* (London: Pearson, 1993).
[40] Bill Ashcroft, Gareth Griffiths, and Helen Tiffin, *The Post-Colonial Studies Reader* (London: Routledge, 2006), p. 2.
[41] Ashcroft, Griffiths, and Tiffin, *The Post-Colonial Studies Reader*, p. 398.

from *The Postcolonial Exotic* by Graham Huggan, was published this century. Rather than update their selection of essays for the second edition to reflect new scholarship published between 1995 and 2005, Ashcroft, Griffiths, and Tiffin instead acknowledge in the headnote to the subsection that, in production and consumption, "conditions change rapidly, and many of the essays here are already outstripped by events."[42] As a result, the 'Production and Consumption' subsection of the second edition of *The Post-Colonial Studies Reader* largely discusses commercial and distribution issues that no longer obtain in the postcolonial cultural industry.

The incorporation of an excerpt from Huggan's *The Postcolonial Exotic* is welcome, and makes discussions of the postcolonial cultural industry and a serious re-evaluation of postcolonial literature's readers possible in the classroom. And its anthologisation in the discipline's most successful reader has increased the study of postcolonial production, circulation, and reception, including the critiques of Sarah Brouillette and Caroline Koegler. But it has also promoted an abbreviated engagement with his work, improving Huggan's citation rate and consecrating his place in the discipline, without always motivating the pursuit of his research questions or the areas he identified for further study. Huggan viewed *The Postcolonial Exotic* "as opening up a field of inquiry—broadly speaking, the sociology of postcolonial literary production—that would then require the kinds of quantitative analysis and empirical endeavour for which I never saw myself as being cut out."[43] This book seeks, among other things, to advance this project of a sociology of postcolonial literary production from the perspective of reception. Yet at times *The Postcolonial Exotic* has been unread, misread, or taken up to reopen paradigmatic debates in the discipline about 'positionality.' In such scholarship, "exoticism becomes a default mode for speaking about colonial/postcolonial otherness, from either the position of the sovereign western subject or the reversed

---

[42] Ashcroft, Griffiths, and Tiffin, *The Post-Colonial Studies Reader*, p. 397. By not substantially updating the 'Production and Consumption' subsection of *The Post-Colonial Studies Reader*, Ashcroft, Griffiths, and Tiffin missed an opportunity to promote the excerpted study of landmark books about reading published in the earlier 2000s, including the following: Wendy Griswold, *Bearing Witness: Readers, Writers, and the Novel in Nigeria* (Princeton: Princeton University Press, 2000), Stephanie Newell, *Literary Culture in Colonial Ghana* (Bloomington: Indiana University Press, 2002), and Isabel Hofmeyr, *The Portable Bunyan: A Transnational History of The Pilgrim's Progress* (Princeton: Princeton University Press, 2004).

[43] Graham Huggan, "Re-Evaluating the Postcolonial Exotic," *Interventions: International Journal of Postcolonial Studies*, 22.7 (2020), pp. 808–24 (p. 809).

perspective of the 'non-west.'"[44] In this way, Huggan's sustained critique of postcolonial studies for its inattention to the circumstances of postcolonial literature's circulation has been translated into the dominant registers of postcolonial studies, and made to serve, rather than challenge, its established protocols and methodologies. Indeed, if Huggan is right that the field's reliance on master theorists like Spivak has led to "the mystification of such historically specific representational processes as cultural 'othering,'"[45] then the critical consecration of Huggan's *The Postcolonial Exotic* as an ahistorical and imprecise critique of othering risks enjoining him to this cause.

The appropriation of *The Postcolonial Exotic* to affirm disciplinary norms, rather than stimulate new interventions in the study of postcolonial print cultures, has in part to do with the limits of the reader form through which many critics and students have been introduced to his work. As Huggan himself writes in the conclusion to *The Postcolonial Exotic* (before the anthologisation of his work), the reader as a genre consecrates the authority of a selected canon of critics, and is "more likely to promote citational fluency than [...] to inculcate disciplinary knowledge."[46] *The Post-Colonial Studies Reader*, he adds, "risks standing in for what it intends to stimulate—further research—plying a trade instead in aphoristic position-takings within the context of a self-ingratiating postcolonial citation cartel."[47] *The Postcolonial Exotic* now belongs to this 'postcolonial citation cartel.' The book has been cited over three thousand times, with 2,880 of those citations arriving since 2006 (the year that the second edition of *The Post-Colonial Studies Reader* was published).

A third edition of *The Postcolonial Studies Reader* is due for publication on 11 July 2024, which at the time of writing lies in the future, but which is probably, as you read, in the past. Ashcroft, Griffiths, and Tiffin have thoroughly revised the reader, including by removing the hyphen from 'post-colonial' in its title. To my surprise, the third edition's 'Production and Consumption' section now contains an excerpt from one of my own early essays, originally published in *Interventions*.[48] Many of the section's most dated essays are out in this latest edition, as is its excerpt from *The*

---

[44] Huggan, "Re-Evaluating the Postcolonial Exotic," p. 810.
[45] Huggan, *The Postcolonial Exotic*, p. 258.
[46] Huggan, *The Postcolonial Exotic*, p. 257.
[47] Huggan, *The Postcolonial Exotic*, p. 256.
[48] Hayley G. Toth, "Reading in the Global Literary Marketplace: Material and Textual Affects," *Interventions: International Journal of Postcolonial Studies*, 23.4 (2021), pp. 636–54.

Postcolonial Exotic, which has been replaced with an excerpt of Huggan's 2020 essay "Re-Evaluating the Postcolonial Exotic." *The Postcolonial Studies Reader*'s inclusion of new material on cultural production and consumption is welcome. It provides Huggan at least with the opportunity to reorient the reception and appropriation of the postcolonial exotic. And if it has the effect of inspiring further research into actual practices and conditions of reading postcolonial literature around the world, or of engendering a shift in the teaching of postcolonial literature to take into account issues of cultural production and consumption, the discipline of postcolonial studies will be better for it. But anthologisation, as Aarthi Vadde has argued, always risks 'monumentalisation,' or the "unif[ication] and beautif[ication] [of] the past into a series of high points."[49] As a form, the anthology can promote uncritical practices of reading that reify the prestige of selected critics. Whether Ashcroft, Griffiths, and Tiffin intend to enshrine a pantheon of postcolonial critics matters less than whether this latest edition of *The Postcolonial Studies Reader* is read and taught as an "encapsulation of an immemorial greatness."[50] For this reason, anthologies like *The Postcolonial Studies Reader* may struggle to facilitate the interrogation of professionalism and practices of distinction that work like my own encourages. The authorising function of the anthology risks assimilating the enterprise of a sociology of postcolonial cultural production and consumption into the dominant paradigms of the discipline and its professionalising logics.

Reading Postcolonial Studies?

The influence of external agents, from government agencies to university administrators to publishers, on how we understand and teach reading in postcolonial studies can make change seem daunting. When the state, university management, and academic publishers in different ways allocate value to the professionalisation of practices of reading postcolonial literature, critics and teachers of postcolonial literature have extra-disciplinary rationales to remain invested in the reproduction of interpretative authority. Yet my point in suggesting that postcolonial studies, like postcolonial literature, is mediated by political and economic pressures, and circulates through mechanisms of distinction and reproduction, is to

---

[49] Aarthi Vadde, "Theories of Anthologizing and Decolonization," in *Decolonizing the English Literary Curriculum*, ed. by Ankhi Mukherjee and Ato Quayson (Cambridge: Cambridge University Press, 2023), pp. 149–66 (p. 155).

[50] Aarthi Vadde, "Theories of Anthologizing and Decolonization," p. 155.

insist that, like postcolonial literature, postcolonial studies can be read. Professional and non-professional readers, including many discussed in this book, have analysed, debated, and critiqued postcolonial literature in relation to its mediating political, economic, and institutional contexts. At times, their reading practices have interrogated the authority of individual texts and the contexts of their reception. In this way, professional and non-professional readers alike model the possibilities of reading. To think of postcolonial studies as something that can be read is to suggest that we as its readers have a part to play in its meaning. Certainly, one of our roles, as reading selves, is to perform a selective approximation of the implied reader of postcolonial studies, and therefore to assimilate the authority of its established disciplinary conventions, including dominant understandings of reading. But, as selves-in-the-world, we are also responsible for holding postcolonial studies to account as a material object that is inseparable from the historical conditions of the present, including the precaritisation of workers in the arts and humanities, and the uneven production and distribution of 'knowledge.' This is not so much a task, as it is a consequence of being a person with knowledge, experiences, and desires from outside the discipline.

Students represent postcolonial studies' largest and most captive audience. Perhaps we could think about the classroom differently—not only as a space in which to train not-yet-professionals in the interpretative and aesthetic repertoire of postcolonial studies, but also as a communal space in which to read the discipline and its claims about reading through the attachments of our selves-in-the-world and their orientation of our reading selves. Students occupy a privileged position as neither professionals nor non-professionals who can code-switch between registers, and therefore identify and denaturalise assumptions about reading in postcolonial studies. This is not to say that our teaching practices should be guided by non-professional critiques of the discipline. It is rather to suggest that students can helps us to see what we as postcolonial critics and teachers take for granted about reading postcolonial literature. Their reading practices can remind us that we "professional readers are also, in other contexts, lay readers."[51] Their practices of reading the discipline can inspire us to read our own participation in postcolonial studies differently, and to revisit and revise the claims we make about our non-professional counterparts.

---

[51] Guillory, "The Ethical Practice of Modernity," p. 34.

Bibliography

Abdallah, Anouar, *For Rushdie: Essays by Arab and Muslim Writers in Defense of Free Speech* (New York: George Braziller, 1994).
Afzal-Khan, Fawzia, "Here Are the Muslim Feminist Voices, Mr. Rushdie!" *Television and New Media*, 3.2 (2002), pp. 139–42.
Ahmad, Aijaz, "The Politics of Literary Postcoloniality," *Race and Class*, 36.3 (1995), pp. 1–20.
—— *In Theory: Classes, Nations, Literatures* (London: Verso, 2000).
Ahsan, M. Manazir, and Abdur Raheem Kidwai, *Sacrilege Versus Civility: Muslim Perspectives on The Satanic Verses Affair* (Leicester: The Islamic Foundation, 1993).
Akhtar, Shabbir, *Be Careful with Muhammad!: The Salman Rushdie Affair* (London: Bellew Publishing, 1989).
Allan, Michael, "Reading with One Eye, Speaking with One Tongue: On the Problem of Address in World Literature," *Comparative Literature Studies*, 44.1–2 (2007), pp. 1–19.
Appignanesi, Lisa, and Sara Maitland, *The Rushdie File* (Syracuse: Syracuse University Press, 1990).
Armstrong, Paul B., "In Defense of Reading: Or, Why Reading Still Matters in a Contextualist Age," *New Literary History*, 42.1 (2011), pp. 87–113.
Asad, Talal, "Ethnography, Literature, and Politics: Some Readings and Uses of Salman Rushdie's The Satanic Verses," *Cultural Anthropology*, 5.3 (1990), pp. 239–69.
—— *Genealogies of Religion: Discipline and Reasons of Power in Christianity and Islam* (Baltimore: John Hopkins University Press, 1993).
—— "Freedom of Speech and Religious Limitations," in *Rethinking Secularism*, ed. by Craig Calhoun, Mark Juergensmeyer, and Johnathan VanAntwerpen (Oxford: Oxford University Press, 2011), pp. 282–97.
Ashcroft, Bill, Gareth Griffiths, and Helen Tiffin, *The Empire Writes Back: Theory and Practice in Post-Colonial Literature* (London: Routledge, 2002).
—— *The Post-Colonial Studies Reader* (London: Routledge, 2006).
—— *Post-Colonial Studies: The Key Concepts* (Abingdon: Routledge, 2007).

Asia Society, "Why Xiaolu Guo Writes in English," YouTube, 9 November 2017 <https://www.youtube.com/watch?v=MOzigblC1mk> [accessed 24 April 2023].

Atia, Nadia, and Kate Houlden, eds, "Introduction," in *Popular Postcolonialisms: Discourses of Empire and Popular Culture* (New York: Routledge, 2019), pp. 1–23.

Attridge, Derek, "Responsible Reading and Cultural Distance," in *Postcolonial Audiences: Readers, Viewers and Reception*, ed. by Bethan Benwell, James Procter, and Gemma Robinson (London: Routledge, 2012), pp. 234–44.

Barthes, Roland, *A Lover's Discourse: Fragments*, trans. by Richard Howard (New York: Hill and Wang, 2001).

Benwell, Bethan, James Procter, and Gemma Robinson, eds, "Not Reading *Brick Lane*," *New Formations*, 73 (2011), pp. 90–116.

—— "Introduction," in *Postcolonial Audiences: Readers, Viewers and Reception* (London: Routledge, 2012), pp. 1–26.

—— "'That May Be Where I Come from but That's Not How I Read': Diaspora, Location and Reading Identities," *Postcolonial Audiences: Readers, Viewers and Reception*, ed. by Bethan Benwell, James Procter, and Gemma Robinson (London: Routledge, 2012), pp. 43–56.

Bhabha, Homi K., "Representation and the Colonial Text: A Critical Exploration of Some Forms of Mimeticism." In *The Theory of Reading*, ed. by Frank Gloversmith (Brighton: The Harvester Press; New York: Barnes and Noble, 1984), pp. 93–122.

Blackman, Malorie, *Noughts & Crosses* (London: Corgi, 2002).

Blackman, Malorie, and Karen Holmes, *Noughts & Crosses*, Pearson Readers edn (Harlow: Pearson Education, 2011).

Blair, Tony, "PM's Article for the *New Nation* Newspaper (27 Nov 06)," *The National Archives*, 27 November 2006 <https://webarchive.nationalarchives.gov.uk/ukgwa/+/http://www.number10.gov.uk/Page10487> [accessed 14 January 2024].

Blanco, Gerardo L., and Abdulghani Muthanna, "Looking for Hope Abroad: The New Global University Beyond Neoliberalism," in *Transformation of the University: Hopeful Futures for Higher Education*, ed. by Søren S. E. Bengtsen and Ryan Evely Gildersleeve (Abingdon: Routledge, 2022), pp. 125–38.

Boehmer, Elleke, *Colonial and Postcolonial Literature: Migrant Metaphors* (Oxford: Oxford University Press, 2005).

—— *Postcolonial Poetics: 21st-Century Critical Readings* (London: Palgrave Macmillan, 2018).

Boehmer, Elleke, and Dominic Davies, "Literature, Planning and Infrastructure: Investigating the Southern City through Postcolonial Texts," *Journal of Postcolonial Writing*, 51.4 (2015), pp. 395–409.

Bold, Melanie Ramdarshan, "Representations of People of Colour Among Children's Book Authors and Illustrators" (BookTrust, 2019).

—— "Representations of People of Colour Among Children's Book Creators in the UK (2020–2021)" (BookTrust, 2022).
Bongie, Chris, *Friends and Enemies: The Scribal Politics of Post/Colonial Literature* (Liverpool: Liverpool University Press, 2008).
Bourdieu, Pierre, *Distinction: A Social Critique of the Judgement of Taste*, trans. by Richard Nice (Cambridge, MA: Harvard University Press, 1984).
Bradford, Clare, "Race, Ethnicity and Colonialism," in *The Routledge Companion to Children's Literature*, ed. by David Rudd (Abingdon, Oxon: Routledge, 2010), pp. 39–50.
Bradshaw, Tim, "Comment on UK Student Numbers at Russell Group Universities," *Russell Group*, 24 July 2023 <https://russellgroup.ac.uk/news/comment-on-uk-student-numbers-at-russell-group-universities/> [accessed 30 October 2023].
Brennan, Timothy, *Salman Rushdie and the Third World: Myths of the Nation* (London: Palgrave Macmillan, 1989).
—— *At Home in the World: Cosmopolitanism Now* (Cambridge, MA: Harvard University Press, 1997).
Bromley, Roger, "Reading the 'Black' in the 'Union Jack': Institutionalising Black and Asian British Writing," in *The Cambridge History of Black and Asian British Writing*, ed. by Susheila Nasta and Mark Stein (Cambridge: Cambridge University Press, 2020), pp. 417–32.
Brouillette, Sarah, *Postcolonial Writers in the Global Literary Marketplace* (Basingstoke: Palgrave, 2011).
—— "On the African Literary Hustle," *Blind Field*, 14 August 2017 <https://blindfieldjournal.com/2017/08/14/on-the-african-literary-hustle/> [accessed 16 April 2019].
—— "The Rise and Fall of the English-Language Literary Novel since World War II," in *After Marx: Literature, Theory, and Value in the Twenty-First Century*, ed. by Colleen Lye and Christopher Nealon (Cambridge: Cambridge University Press, 2022), pp. 116–30.
—— "Reading After the University," *Public Books*, 23 November 2022 <https://www.publicbooks.org/reading-after-the-university-english-departments/> [accessed 2 February 2024].
Bullen, Chiara, "'Your Bookshelf Is Problematic': Progressive and Problematic Publishing in the Age of COVID-19," in *Bookshelves in the Age of the COVID-19 Pandemic*, ed. by Corinna Norrick-Rühl and Shafquat Towheed (Sham: Palgrave Macmillan, 2022), pp. 69–92.
Bush, Ruth, and Madhu Krishnan, "Print Activism in Twenty-First-Century Africa," *Wasafiri*, 31.4 (2016), pp. 1–2.
Butler, Catherine, "Counterfactual Historical Fiction for Children and Young Adults," in *The Edinburgh Companion to Children's Literature*, ed. by Clémentine Beauvais and Maria Nikolajeva (Edinburgh: Edinburgh University Press, 2017), pp. 179–93.

Butler, Pamela, and Jigna Desai, "Manolos, Marriage, and Mantras: Chick-Lit Criticism and Transnational Feminism," *Meridians*, 8.2 (2008), pp. 1–31.

Carby, Hazel V., "Schooling in Babylon," in *The Empire Strikes Back: Race and Racism in 70s Britain*, ed. by the Centre for Contemporary Cultural Studies (London: Routledge, 1982), pp. 181–209.

Chambers, Clare, and Susan Watkins, introduction to the "Online Special Issue: *The Satanic Verses*," *Journal of Commonwealth Literature*, n.d. <http://journals.sagepub.com/page/jcl/collections/online-special-issue-satanic-verses> [accessed 24 November 2023].

Chapman, Susan, and others, *What Literature Texts Are Being Taught in Years Seven to Nine?* (United Kingdom Literacy Association, 2021).

Chigwedere, Yuleth, "The Wretched of the Diaspora: Traumatic Dislocation in Brian Chikwava's *Harare North*," *Journal of the African Literature Association*, 11.2 (2017), pp. 169–82.

Chikwava, Brian, *Harare North* (London: Vintage, 2010).

Cirin, Rob, *Do Academies Make Use of Their Autonomy?* (Department for Education, 2014).

Cleary, Joe, "The English Department as Imperial Commonwealth, or The Global Past and Global Future of English Studies," *boundary 2*, 48.1 (2021), pp. 139–76.

Cole, Teju, "Far Away from Here," *The New York Times Magazine*, 23 Sept 2015 <https://www.nytimes.com/2015/09/27/magazine/far-away-from-here.html> [accessed 28 February 2024].

Comunian, Roberta, Alessandra Faggian, and Sarah Jewell, "Embedding Arts and Humanities in the Creative Economy: The Role of Graduates in the UK," *Environment and Planning C: Government and Policy*, 32.3 (2014), pp. 426–50.

Cooke, Dominic, *Noughts & Crosses* (London: Nick Hern Books, in association with the Royal Shakespeare Company, 2007).

—— *Noughts & Crosses* (Oxford: Oxford University Press, 2008).

Csáky, Taissa, *Noughts & Crosses* information pack (Royal Shakespeare Company, 2008).

Darnton, Robert, "What is the History of Books?" *Daedalus*, 111.3 (1982), pp. 65–83.

Davies, Dominic, personal communication, 24 October 2023.

Davis, Caroline, *African Literature and the CIA: Networks of Authorship and Publishing* (Cambridge: Cambridge University Press, 2020).

Department for Education, *English Language GCSE Subject Content and Assessment Objectives* (HM Government, 2013).

Department for Education, *English Literature GCSE Subject Content and Assessment Objectives* (HM Government, 2013).

Devadas, Vijay, and Chris Prentice, "Introduction: Postcolonial Popular Cultures," *Continuum: Journal of Media & Cultural Studies*, 25.5 (2011), pp. 687–93.

DNA Web Team, "Hadi Matar Breaks Silence on Salman Rushdie Attack, Says Read Only Two Pages of *The Satanic Verses*," *DNA*, 18 August 2022 <https://www.dnaindia.com/world/report-hadi-matar-breaks-silence-on-salman-rushdie-attack-says-read-only-2-pages-of-the-satanic-verses-2977430> [accessed 28 February 2024].

Doloughan, Fiona, "Text Design and Acts of Translation: The Art of Textual Remaking and Generic Transformation," *Translation and Interpreting Studies*, 4.1 (2009), pp. 101–15.

—— "The Construction of Space in Contemporary Narrative," *Journal of Narrative Theory*, 45.1 (2015), pp. 1–17.

—— "Translation as a Motor of Critique and Invention in Contemporary Literature: The Case of Xiaolu Guo," in *Multilingual Currents in Literature, Translation and Culture*, ed. by Rachael Gilmour and Tamar Steinitz (New York: Routledge, 2017), pp. 150–67.

Donadio, Rachel, "Fighting Words on Sir Salman," *The New York Times*, 15 July 2007 <https://www.nytimes.com/2007/07/15/books/review/15donadio.html> [accessed 29 October 2019].

Driscoll, Beth, and DeNel Rehberg Sedo, "Faraway, So Close: Seeing the Intimacy in Goodreads Reviews," *Qualitative Inquiry*, 25.3 (2018), pp. 248–59.

Duri, Fidelis Peter Thomas, "'Green Bombers,' Torture and Terror: Political Security and the Nazi Legacy in Zimbabwe, 2001-2009," in *Development Naivety and Emergent Insecurities in a Monopolised World: The Politics and Sociology of Development in Contemporary Africa*, ed. by Munyaradzi Mawere (Bamenda: Langaa RPCIG, 2018), pp. 35–76.

Dutrion, Marianne, "A propos d'*Harare North*. Une conversation avec Brian Chikwawa," *Malfini*, 4 October 2012 <http://malfini.ens-lyon.fr/document.php?id=170> [accessed 8 July 2019].

Edoro, Ainehi, and Bhakti Shringarpure, "Why is the Cultural Life of *Black Panther* So Derivative?" *Africa Is a Country*, 26 February 2018 <https://africasacountry.com/2018/02/africa-is-a-country-in-wakanda> [22 December 2023].

Elshayyal, Khadijah, *Muslim Identity Politics: Islam, Activism and Equality in Britain* (London: I.B. Taurus, 2018).

Emre, Merve, "Introduction to the New Edition," in *Cultural Capital: The Problem of Literary Canon Formation*, by John Guillory (Chicago: University of Chicago Press, 2023).

"*Endgame* Publishes 20 Years after *Noughts & Crosses*," *The Agency*, n.d. <https://theagency.co.uk/childrens-books/endgame-publishes-20-years-after-malorie-blackmans-noughts-crosses> [accessed 19 December 2023].

Entry "read," *Oxford English Dictionary*, n.d. <https://www.oed.com/view/Entry/158851?rskey=IUqUpA&result=3> [accessed 7 January 2022].

"Episode 1," *Noughts + Crosses*, dir. Julian Holmes and Koby Adom, season 1, episode 1 (BBC, 2020).

The Ezra Klein Show, "Salman Rushdie Is Not Who You Think He Is," *The New York Times*, 26 April 2024 <https://www.nytimes.com/2024/04/26/opinion/ezra-klein-podcast-salman-rushdie.html> [accessed 14 May 2024].

Falconer, Rachel, "Cross-Reading and Crossover Books," in *Children's Literature: Approaches and Territories*, ed. by Janet Maybin and Nicola J. Watson (Basingstoke: Palgrave Macmillan in association with the Open University, 2009), pp. 366–79.

Featherstone, Simon, *Postcolonial Cultures* (Edinburgh: Edinburgh University Press, 2005).

—— "Postcolonialism and Popular Cultures," in *Oxford Handbook of Postcolonial Studies*, ed. by Graham Huggan (Oxford: Oxford University Press, 2015), pp. 380–95.

Ferri, Guiliana, "The Master's Tools Will Never Dismantle the Master's House: Decolonising Intercultural Communication," *Language and Intercultural Communication*, 22.3 (2022), pp. 381–90.

Finn, Ed, "The Social Lives of Books" (PhD dissertation, Stanford University, 2011).

Fischer, Michael M. J., and Mehdi Abedi, "Bombay Talkies, the Word and the World: Salman Rushdie's *Satanic Verses*," *Cultural Anthropology*, 5.2 (1990), pp. 107–59.

Flood, Alison, "Malorie Blackman: Developing Negatives," *The Guardian*, 10 November 2008 <https://www.theguardian.com/books/2008/nov/10/malorie-blackman-double-cross-noughts-crosses> [29 February 2024].

Fraser, Robert, *Book History through Postcolonial Eyes: Re-Writing the Script* (Abingdon: Routledge, 2008).

Frost, Caroline, "'I Don't Like Him': Salman Rushdie's Alleged Attacker Claims He's Only Read Two Pages of *Satanic Verses*," *Deadline*, 19 August 2022 <https://deadline.com/2022/08/salman-rushdie-alleged-attacker-hadi-matar-read-two-pages-satanic-verses-1235096009/> [accessed 28 February 2024].

Gabriel, John, *Racism, Culture, Markets* (London: Routledge, 1994).

García, Carmen Aguilar, and others, "Fifth of UK Universities' Income Comes from Overseas Students, Figures Show," *The Guardian*, 14 July 2023 <https://www.theguardian.com/education/2023/jul/14/overseas-students-uk-universities-income> [accessed 30 October 2023].

Gikandi, Simon, "Poststructuralism and Postcolonial Discourse," in *The Cambridge Companion to Postcolonial Literary Studies*, ed. by Neil Lazarus (Cambridge: Cambridge University Press, 2004), pp. 97–119.

Gillborn, David, "Tony Blair and the Politics of Race in Education: Whiteness, *Doublethink* and New Labour," *Oxford Review of Education*, 34.6 (2008), pp. 713–25.

Gilmour, Rachael, "Living between Languages: The Politics of Translation in Leila Aboulela's *Minaret* and Xiaolu Guo's *A Concise Chinese-English Dictionary for Lovers*," *Journal of Commonwealth Literature*, 47.2 (2012), pp. 207–27.

—— *Bad English: Literature, Multilingualism, and the Politics of Language in Contemporary Britain* (Manchester: Manchester University Press, 2020).
Grant, Damian, *Salman Rushdie* (Devon: Northcote House, 1999).
Gregory, Frances, *Oxford Rollercoasters: Noughts & Crosses* (Oxford: Oxford University Press, 2008).
Griswold, Wendy, *Bearing Witness: Readers, Writers, and the Novel in Nigeria* (Princeton: Princeton University Press, 2000).
Guardian Research Department, "November 1997: Rushdie and le Carré in Literary Spat," *The Guardian*, 12 November 2012 <https://www.theguardian.com/theguardian/from-the-archive-blog/2012/nov/12/salman-rushdie-john-le-carre-archive-1997> [accessed September 2017].
Guillory, John, *Cultural Capital: The Problem of Literary Canon Formation* (Chicago: Chicago University Press, 1993).
—— "The Ethical Practice of Modernity," in *The Turn to Ethics*, ed. by Majorie Garber, Beatrice Hanssen, and Rebecca L. Walkowitz (New York: Routledge, 2000), pp. 29–46.
Gunew, Sneja, *Post-Multicultural Writers as Neo-Cosmopolitan Mediators* (Anthem Press, 2017).
Gunning, Dave, "Dissociation, Spirit Possession and the Languages of Trauma in Some Recent African-British Novels," *Research in African Literatures*, 46.4 (2015), pp. 119–32.
Guo, Xiaolu, *A Concise Chinese-English Dictionary for Lovers* (London: Vintage, 2008).
—— *A Lover's Discourse* (London: Vintage, 2020).
Guo, Xiaolu, and Maya Jaggi, "Xiaolu Guo: 'Growing up in a Communist Society with Limited Freedom, You're a Spiky, Angry Rat,'" *The Guardian*, 30 May 2014 <https://www.theguardian.com/books/2014/may/30/xiaolu-guo-communist-china-interview> [accessed 24 April 2023].
Györke, Ágnes, "Rushdie and Globalization," in *Rushdie in Context*, ed. by Florian Stadtler (Cambridge: Cambridge University Press, 2023), pp. 182–92.
Hall, Stuart, "Notes on Deconstructing the Popular," in *Cultural Resistance Reader*, ed. by Stephen Duncombe (London: Verso, 2002), pp. 185–92.
Hampton-Reeves, Stuart, "New Artistic Directions: An Interview with Michael Boyd," *Shakespeare* 1.1–2 (2005), pp. 91–98.
Harris, Ashleigh, "Awkward Form and Writing the African Present," *The Salon*, 7 (2014), pp. 3–8.
Hofmeyr, Isabel, *The Portable Bunyan: A Transnational History of The Pilgrim's Progress* (Princeton: Princeton University Press, 2004).
Hogg, Christopher, *Adapting Television Drama: Theory and Industry* (London: Palgrave, 2021).
Horta, Paulo Lemos, "'The Most Secret Memory of Men': Global South Print Culture between Bolaño and Mbougar Sarr," in *The Bloomsbury Handbook of Postcolonial Print Cultures*, ed. by Toral Jatin Gajarawala and others (London: Bloomsbury, 2023), pp. 153–65.

Huchu, Tendai, *The Maestro, the Magistrate and the Mathematician* (Bulawayo: 'amaBooks, 2014).
Huggan, Graham, *The Postcolonial Exotic* (London: Routledge, 2001).
—— *Interdisciplinary Measures* (Liverpool: Liverpool University Press, 2008).
—— "A Preface: Reflections on the Postcolonial Exotic," in *Postcolonial Audiences: Readers, Viewers and Reception*, ed. by Bethan Benwell, James Procter, and Gemma Robinson (London: Routledge, 2012), pp. xiii–xvi.
—— "Re-Evaluating the Postcolonial Exotic," *Interventions: International Journal of Postcolonial Studies*, 22.7 (2020), 808–24.
Hurley, Bevan, "Salman Rushdie Moderator Henry Reese Reveals Black Eye and Knife Wound from Attack on Author," *Independent*, 18 August 2022 <https://www.independent.co.uk/news/world/americas/salman-rushdie-henry-reese-attack-author-b2147766.html> [accessed 28 February 2023].
Hwang, Eunju, "Love and Shame: Transcultural Communication and Its Failure in Xiaolu Guo's *A Concise Chinese-English Dictionary for Lovers*," *ariel: A Review of International English Literature*, 43.4 (2013), pp. 69–95.
Innes, C. L., *The Cambridge Introduction to Postcolonial Literatures in English* (Cambridge: Cambridge University Press, 2007).
Iser, Wolfgang, *The Implied Reader: Patterns of Communication in Prose Fiction from Bunyan to Beckett* (Baltimore: Johns Hopkins University Press, 1974).
—— *The Act of Reading: A Theory of Aesthetic Response* (Baltimore: Johns Hopkins University Press, 1978).
—— *The Range of Interpretation* (New York: Columbia University Press, 2000).
Jeffries, Stuart, "Lie Back and Think of Jesus," *The Guardian*, 5 September 2006 <https://www.theguardian.com/world/2006/sep/05/gender.religion> [accessed 29 February 2024].
Keenan, Siobhan, "The Royal Shakespeare Company at 50," *Shakespeare*, 8.2 (2012), pp. 195–201.
Koegler, Caroline, *Critical Branding: Postcolonial Studies and the Market* (New York: Routledge, 2018).
Krishnan, Madhu, *Contemporary African Literature in English: Global Locations, Postcolonial Identifications* (Basingstoke: Palgrave Macmillan, 2014).
Lakshmi, Vijay, "Rushdie's Fiction: The World Beyond the Looking Glass," in *Reworlding: The Literature of the Indian Diaspora*, ed. by Emmanuel S. Nelson (New York: Greenwood Press, 1992), pp. 149–55.
La'Porte, Victoria, *An Attempt to Understand the Muslim Reaction to* The Satanic Verses (Lewiston: Edwin Mellen Press, 1999).
Lascelles, Amber, "Black Feminism in a Neoliberal World: Resistance in Contemporary Black Women's Fiction" (PhD thesis, University of Leeds, 2020).

—— "We Should All Be *Radical* Feminists: A Review of Chimamanda Ngozi Adichie's Contribution to Literature and Feminism," *Journal of Postcolonial Writing*, 57.6 (2021), pp. 893–99.

Lawton, Georgina, "Malorie Blackman: 'Don't Apologise to Anyone for Living, or Being,'" *gal-dem*, 19 August 2019 <https://web.archive.org/web/20240415052053/https://gal-dem.com/malorie-blackman-dont-apologise-to-anyone-for-living-or-being/> [accessed 2 January 2024].

Lazarus, Neil, "Introducing Postcolonial Studies," in *The Cambridge Companion to Postcolonial Literary Studies*, ed. by Neil Lazarus (Cambridge: Cambridge University Press, 2004), pp. 1–18.

—— "Afterword," *African Identities* (Special Issue: Marxism and African Literatures: New Interventions), 18.1–2 (2020), pp. 182–92.

Leitch, Vincent B., "Ideology of Headnotes," *On Anthologies: Politics and Pedagogy*, ed. by Jeffrey Di Leo (Lincoln: University of Nebraska Press, 2004), pp. 372–83.

Long, Elizabeth, *Book Clubs: Women and the Uses of Reading in Everyday Life* (Chicago: Chicago University Press, 2003).

Lyngstad, Marit Elise, "Integrating Competence and *Bildung* through Dystopian Literature: Teaching Malorie Blackman's *Noughts & Crosses* and Democracy and Citizenship in the English Subject," *Utbildning & Lärande*, 15.2 (2021), pp. 11–26.

Macpherson, William, *Inquiry into the Matters Arising from the Death of Stephen Lawrence on 22 April 1993 to Date, Order Particularly to Identify the Lessons to be Learned for the Investigation and Prosecution of Racially Motivated Crimes* (London: Home Office, 1998).

Mahfouz, Sabrina, *Noughts & Crosses* (London: Nick Hern Books, in association with Pilot Theatre, 2020).

Malik, Kenan, "Exploding the Fatwa Myths," *The Guardian*, 9 February 2009 <https://www.theguardian.com/commentisfree/2009/feb/09/religion-islam-fatwa-khomeini-rushdie> [accessed 12 February 2024].

—— *From Fatwa to Jihad: The Rushdie Affair and Its Legacy* (London: Atlantic Books, 2009).

Marais, Mike, "J. M. Coetzee's 'Disgrace' and the Task of the Imagination," *Journal of Modern Literature*, 29.2 (2006), pp. 75–93.

Massie, Graeme, "Salman Rushdie Attack Suspect Says He Only Read Two Pages of *Satanic Verses*," *Independent*, 17 August 2022 <https://www.independent.co.uk/news/world/americas/crime/salman-rushdie-attack-hadi-matar-satanic-verses-b2147081.html> [accessed 28 February 2024].

McCann, Fiona, "Uncommonly Other in Belfast, London and Harare: AlieNation in Robert McLiam Wilson's *Ripley Bogle* and Brian Chikwava's *Harare North*," *Commonwealth Essays and Studies*, 37.1 (2014), pp. 67–78.

McDonald, Peter D., "The Ethics of Reading and the Question of the Novel: The Challenge of J. M. Coetzee's *Diary of a Bad Year*," *NOVEL: A Forum on Fiction*, 43.3 (2010), pp. 483–99.

McGurl, Mark, *Everything and Less: The Novel in the Age of Amazon* (London: Verso, 2021).
McLeod, John, "Postcolonial Studies and the Ethics of the Quarrel," *Paragraph*, 40.1 (2017), pp. 97–113.
McLoughlin, Seán, "The State, New Muslim Leaderships and Islam as a Resource for Public Engagement in Britain," *European Muslims and the Secular State*, ed. by Jocelyne Cesari and Seán McLoughlin (London and New York: Routledge, 2005), pp. 55–69.
Miller, J. Hillis, "The Ethics of Reading," *Style*, 21.2 (1987), pp. 181–91.
Modood, Tariq, "Religious Anger and Minority Rights," *The Political Quarterly*, 60.3 (1989), pp. 280–84.
Moi, Toril, "Rethinking Character," in *Character: Three Inquiries in Literary Studies*, ed. by Amanda Anderson, Rita Felski, and Toril Moi (Chicago: University of Chicago Press, 2019), pp. 27–75.
Mondal, Anshuman A., "'Representing the Very Ethic He Battled': Secularism, Islam(ism) and Self-transgression in *The Satanic Verses*," *Textual Practice*, 27.3 (2013), pp. 419–37.
Mongia, Padmini, *Contemporary Postcolonial Theory: A Reader* (Abingdon: Routledge, 1997).
Morey, Peter, *Islamophobia and the Novel* (New York: Columbia University Press, 2018).
—— "Rushdie and Globalization," in *Rushdie in Context*, ed. by Florian Stadtler (Cambridge: Cambridge University Press, 2023), pp. 318–28.
Muchemwa, Kizito Z., "Old and New Fictions: Rearranging the Geographies of Urban Space and Identities in Post-2006 Zimbabwean Fiction," *English Academy Review*, 27.2 (2010), pp. 134–45.
Mukherjee, Ankhi, and Ato Quayson, eds, "Introduction," in *Decolonizing the English Literary Curriculum* (Cambridge: Cambridge University Press, 2023), pp. 1–20.
Murray, Padmini Ray, and Claire Squires, "The Digital Publishing Communications Circuit," *Book 2.0*, 3.1 (2013), pp. 3–23.
Murray, Simone, *The Digital Literary Sphere: Reading, Writing, and Selling Books in an Internet Era* (Baltimore: John Hopkins University Press, 2018).
Musanga, Terrence, "'Ngozi' (Avenging Spirit), Zimbabwean Transnational Migration, and Restorative Justice in Brian Chikwava's *Harare North* (2009)," *Journal of Black Studies*, 48.8 (2017), pp. 775–90.
Nadiminti, Kalyan, "The Global Program Era: Contemporary International Fiction in the American Creative Economy," *NOVEL: A Forum on Fiction*, 51.3 (2018), pp. 375–98.
Nakamura, Lisa, "'Words with Friends': Socially Networked Reading on 'Goodreads,'" *PMLA*, 128.1 (2013), pp. 239–43.
Nasta, Susheila, "Editorial: The Scramble for New Literatures," *Wasafiri*, 10.20 (1994), pp. 3–4.

Ndlovu, Isaac, "Language and Audience in Brian Chikwava's *Harare North* (2009)," *English Academy Review*, 33.2 (2016), pp. 29–42.

—— "Writing and Reading Zimbabwe in the Global Literary Market: A Case of Four Novelists," *Journal of Postcolonial Writing*, 57.1 (2021), pp. 106–20.

Ndlovu-Gatsheni, Sabelo J., *Coloniality of Power in Postcolonial Africa: Myths of Decolonization* (Dakar: Council for the Development of Social Science Research in Africa, 2013).

Neves, Johnathan, and Rose Stephenson, *Students Academic Experience Survey 2023* (Higher Education Policy Institute, 2023).

Newell, Stephanie, *Literary Culture in Colonial Ghana* (Bloomington: Indiana University Press, 2002).

—— *West African Literatures: Ways of Reading* (Oxford: Oxford University Press, 2006).

Norris, Sharon, "The Booker Prize: A Bourdieusian Perspective," *Journal for Cultural Research*, 10.2 (2006), pp. 139–58.

"Noughts & Crosses," Royal Shakespeare Company, n.d. <https://www.rsc.org.uk/noughts-and-crosses> [accessed 23 February 2024].

Noxolo, Patricia, "Towards an Embodied Securityscape: Brian Chikwava's *Harare North* and the Asylum Seeking Body As Site of Articulation," *Social & Cultural Geography*, 15.3 (2014), pp. 291–312.

Nugent, Annabel, "Malorie Blackman: 'I Didn't Read a Book That Featured a Black Protagonist until I Was 21,'" *Independent*, 6 December 2020 <https://www.independent.co.uk/arts-entertainment/books/features/malorie-blackman-interview-noughts-and-crosses-b1765578.html>.

Nyman, Jopi, "A Post-Colonial Canon? An Explorative Study of Post-Colonial Writing in University-Level Courses," in *Diasporic Literature and Theory— Where Now?*, ed. by Mark Shackleton (Newcastle: Cambridge Scholars Publishing, 2008), pp. 36–56.

Oboe, Annalisa, "Language, Eros and Culture in Xiaolu Guo's *A Concise Chinese-English Dictionary for Lovers*," in *The Tapestry of the Creative Word in Anglophone Literatures*, ed. by Antonella Riem Natale, and others (Udine: Forum Editrice Universitaria Udinese, 2013), pp. 267–79.

Ommundsen, Wenche, "From China with Love: Chick Lit and The New Crossover Fiction," in *China Fictions/English Language: Literary Essays in Diaspora, Memory, Story*, ed. by A. Robert Lee (Amsterdam: Rodolpi, 2008), pp. 327–45.

OpenLearn, "Writing Across Cultures," *Medium*, 9 July 2017 <https://openlearn.medium.com/writing-across-cultures-fd191d0c0a33> [accessed 12 June 2023].

Oyedeji, Koye, "Out of the Frying Pan... (Literary London Still Has a Colonial Welcome for its Postcolonial Migrants)," *Wasafiri*, 28.4 (2013), pp. 47–52.

Pardey, Hannah, "Middlebrow 2.0: The Digital Affect and the New Nigerian Novel," in *Imperial Middlebrow*, ed. by Christopher Ehland and Jana Gohrisch (Leiden: Brill, 2020), pp. 218–39.

Parekh, Bhikhu, "Between Holy Text and Moral Void," *New Statesman and Society*, 24 March 1989, pp. 29–33.

—— "The Rushdie Affair and the British Press," in *Text Wars: Communication, Censorship, Freedom and Responsibility*, ed. by Hilda David and Francis Jarman (Oxford: Oxford University Press, 2021), pp. 62–85.

Parry, Benita, "The Institutionalization of Postcolonial Studies," in *The Cambridge Companion to Postcolonial Literary Studies*, ed. by Neil Lazarus (Cambridge: Cambridge University Press, 2004), pp. 66–80.

"Past Lives and Present Tensions," *The Guardian*, 4 April 2002 <https://www.theguardian.com/books/2002/apr/04/buildingachildrenslibrary.booksforchildrenandteenagers1> [accessed 14 January 2023].

Pianzola, Federico, "Sociality and Seriality in Digital Reading: Two Extra Memos for this Millennium," in *The Routledge Companion to Literary Media*, ed. by Astrid Ensslin, Julia Round, and Bronwen Thomas (Abingdon: Routledge, 2023), pp. 479–89.

Pipes, Daniel, *The Rushdie Affair: The Novel, the Ayatollah, and the West* (New York: Birch Lane Press, 1990).

Poon, Angelia, "Becoming a Global Subject: Language and the Body in Xiaolu Guo's *A Concise Chinese-English Dictionary for Lovers*," *Transnational Literature*, 6.1 (2013), pp. 1–9.

Potts, Deborah, "'Restoring Order'? Operation Murambatsvina and the Urban Crisis in Zimbabwe," *Journal of Southern African Studies*, 32.2 (2006), pp. 273–91.

Price, Leah, "Reading: The State of the Discipline," *Book History*, 7 (2004), pp. 303–20.

Procter, James, "'The Ghost of Other Stories': Salman Rushdie and the Question of Canonicity?" in *A Black British Canon?*, ed. by Gail Low and Marion Wynne-Davies (Basingstoke: Palgrave Macmillan, 2006), pp. 35–49.

—— "Reading, Taste and Postcolonial Studies," *Interventions: International Journal of Postcolonial Studies*, 11.2 (2009), pp. 180–98.

Procter, James, and Bethan Benwell, *Reading Across Worlds: Transnational Book Groups and the Reception of Difference* (Basingstoke: Palgrave Macmillan, 2015).

Pucherová, Dobrota, "'A Continent Learns to Tell its Story at Last': Notes on the Caine Prize," *Journal of Postcolonial Writing*, 48.1 (2012), pp. 13–25.

—— "Forms of Resistance against the African Postcolony in Brian Chikwava's *Harare North*," *Brno Studies in English*, 41.1 (2015), pp. 157–73.

Ramone, Jenni, *Postcolonial Literatures in the Local Literary Marketplace* (London: Palgrave Macmillan, 2020).

Ranasinha, Ruvani, "The Fatwa and its Aftermath," in *The Cambridge Companion to Salman Rushdie*, ed. by Abdulrazak Gurnah (Cambridge: Cambridge University Press, 2007), pp. 45–59.

—— *South Asian Writers in Twentieth-Century Britain: Culture in Translation* (Oxford: Oxford University Press, 2007).

Reinelt, Janelle, "Toward a Poetics of Theatre and Public Events: In the Case of Stephen Lawrence," *The Drama Review*, 50.3 (2006), pp. 69–87.

Remnick, David, "The Defiance of Salman Rushdie," *The New Yorker*, 6 February 2023 <https://www.newyorker.com/magazine/2023/02/13/salman-rushdie-recovery-victory-city> [accessed 28 February 2023].

Rigby, Phil, "English Teachers and English Teaching," in *Teaching English: Developing as a Reflective Secondary Teacher*, ed. by Carol Evans, and others (London: SAGE Publications, 2009), pp. 1–26.

Rogers, Asha, "Crossing 'Other Cultures'? Reading Tatamkhula Afrika's 'Nothing's Changed' in the NEAB Anthology," *English in Education*, 49.1 (2015), pp. 80–93.

—— *State-Sponsored Literature: Britain and Cultural Diversity after 1945* (Oxford: Oxford University Press, 2020).

Rose, Johnathan, *The Intellectual Life of the British Working Classes* (New Haven: Yale University Press, 2001).

RSC Annual Report and Accounts, 2007/2008, Royal Shakespeare Company, 22 September 2008 <https://www.rsc.org.uk/annual-review/previous-annual-reviews> [accessed 12 January 2024].

Rushdie, Salman, "The Book Burning," *The New York Review of Books*, 2 March 1989, n.p.

—— "My Book Speaks for Itself," *The New York Times*, 17 February 1989, p. 39.

—— *Imaginary Homelands: Essays and Criticism 1981-1991* (London: Granta, 1991).

—— *The Satanic Verses* (London: Vintage, 2006).

—— *Joseph Anton: A Memoir* (London: Vintage, 2013).

Ruthven, Malise, *A Satanic Affair: Salman Rushdie and the Rage of Islam* (London: Chatto & Windus, 1990).

—— *A Fury for God: The Islamist Attack on America* (London: Granta, 2002).

Saha, Anamik, "The Rationalizing/Racializing Logic of Capital in Cultural Production," *Media Industries*, 3.1 (2016), pp. 1–16.

Said, Edward, *Culture and Imperialism* (London: Chatto & Windus, 1993).

Said, Edward, and others, "Antithetical to Islam," *The New York Review of Books*, 17 February 1989 <http://www.nytimes.com/1989/02/17/opinion/l-antithetical-to-islam-121589.html> [accessed 17 January 2017].

"Salman Rushdie Attacker: 'I Only Read Two Pages of His Book,'" *Al Bawaba*, 18 August 2022 <https://www.albawaba.com/node/salman-rushdie-attacker-%E2%80%98i-only-read-two-pages-his-book-1487905> [accessed 28 February 2024].

Sands-O'Connor, Karen, "Smashing Birds in the Wilderness: British Racial and Cultural Integration from Insider and Outsider Perspectives," *Papers: Explorations into Children's Literature*, 13.3 (2003), pp. 43–50.

—— *Children's Publishing and Black Britain, 1965–2015* (New York: Palgrave Macmillan, 2017).

Scott, Helen, "Was There a Time Before Race? Capitalist Modernity and the Origins of Racism," in *Marxism, Modernity and Postcolonial Studies*, ed. by Crystal Bartolovich and Neil Lazarus (Cambridge: Cambridge University Press, 2002), pp. 167–82.

Sedgwick, Eve Kosovsky, *Touching Feeling: Affect, Pedagogy, Performativity* (Durham: Duke University Press, 2002).

Sedo, DeNel Rehberg, "'I Used to Read Anything That Caught My Eye, But...': Cultural Authority and Intermediaries in a Virtual Young Adult Book Club," in *Reading Communities from Salons to Cyberspace*, ed. by DeNel Rehberg Sedo (New York: Palgrave Macmillan, 2011), pp. 101–22.

Senior, Claire, *Getting the Buggers to Read* (London: Continuum, 2005).

Shi, Flair Donglai, "Reborn Translated: Xiaolu Guo as World Author," *Kritika Kultura*, 36 (2021), pp. 166–94.

—— "Translating the Translational: A Comparative Study of the Taiwanese and Mainland Chinese Translations of Xiaolu Guo's *A Concise Chinese-English Dictionary for Lovers*," *Translation and Literature*, 30 (2021), pp. 1–29.

Sinkyin, Dan, and Edwin Roland, "Against Conglomeration," *Journal of Cultural Analytics*, 6.2 (2021), pp. 72–107.

"Sir Salman Rushdie Attack Suspect 'Only Read Two Pages' of *Satanic Verses*," *BBC*, 18 August 2022 <https://www.bbc.co.uk/news/entertainment-arts-62588666> [accessed 28 February 2024].

Siziba, Gugulethu, "Reading Zimbabwe's Structural and Political Violence through the Trope of the Unnameable and Unnamed in Brian Chikwava's *Harare North*," *Literator*, 38.1 (2017), pp. 1–9.

Spivak, Gayatri Chakravorty, *An Aesthetic Education in an Era of Globalization* (Cambridge, MA: Harvard University Press, 2012).

Spowage, Kate, "Against the Game: Sid Meier's *Civilization* and Vernacular Theories of Language," *Language in Society*, forthcoming.

Spowage, Kate, and Hayley G. Toth, 'Reading and Ideology: The Case of the Free Public Libraries Movement,' *Journal of Political Ideologies*, 29.3 (2024), pp. 513–32.

Spyra, Ania, "On Labors of Love and Language Learning: Xiaolu Guo Rewriting the Monolingual Family Romance," *Studies in the Novel*, 48.4 (2016), pp. 444–61.

Squires, Claire, "Too Much Rushdie, Not Enough Romance? The UK Publishing Industry and BME (Black Minority Ethnic) Readership," in *Postcolonial Audiences: Readers, Viewers and Reception*, ed. by Bethan Benwell, James Procter, and Gemma Robinson (London: Routledge, 2012), pp. 99–111.

Srivastava, Neelam, "Anthologizing the Nation: Literature Anthologies and the Idea of India," *Journal of Postcolonial Writing*, 46.2 (2010), pp. 151–63.

Staunton, Irene, "'Sorry: No Free Reading'," *African Research and Documentation*, 69 (1995), pp. 17–22.

Strike, Tony, "Taking the Long View on Student Number Control," *Association of Heads of University Administration (AHUA)*, 16 April 2020 <https://www.ahua.ac.uk/taking-the-long-view-on-student-number-control/> [accessed 30 October 2023].

Syed, Ghazal Kazim, and others, "Developing UK and Norwegian Undergraduate Students' Conceptions of Personal Social Issues in Young Adult Fiction through Transnational Reflective Exchange," *English in Education*, 55.1 (2021), pp. 53–69.

Toth, Hayley G., "Spivak's Planetarity and the Limits of Professional Reading," *Comparative Critical Studies*, 17.3 (2020), pp. 459–78.

—— "Reading in the Global Literary Marketplace: Material and Textual Affects," *Interventions: International Journal of Postcolonial Studies*, 23.4 (2021), pp. 636–54.

—— "Bad Reading / Bad Gaming," *Post45 Contemporaries*, 8 April 2024 <https://post45.org/2024/04/bad-reading-bad-gaming/> [accessed 9 May 2024].

Trivedi, Harish, "Salman Rushdie and Postcolonialism," in *Salman Rushdie in Context*, ed. by Florian Stadtler (Cambridge: Cambridge University Press, 2023), pp. 293–304.

Vadde, Aarthi, "Theories of Anthologizing and Decolonization," in *Decolonizing the English Literary Curriculum*, ed. by Ankhi Mukherjee and Ato Quayson (Cambridge: Cambridge University Press, 2023), pp. 149–66.

Vago, Steven, and Ben Kesslen, "Salman Rushdie Attacker Praises Iran's Ayatollah, Surprised Author Survived: Jailhouse Interview," *New York Post*, 17 August 2022 <https://nypost.com/2022/08/17/alleged-salman-rushdie-attacker-didnt-think-author-would-survive/> [accessed 28 February 2023].

Venuti, Lawrence, *The Translator's Invisibility: A History of Translation* (London: Routledge, 2004).

Walkowitz, Rebecca L., *Born Translated: The Contemporary Novel in an Age of World Literature* (New York: Columbia University Press, 2015).

Waring, Wendy, "Is This Your Book? Wrapping Postcolonial Fiction for the Global Market," *Canadian Review of Comparative Literature/ Revue Canadienne de Littérature Comparée*, 22.3–4 (1995), pp. 455–66.

Weldon, Fay, *Sacred Cows* (London: Chatto & Windus, 1989).

Wicomb, Zoë, "Heterotopia and Placelessness in Brian Chikwava's *Harare North*," in *The Globalization of Space*, ed. by Mariangela Palladino and John Miller (Abingdon: Routledge, 2016), pp. 49–64.

Wilkie-Stibbs, Christine, "The 'Other' Country: Memory, Voices, and Experiences of Colonized Childhoods," *Children's Literature Association Quarterly*, 31.3 (2006), pp. 237–59.

Williams, Patrick, and Laura Chrisman, *Colonial Discourse and Post-Colonial Theory: A Reader* (London: Pearson, 1993).

Wilson, Richard, "NATO's Pharmacy: Shakespeare by Prescription," in *Shakespeare and National Culture*, ed. by John J. Joughin (Manchester: Manchester University Press, 1997), pp. 58–80.

Young, John K., *Black Writers, White Publishers: Marketplace Politics in Twentieth-Century African American Literature* (Jackson: University of Mississippi Press, 2006).

Index

Achebe, Chinua 167, 168n7, 178
A Concise Chinese-English Dictionary for Lovers 17, 19, 29, 31, 33, 73–98, 110, 175
  see also Guo, Xiaolu
Adichie, Chimamanda Ngozi 138, 168
Ahsan, Muhammad Manazir (Director of the Islamic Foundation of Leicester) 44–46
Akhtar, Shabbir 57–58, 68
Al-Ghamdi, Mughram (convenor of UK Action Committee on Islamic Affairs) 45
  see also UK Action Committee on Islamic Affairs (UKACIA)
A Lover's Discourse 17
A Lover's Discourse: Fragments 17
Amazon 4, 28–30, 82–85, 88, 90–92, 95, 104–6, 109–10, 113–14, 151
Americanah 138
anthologies 35, 166, 178–82
  see also *The Post-Colonial Studies Reader*
anticolonial 10, 15, 177
Appignanesi, Lisa see *The Rushdie File*
Armstrong, Paul B. 15, 24
Arts Council England 145
Ashcroft, Bill 2, 179–82
Ashraf, Syed Ali 56–57, 68–69
A Time to Kill 157–58, 161
Attridge, Derek 3–4, 7, 125

Barthes, Roland 17–18
Be Careful with Muhammad!: The Salman Rushdie Affair see Akhtar, Shabbir
Benwell, Bethan 6, 34, 54–55, 87–90, 97, 111, 129, 176
Bhabha, Homi 167n3, 178
Blackman, Malorie 131–33, 141–43, 145, 148, 150, 152, 156
  see also *Noughts & Crosses*
Black Panther (2018 film) 136, 138
Blair, Tony see UK government
Boehmer, Elleke 7–8, 125
Bogle-L'Ouverture 9
Bongie, Chris 88, 135–37
book covers see paratexts
Booker Prize see prizes
Bourdieu, Pierre 4–5, 18, 162
Bradford book burning demonstration (14 January 1989) 47–48, 50–51
Bradford Council of Mosques see Bradford book burning demonstration (14 January 1989)
Brouillette, Sarah 5–6, 8, 10n34, 11–13, 81, 105n16, 127, 176, 180
Bulawayo, NoViolet 12

Caine Prize for African Writing see prizes
canonisation 23, 97
  Americanah's canonisation 138

canonical literature 2, 150
critical canon 181
    see also anthologies
Rushdie's canonisation of post-nationalism 61
Rushdie's "self-canonisation" 51
postcolonial canon 178
postcolonial writing as 'non-canonical' 169
capitalism 9n28, 10, 15, 127, 138–40, 156, 174
censorship 44, 51, 53–54, 73–74
Chatto & Windus 31
Chautauqua Institution see Rushdie, Salman
Chikwava, Brian 33–34, 101–2, 105, 107, 109, 125
    see also Harare North
City of Asylum 37
Comedy of Errors, The 147
Concrete Revolution, The 73
conventionalisation in literature and criticism 1, 11, 17, 30, 60, 86–87, 89, 112–14, 124, 169, 183
cultural capital 4, 8, 15, 23, 28, 44, 46–47, 97, 114
    see also Guillory, John

Dahl, Roald 51
damnés de la terre, Les see Wretched of the Earth, The
distinction 3–5, 7, 18, 30, 41, 72, 100, 125, 130, 136–37, 140, 175–76, 182
    see also Bourdieu, Pierre
Doloughan, Fiona 76, 86
Doubleday 31

education 4, 24
    international students 83, 172–74
    primary school 148n67
    racism 131–33, 132
    relationship to Noughts & Crosses 35, 131–34, 145–53, 156–57, 161–62
    relationship to postcolonial studies 1, 4–5, 35–36, 169, 171, 173, 175, 178–83
    relationship to reading 110, 153, 157
    represented in literature 74, 102, 107, 131–32
    secondary school 132–33, 144, 147–50, 153, 166n1, 171n16
    university 1, 4–5, 35–36, 169, 171–75, 178–83
English
    author attitudes toward writing in English 73–74, 102
    literature in English 2, 4, 10–11, 14, 33, 81, 84, 102, 170
    politics of English names 154
    reader attitudes toward representations of 'non-standard' English 76–78, 84, 91, 93–96, 99–100, 104–10
    readers see readers
    relationship to world literature 173
    representations of language learning 31, 74–75, 107
    see also pidgin

Fanon, Frantz 79
Faruqi, Muhammad Hashir (editor of Impact International) 45–46
fatwā 32, 48–51, 54, 57, 62, 67
Featherstone, Simon 137, 176–78

Gandhi, Rajiv (Prime Minister of India, 1984–1989) 42–44, 53
global literary marketplace 13, 77
global literature see world literature
Goodreads 17–18, 27–30, 82–86, 90, 92–94, 96, 104, 106–9, 113–14, 116–19, 123–25, 127, 151–58
Griffiths, Gareth 2, 179–82
Guillory, John 3–4, 22, 29, 112
Gunew, Sneja 76, 81
Guo, Xiaolu 17, 19, 33, 73–77, 82, 88, 92–98
    see also A Concise-Chinese English Dictionary for Lovers
Gurnah, Abdulrazak 178

Hall, Stuart 35, 134, 140–41
Harare North 31, 33–34, 99–110, 112–20, 122–27, 129, 175
  see also Chikwava, Brian
higher education *see* education
Huchu, Tendai 99
Huggan, Graham 4, 8, 13, 176, 179, 180–82

identity *see* reading
Impact International 45–46, 56, 68
  see also Faruqi, Muhammad Hashir (editor of *Impact International*)
indeterminacy 16, 20, 26, 70, 104, 121–22, 127–28, 153
Iser, Wolfgang 16–24, 26, 140
Islamic Foundation of Leicester *see* Ahsan, Muhammad Manazir (Director of the Islamic Foundation of Leicester)

Johnathan Cape 31, 101
Joseph Anton: A Memoir 53, 64

Khamenei, Ali (the second Supreme Leader of Iran, 1989–present) 66–68
Khomeini, Ayatollah (the first Supreme Leader of Iran, 1979–89) *see* fatwā
Knife: Mediations After an Attempted Murder 39

labour (of reading) 1, 3, 7, 15, 27, 112, 127, 129
language *see* English; pidgin
Le Carré, John 51
literary fiction 18, 32, 47, 59–61, 66, 68, 137–38
  difficulty 33–34, 68, 89, 97, 135 *see also* reading
literary prizes *see* prizes
London 45n19, 46, 62, 73, 132, 142
  City, University of London 169

publishers 9
readers from London *see* readers
represented in literature 31, 65, 68, 70, 74, 84–86, 93, 101–2, 106, 113, 116, 117–18, 120, 123

Macpherson report, The *see* Stephen Lawrence, the murder of
Maestro, the Magistrate and the Mathematician, The 99
Maitland, Sara *see The Rushdie File*
Malik, Kenan 43, 53
Marxism 8–9
  see also capitalism
Matar, Hadi 37–38
McDonald, Peter D. 22
Midnight's Children 71
Murray, Simone 28, 114

Nasta, Susheila 166–67
New Beacon Books 9
New York Times, The 39, 43, 51, 64n108, 94
Noble Prize for Literature *see* prizes
non-understanding 26, 33–34, 56, 100–1, 111–12, 115, 121, 124–30
Noughts & Crosses 31, 35, 131–34, 141–62, 175
  see also Malorie Blackman
Noughts + Crosses (BBC television adaptation) 31, 141, 152, 158–62

Orange Prize *see* prizes
Orientalism 177–78

paratexts 11, 19, 25, 34, 76, 81, 95, 105–6, 141
Parekh, Bhikhu 55n70, 57–58, 61
Peepal Tree Press 9
Penguin (publisher) 10, 31, 46–47, 138
Pianzola, Federico 27–28
pidgin 34, 104–7, 109
Pinter, Harold 44, 49
post-92 universities 169

Post-Colonial Studies Reader, The 179–82
   see also anthologies
Présence Africaine 9
prizes 10, 60, 96–97
   Booker Prize 43, 47, 55, 60
   Caine Prize for African Writing 34, 105
   Nobel Prize for Literature 167, 178
   Orange Prize 96
   Whitbread Prize 47, 59–60
Procter, James 6–7, 14, 34, 54–55, 61, 87–90, 97, 111, 129, 176
publishers 8–12, 14, 22, 28–29, 31, 60, 76, 78, 80, 98, 132–33, 138, 143–44, 148, 150, 161, 176–82
   relationship to the Rushdie affair 44, 46, 49, 53, 62
Puri, Nisha 59

Rajan, Rajeswari Sunder 8
Ramone, Jenni 25, 110n22
Ranasinha, Ruvani 11, 50
Random House 31, 101, 138, 177
readers
   addressed 33, 75–81, 85–86, 95–97
   African 34, 106–10, 129
   Black 159–61, 163
   Chinese 83, 85
   English/English-speaking 71, 76–78, 82, 85–86, 97–98, 102, 111, 121
   European 3–4, 79
   implied 12–13, 22, 24, 33, 55, 67, 76, 78, 81, 98, 128–29, 134, 149, 183
   see also Iser, Wolfgang
   London-based 82–83, 85, 117–18
   market 81, 86, 129
   migrant 83–84
   native 75–77, 79–82, 97
   non-African 34, 105–6, 110
   non-readers 26, 32, 38–39, 42–44, 52–56, 129
      see also Shahabuddin, Syed

   non-Zimbabwean 100, 105–7, 109–11
   Western 3–4, 33, 54–55, 75–77, 80–83, 92, 97, 104, 108, 129, 138–40
   Zimbabwean 34, 107–10, 129
reading
   contrapuntal reading 2–3
   diagnostic reading 15, 100, 115, 118–22, 124–25
   difficulty 33–34, 68, 99–113, 123, 126–27, 129–30
   gendered reading 31, 82–83, 92–95, 111
   identification 33, 75, 77, 79, 82–98, 104, 114–17
   not reading 26, 32, 38–39, 42–44, 52–56, 129
   partial reading 7, 20, 26, 34, 55–56, 66, 69, 100, 111–12, 115, 122, 124–25, 146
   pleasure 20, 83–84, 95–96, 105, 112–13, 126–27, 152, 155–56
   realist reading 33, 89–98, 100, 109–11, 115–18, 122–25
   relatability 69, 84, 90–91, 114
   relationship to identity 18, 31–34, 42, 46, 52, 54–55, 64
   reparative reading 33, 90, 98
   responsible reading 2–4, 7
      see also Attridge, Derek
   revelatory reading 100, 115, 122–25
   selective reading *see* partial reading
   symptomatic reading 2–3, 7–8, 14–15, 79–80, 118–22
recursion 19–21, 26–27, 56, 66, 80, 153
Reese, Henry 37
Research Excellence Framework 168, 174
Robinson, Gemma 6, 34, 54–55, 111, 176
Romeo and Juliet 144, 150, 162
Royal Shakespeare Company 145–47, 161
Royal Society of Literature (RSL) 67

Rushdie File, The 40, 59
Rushdie, Salman 10–11, 31–32, 37–44, 46, 48–54, 56–64, 66–72, 170, 178
    attack on the author (2022) 32, 37–39, 72
    see also *Satanic Verses, The*

Sacred Cows see Weldon, Fay
Said, Edward 2, 49–50, 177–78
Samuels, Diane 37
Satanic Verses, The 31–32, 38–72, 129, 175
    petition to ban the novel 32, 42–44, 53–54
    representation of the Prophet Muhammad 32, 40, 44, 56–58, 62–64, 67–70
    see also Rushdie, Salman
school see education
Shahabuddin, Syed 42–44, 46, 52–53, 55
Shakespeare, William 144–45, 146n61, 150
Shi, Flair Donglai 76–78
social media 22, 27–30, 35, 38, 114
    see also Amazon; Goodreads; YouTube
Spivak, Gayatri Chakravorty 9, 22, 49–50, 178, 181
Srivastava, Neelam 8, 169–70
Stephen Lawrence, the murder of 35, 142–46, 150, 162

taste 5, 18, 55, 58–59, 65–66, 76, 124, 134, 136, 138, 153
    see also Bourdieu, Pierre; distinction
teaching see education

Third World Literature 60–62, 66
Third World Press 9
Tiffin, Helen 2, 179–82
translation 12, 33, 41, 74, 77, 80, 84, 98, 102, 109
    as a conceptual metaphor for reading 17, 19, 21, 23, 26, 79–80, 85, 90, 115
    theory 33, 78–81
    see also Venuti, Lawrence
translational literature 33, 74–77, 81

UK Action Committee on Islamic Affairs, The (UKACIA) 44–46, 51
UK government
    approach to higher education 171–72, 175
    relationship to *The Satanic Verses* 49, 60
    Tony Blair 142, 150–51

Venuti, Lawrence 33, 78–80
Viking (publisher) 31, 46–47

Walkowitz, Rebecca L. 77–78
Walsh, John 69–70
Wasafiri 107, 166
Weldon, Fay 48–49, 59–61, 63
We Need New Names 12–13
Whitbread Award see prizes
world literature 77–78, 81, 97, 173–74
Wretched of the Earth, The 79

YouTube 37–38

Zimbabwean African National Union Patriotic Front (ZANU-PF) 101, 103

www.ingramcontent.com/pod-product-compliance
Lightning Source LLC
Chambersburg PA
CBHW071816290825